Naga-Ahom Relations in Pre-Colonial Period

Naga-Ahom Relations in Pre-Colonial Period

N. Nyejat Konyak

GenNext Publication

Published by

GenNext Publication
5, Ansari Road
Daryaganj, New Delhi-110002
Phone: 011-47034999, 9811692060
E-mail: gennextpublication@hotmail.com

Distribution Network
gyanbooks.com
India, USA, Canada, UK, Australia, France

ISBN: 978-93-5663-637-8 (PB)
First Published, 2024

Printed at: Gyan Press, Delhi.

Naga-Ahom Relations in Pre-Colonial Period

Author: N. Nyejat Konyak

Contents

	Abbreviation	7
	Glossary	9
I.	Introduction	13
II.	Early Contact and Political Relations	55
III.	Economic Relations	103
IV.	Socio-Cultural Relations	145
	Conclusion	193
	Works Cited Bibliography	201
	Appendices	223
	Maps and Photo	233
	Index	243

Abbreviation

AAH	An Account of Assam
AAHAB	An Account of Assam and her Administration
AB	Ahom Buranji, (tr. & ed.) G.C. Barua
AAR	Anglo-Assamese Relations 1771-1826
AHA	A History of Assam
ABHT	Atan Burangohain and His Times
APS	Ahom Political System
ATRAPS	Ahom Tribal-Relations: A Political Study
ACHA	A Comprehensive History of Assam
DAB	Deodhai Assam Buranji
DAB	A Descriptive Account of Assam
DHAS	Department of Historical and Antiquarian Studies
IHC	Indian History Congress
JB	Jayantia Buranji
JASB	Journal of Asiatic Society of Bengal
JRASB	Journal of Royal Asiatic Society of Bengal
MECA	Medieval and Early Colonial Assam
NEIHA	North East India History Association
RAW	Welsh's Report on Assam
RAM	Mills Report on Assam
SAB	Satsari Asam Buranji
TB	Tungkhungia Buranji
TIK	The Tai and the Tai Kingdom

Glossary

Angh/Wangham/ Longwang	Traditional chieftainship among the Konyak-Wancho-Nocte
Ariju	A house where all the social welfare of the village is discussed. All male members of the village when they reach 13 to 14 year of age, they were obligatory to sleep at Ariju (morung), until they get married and learn the socio-cultural and political affairs.
Ali	Road/embankment.
Asu	It is a term used for a span of life about 100 to 130 years (i.e., Ao dialect).
Bahatiyas	Peasant-*paik's* residing in the foothill areas of Assam who were assigned to the hill tribes by the Assam rulers for rendering service to pay a stipulated tribute in kind called *posa* to their hill masters.
Bailung	An Ahom priest mainly engaged in astrological calculations. Only the priestly clan maintain the genealogy of the Ahom Royal families.
Beepuri	They acted as both itinerant private dealer and the intermediary trader between the primary producer and any traders (both hills and plains)
Bigha	Unit of land measurement equal to 14,400 sq.ft. adopted by the Ahom rulers.
Bihu	Festivals of the Assamese. There are three Bihus in Assam: The Bohag Bihu or Rongali Bihu, the Kati Bihu or Kangali Bihu, the Magh Bihu or Bhogali Bihu.

Bheel	A pond, a small lake fishery.
Buranji	Initially chronicles (Ahom Buranjis) were written in Tai language. However, when the Ahom came into contact with non-tai Indians speaker and were greatly influenced by their language, culture and traditions, through prolonged lingo-cultural admixture from the time of Ahom king Kuhung Mung. Later on from 16th century linguistic assimilate began to maintain the transcript chronicle into Assamese language.
Chabili	Traditional currency consisted of narrow strips of iron used by the Ao people for their transactions.
Cowrie	A sea shell used as coin in medieval Assam by the Nagas
Charit/Charit Puthi	Biography of the medieval Vaishnava saints of Assam
Charaideo	Ahom first capital, latter converted into religious metropolis by the Ahom Kings, also the royal families was buried at Charaideo.
Chowki/Chawkys	An frontier outpost duly fortified, a customs house.
Dao	A long knife or a short sword with a long handle used by the Nagas.
Dasa	Slave.
Deodhai	A Ahom priest who offered worship to the deities (Bailung, Turung, and Mohan are the priestly clans)
Duar	A pass or gate.
Khaiyas	Cultivator or peasant
Kataki's	Envoys of the Ahom Government
Khat	Landing place on the bank of a river, a tax for using such a place for trade.
Khel	An association or guild of Assamese subjects rendering specific services to the state, under a hierarchy officers namely, Phukans, Barua, Rajkhowa
Garh	Embankment.
Ghat	Landing place on the bank of a river, a revenue was collect for using such a place for trade.

Genna	Taboos, which means, 'forbidden' days among the Nagas'.
Hat	Weekly or bi-weekly markets in an open space at the foothills.
Hatkhowa	A lessee or collector of taxes in a hat or market.
Hati Baruah	Superintendent of elephant.
Japi	A broad, circular bamboo-made cover used as sun-shade or in rain.
Mithun or Mithan	A species of Indian bison which are used during the feast of merit event by the Nagas, also use as a mode of currency.
Moamariya	Disciples of the *Moamariya* or *Mayamara*satra.
Morung	Ariju (bachelor dormitory for male) where the youth of Nagas from the age of 12 to 13-year-old go to Morung and learned the traditional knowledge skills and customs which were transmitted from generation to generatio. Until they get married they have to slept at the morung.
Paik	An Assemese peasant who rendered periodic labour state service under Ahom administration.
Pura	Unit of measurement of lands, rice, pulses etc.
Putu	Generation or Council of village elders consisting of about 25 to 30 years tenure of administration.
Tatar	Member of elder's council in a village polity (Ao dialect)
Dankhawali	A families genealogical register maintain by the Ahom priestly clan

1

Introduction

It is in the Ahom *Buranjis*[1] or chronicles that references to the Nagas are mentioned as it was through the area inhabited by the Wancho, Nocte, Tangsa and Konyak Naga tribes[2] that the Ahoms[3] had to pass to come to Assam during the thirteenth century. The *Buranjis* refer to the Nagas by various names depending on the village or area of their habitation, such as Paniphatias, Torphatias, Doyingias, Hatigurias, Assiringias, Dopdarias, Namsangias, Borduarias, Tablungias, Jaktungias, Moolungias, Paniduarias etc. These names do not relate to the names used in the present time. The names mentioned in the *Buranjis* have been identified with the present Naga groups or villages by taking into account the oral, colonial and archaeological sources.

The Nagas mentioned in the Ahom chronicles are with reference to the Wancho, Tangsa, Nocte, Konyak, Phom, Ao, Lotha and Rengma residing in present day Arunachal Pradesh and Nagaland. Later the name Nagas was mentioned by British officials in the old maps of Assam. During the Ahom period the *duar*'s immediately bordering the plains through which the different Naga groups interacted with the plains were categorised by different names given to them by the Ahom; hence the colonial officials also followed this tradition by mentioning the Nagas as 'Dup-duar-ias' 'Pani-duar-ias' 'Hatigorias,' etc. Assamese names were also given to villages; the hillmen who went down to the plains and had frequent contact with the Assamese are aware of these names and even described themselves by these Assamese names to an outsider visiting them. During the Burmese invasions, many villages were looted and burned. These have been since rebuilt and new names given to them, the old ones being frequently retained.[4] Initial history of contact refers to conflict and hostilities between the Naga and the Ahom. The

Ahoms adopted a liberal social and political outlook in dealing with the Nagas. Besides, from the economic point of view, the Ahoms considered the Naga areas important due to the presence of salt springs.[5] The Ahoms adopted a liberal social and political outlook in dealing with the Nagas.

The Naga raids on the plains, as well as fighting for the salt springs were some of the issues over which there was frequent warfare between the Naga-Ahom, followed by periods of peace and tranquillity.[6] In the later period, some of these Naga tribes came to enjoy grants of land (*khats*) and fishing waters (*bheels*) in the plains obtained from the Ahom kings.[7] Naga *katakis* appointed by Ahom rulers acted as a channel of communication between the Naga and the Ahom.[8] Some of the Ahom rulers are known to have married Naga women. Moreover, the custom of adoption and matrimonial alliances with the hill tribes was practised during the Ahom regime. Sometimes the adopted children were even placed in high positions. As a result of this relationship, a common lingua-franca known as Nagamese[9] for the Naga developed. In times of danger or foreign invasions, such as the Koch, Mughal, and Burmese invasions, many Ahoms also took shelter in the Naga villages (Konyak and Ao).

The above account, based on the available literature indicates the existence of mutual relation between the Naga and the Ahom. The relations are stated to have developed out of the mutual needs of both for maintaining their political and economic ends.

History writing in North-East India, with certain exception, continues to be chained to its colonial framework set by Edward Gait.[10] In consequence most studies of the medieval period in Assam have tended to focus on the dynastic and political history of major kingdoms or states like the Ahom, Koch, Meitei or Kachari etc. Such history has been largely descriptive and valley centric which has left out the history of the interaction between the hill tribes and valley plains. Account of Naga-Ahom relation has been limited to description of Naga raids and Ahom counter punitive measures and to some extent on trade relations. But even here the contact appears to be limited only to the foothill *khats* and markets. However, oral sources found among the Konyak and Ao Nagas for example indicate a more extensive interaction and influence. The Ahom state based in the valley and the tribes[11] living beyond were connected by way of geographical proximity, economic interdependence, trade, cultural relations etc. which affected equally. There is a need to go further beyond the merely descriptive portrayal of Naga-Ahom relations and examine it in its entirety-integrating the political and socio-economic factors and influences that formed the basis of the relationship.

For this there is also a need to integrate oral sources with archival sources. It was only in the 19th century that oral traditions became an area of knowledge and enquiry.[12] Until recently Naga history had been written largely from chronicles or *Buranjis* Persian sources, colonial ethnography, and official records of the British etc. For a study of the past history of the Nagas, a pre-literate society who did not have a script of their own until the nineteenth century, the incorporation of oral tradition is very much needed. It is a well-known fact that northeast India is a treasure-trove of oral traditions.[13] Hence oral traditions have become handy in the reconstruction of their history.

The book examines the relation of the three major Naga tribes, the Konyak,[14] Ao, and Lotha, with the Ahom State during the pre-colonial period. These three tribes owing to their geographical location bordering the Brahmaputra Valley had a much more extensive contact with the Ahoms than other tribes. The area inhabited especially by the Lower Konyak Naga also extended beyond the present state of Nagaland to areas presently located in Arunachal Pradesh.

Understanding the term 'Nagas'

According to B.B. Goswami, Nagas belong to various ethnic compositions of northeast India and three language families, the Mon-Khmer, the Tibeto-Burman and the Siamese-Chinese family. To the Tibeto-Burman family belong the Nagas, the Kuki-Chin and the Bodo who are 'distributed all over the hills and plains of Assam.'[54] Ethnologically, the hill tribes of the northeast frontier are primarily of the Tibeto-Mongoloid stock with a sprinkling of Austric and Dravidian blood. Verrier Elwin states that Nagas are ethnically an Indo-Mongoloid folk, inhabited in the northeast hills of India, divided into over a dozen languages and dialects.[55] For instance, the Ao speaks Ao, the Konyak speaks Konyak and Wancho. Furthermore, most tribes are divided into sub-tribes having their dialects. Ao is divided into Chongli and Mongsen, having diverse dialect differentiations. This language diversity has led some to believe that the Nagas are not of a common origin.

The Census of India 1911, also states that 'they (Nagas) are mostly Mongolian both in physical type and language and in customs they are in some ways, like the hillmen and islanders of South East Asia.[56] The oral traditions, which are surviving to this day, also amply prove their migration to the present habitat from the east, though at different periods through different routes. Therefore, they are not autochthonous people.[57] Whatever might have been the route of their migration or their original home; Naga appears closely a kin to the communities of Indo-China, Malaya, Indonesia, Taiwan, and the Philippines Islands. W.C. Smith, a Christian missionary and a sociologist, enumerated twelve characteristics of the Nagas that are common with the Indonesians, the people of Malaya and the Island of Indonesia. Some of these are the practice of head-hunting, common sleeping houses for unmarried men and women, disposal of death in raised platforms, tattooing by pricking, hilly residences etc. this shows that at one time or other, the Nagas were closely connected with the tribes of South-East Asia, particularly with the Dyaks of Borneo, the Baltaks of Sumatra, Igorots, Ifugaos, and of Philippines and some tribes of Formosa.[58]

The nomenclature and the term 'Nagas' implies a conglomeration and blanket term for different groups/tribes in Assam, Arunachal, Manipur and Nagaland who had identified and associated themselves as 'Nagas.' It was a colonial construct which was further reinforced by R. Woodthorpe.[59]

While the term 'Nagas' remains obscure, the etymological derivation has also been varied. The Ahom used the word '*Noga*,' derived from the Assamese language, meaning people inhabiting the hills. By the late 18*th* century and dawn of the 19*th* century, the British administrators used the word '*Naga*,' a generic term for people inhabiting the 'Naga Hills' and thus also popularised it simultaneously. Another more logical and plausible explanation for this etymological and popular acronym can be traced to the Tibeto-Burman word '*Na-ka*,' which means 'folk with the piercing of the earlobes.[60] The Konyak Naga also uses the word '*Na-kha*' or '*Na-ka*,' meaning 'pierced earlobes'. However, to define and give the term to the people about their physical characteristics and cultural entity can also betray the supposed logic. For instance, the Bontoc and Ifugaos of the Philippines have a culture of piercing their ears but are not known by the term '*Naga*'. Similarly, the Mikirs, Garos, and Akas of northeast India have a similar practice of piercing their earlobes but are not referred to with the same or similar term. Therefore, the term '*Naga*' remains obscure in its real sense.[61]

Today, the hill tribes commonly referred to as '*Naga*' dwell in the northern hill ranges bounded by the Hawkong valley in the north-east; China to the north; the Brahmaputra valley in the north-west; Manipur to the south and the valley of Chindwin River to the east.[62] This tract of hill tribes extends for about two hundred and fifty miles long by a hundred to fifty miles broad from 93° to 96° East longitude and about 25° to 27° North latitude.[63] It is a land of diverse culture, inhabited by families of the pan Mongolian race.[64]

The Nagas have a vibrant oral tradition. During the pre-colonial period, like most of the tribal communities of the northeastern region, they shared a common feature of having only the spoken language with no script of their own. Only in the late 19th century, when the region was annexed and brought into the fold of British colonial rule, the local languages began to be transcribed using the Roman script. The Naga claim that they had recorded their history on animal skin, which, unfortunately, was eaten by insects. Since then, their history and traditions have been preserved in their memories and disseminated orally through songs, myths, folktales, and their material culture. To represent the Naga pre-colonial past, researchers must uncover their past through oral sources and their material artefacts. Therefore, it becomes necessary to decode the past by innovative and unconventional methods; in using oral sources, Jan Vansina's text is a crucial methodological intervention of how oral traditions can aid in reconstructing the history of pre-literate society. Vansina argues for the equal value of the oral sources of history with the written records.[65]

Likewise, the Naga tribes during the pre-colonial period had multiple social and cultural interactions, intertwined in diverse sources. These records, which are reposed in the material, oral and written texts, must be studied conjunctively and comparatively to understand the Naga past.

Oral tradition as a source in reconstructing Migrations of the Nagas

The origin myths of the Nagas are associated with common myths of origin and references to stones or a wide opening space. These account that migrations of the Nagas took place in three successive phases and waves. The first was the Angami, Chakhesang, Lotha, Rengma, Sema, and the Zeliang, who crossed the Chindwin River and came to the place known as '*Samsok*' which literally means a 'parting place.'[66] The second wave of migration consisted of the Aos, Chang, Khiamunggan, Sangtam, Tikhir, and the Yimchunger who crossed the Patkai range along the course of the Tizzy River and entered the present settlements.[67] The third wave consisted of Konyaks and the Sumi who went up along the river Tunai (Chindwin) and some of them moved towards the western side following the Hangnu River.[68] Similar another legend accounts of a specific stoppage or a space through which the different groups passed. For the Aos, they believed they originated from '*Longterok,*' literally meaning 'six stones,' which are now in Chungliyimti, situated about 25 kms from Mokokchung in the Sangtam area under the Tuensang district of Nagaland. These stones were again categorised individually into males namely *Tongpok, Longphok,* and *Longchakrep* and female namely *Longkakpokla, Yongmenala,* and *Elongse* of which the Christian missionaries destroyed the biggest female stone in a fit of iconoclastic zeal.[69] According to this myth, Tonpok with his sister Lendina of the Imsong clan was the first to emerge from Lonterok (six stones), followed by Longpok with his sister Yongmela of Longkumer clan and Longjakrep with sister Elong she of the Jamir clan.[70] Similarly the myths of origin can be found among the Angami, Zeliangrong, Lotha, and Konyak. For the Konyak, they believed that they passed through '*Longphang tinu*' meaning 'behind large stone of a big river.'[71] Therefore if one looks at the myth of origin, the significance of stones is explicit. However, apart from the myth of origins, stones are associated with different social aspects in the Naga society.

Each Naga group emphasises their origins from a 'stone' or 'cave'. The memory of migrations and settlements is also and often related to erecting stone monuments during these migrations. Therefore, the history of the Nagas, and in particular, the 'stone monuments' cannot be analysed without incorporating the myths of origin. Myth becomes essential when the claimant/group asserts and reflects through material cultures. For instance, the Mao Nagas believed that their common ancestors emerged from the earth, and a stone was erected at Maikel to mark the place of their emergence[72] and dispersion to other settlements. Oral tradition encompasses cultural information about the past carefully preserved. Integrating oral tradition in study of the past is challenging, nonetheless valuable insights have been provided through such a method.

The legend of Chakhesang Nagas tells of their encounter with a magical slab stone with the miraculous power of turning and converting a grain stalk into four-grain stalks. They named the stone '*Tso-Tawo*' meaning 'the spirit stone' and thus decided to settle in the present place.[73] The legends and elders of various Naga tribes like the Tangkhuls, Maos, Manipur, Sema, and Lotha named adjacent areas as their place of origin in stone caves.[74]

One of the Naga myths tells about the migration of the Nagas as hailing from the mainland of China who migrated to Myanmar along the rivers and corridors. They migrated to the southern seas of Myanmar along the rivers and lived near the seas coast of Moulmein (Myanmar) for generations before they retreated to Irrawaddy and Chindwin valleys. They lived for generations at Irrawaddy valley; however, they were driven out to the hills by more advanced races in warfare. The Nagas then migrated to Manipur and finally reached *Makhel* (place from which the Naga dispersed), a historical site in Senapati, Manipur district. The following myth shows how the village *Makhel* is associated with the origins and migrations of Mao Nagas, and Manipur tribes.[75]

The other determinant factor for the obsession with the fertility of agriculture, cattle, and human amongst the Nagas, particularly the Konyaks could be associated with a poor harvest. Famines, hunger and scarcity, in the past is a popular lore among the Konyak to these day. Among other reasons, two factors could be attributed to the concept of fertility and good harvest. Firstly, this can be attributed to the nature of the hilly and rugged terrain which made jhum cultivation the dominant mode of cultivation. Secondly, the warring nature and disputes between villages could have restricted the inhabitants from freely going and cultivating the land from fear of surprise raids.

The Nagas occasionally launched fierce raids on the plains, though it was not the aims of Nagas to conquest the territory of the plains. From colonial sources, we get an idea of Naga warfare.

> "It indicates that their defences were well conceived, and the natural strength of their villages and jungles would enable a bold enemy possessed of only the most inferior weapons to inflict much loss upon any attacking forces. However, the Nagas would neither conceal themselves for a rush at close quarters nor attack before they came under confrontation."[76]

The Nagas relied mostly on a night attack, ambuscades, booby traps, and stone shoots, etc., on which they expended great labour. Their weapons are a long, straight, dao, spears, and bows and arrows, the latter being prepared for war with a dab of poison paste sometimes made of pig's blood and aconite or the juice of the croton plant, which is put on just behind the arrow head.[77]

The warring nature of the Nagas in the past had nothing to do with territorial expansion; but more with prestige which is then related to soil fertility, cattle, and human fertility. The fertility of humans and the desire for population growth could also throw light on the frequent loss of lives, and thus more people could enhance the security of the settlements, and these elements are represented through achievement in war and the eligibility to erect the stones.[78] Therefore, the oral tradition of origins and settlement has remained a significant and persuade in the archaeological investigation. The incorporation of folklore to understand social relation and interaction of the past have been an important objective. Even though each village has its own account of origin and migration of their people, the familiar story among the Nagas of their origin and emergence from stone is one of their most unifying beliefs and traditions.

Socio-Political Structure of the Nagas

The Nagas are of mixed cultural origin. According to Smith,[79] there were no hierarchy in Naga society during the olden days. There were only different ethnic groups with varied styles of political and socio-economic organisations. The mode of production was subsistence-oriented and was based on a communal system of labour utilisation which was either voluntary or obligatory or both. Each tribe was a distinctive unit, generally managed by the tribe-elders or the chiefs.[80] The customary laws and traditions were the code of conduct.[81] A person's identity was inseparable from that of his family, clan, *khel* and village.[82]

Traditionally, the Naga villages were predominantly an autonomous structure. Village arrangements and architecture were different in each tribe; for instance, the Lotha built smaller and meandered-looking-dwelling houses, the Ao and Konyak built houses which was of bamboo and standing high off the ground on piles. It comprised of several wards or areas (known as *zong* among the Konyak), usually occupying a strategically favourable position. For security reasons, it was always safeguarded by ditches and bamboo barricades. Among the Konyak they assigned five to six men clan wise to guard the village *Morung* (dormitory) and to help the chiefs in doing his chores. Inter-village feuds were common and if any unfortunate circumstance appears then the villagers would have retaliated any dishonest act committed by any person or a culprit in seeking vengeance.

The Nagas strictly followed and practiced their customary tradition. Violation of the rule of incests was a severe social offence and the punishment for this among many tribes was expulsion or excommunicate of the couple from the village for life. Theft was always punished by exacting from the thief the value of the property stolen (among the Konyak-Wancho-Nocte), the fine being paid to the victim of the thief, whose possessions was also returned to him/her if recovered.[83]

We can refer from colonial records the general practice of slavery among the Nagas. The Eastern Nagas kidnapped slaves from Burma and Assam for human sacrifices if they needed to end epidemics (small-pox), drought, and famines in their village.[84] Among the Konyak, the slaves captured from plains and Burma were killed occasionally for rituals and as war trophies. Some Nagas often sold 'even their children and kinsmen into slavery' to repay their debts.[85] Early British records of slaves described them as an indeterminate number of 'broken men' and 'runaways' in the Naga hills, who were loosely defined as 'slaves'. The Konyak considered a big Burmese *gong* or *Lah* as equivalent to one 'broken man' for exchange. However, such a medium of exchange was not in plentiful supply as it involved costly items.[86] Often the Nagas sold off habitual thieves or criminals to adjoining tribal segments or the Ahoms, for they had no customs or moral sanction of executing their erstwhile kinsmen.[87]

It was the typical practice of the Konyak and Ao Nagas to give children into slavery for debts ranging from the value of a pig, or even less, to the value of six or seven cows. As recorded by Butler on the Naga slaves, a male slave was worth one cow and three conch shells, a female slave three cows and four or five conch shells.[88] Hornell also recorded that a male slave at that time was worth one cow and three conch shells, and a female slave much more valuable. A cow was valued at ten conch shells, a pig and a goat at two each; a fowl was worth only one packet of salt.[89] Based on British colonial, sources the Ahoms procured some slaves from the Ao, Lotha, and Konyak Nagas.[90]

Among the Aos slavery existed in the forms of an institution which in the domestic form prevails widely throughout the tribe. Some rich men are said to possess as many as 10 or 20 slaves. Slaves are not allowed to marry, nor to possess property, and children borne by female slaves are usually put to death.[91]

One of the notable features of Konyak society was that the Konyak women used to take part in war and slaying of enemy heads during the head hunting days. There were women warriors among the Konyak in the olden days that held a high social position. Besides, most of the *jhum* works (men only do cutting down of trees/clearing jungles) and trading were done by the women, the women in fact ran the household in the families.[92]

The geographical landscape of the Naga being one of hilly terrains intercepted by valley and rivulets; this natural configuration resulted in the formation of isolated villages having pockets of habitations at intervals with clan settlement life chained to clan consciousness and there by generated intra and inter-tribal conflicts and dispersed identities. The same is reflected in their relations with Ahoms as observed in the next chapter.

In the following pages we discuss the socio-economic and political structure of the Ao, Konyak and the Lotha in order to contextualise their relationship with the Ahoms. For this purpose, besides oral sources, information given by early colonial ethnographers and officials has been used as they provide the earliest written observations of their encounters and observations relating to the Naga. During the Ahom days, the Nagas were given a name based on the area they visited the plains. During the colonial period, Naga was termed under various names like Konyak, Phom, Wancho, Nocte, Tutsa, Tangsa, etc. Terms such as Eastern Nagas, Nagas of Sibsagar, Boree Nagas, Abori Nagas, Patkai Nagas etc., were also used by the British in their writings.

Role of Naga Chief in Naga-Ahom relations

The Lotha and the Konyak tribes have hereditary chiefs. Among the Konyaks and Lhotas the chiefs were called *Angh/wanghampa* and *pvuti*, and were given great respect and are considered sacrosanct.[93] The chiefs governed with the council of elders representing the clans. The Aos did not have a hereditary chief; they had a council of elders-comprised of members who represented the different clans in the village. The council used to be the traditional body of governance with effective authority to make and implement the decisions.

The central institution in the Naga village was the '*Morung*,' (dormitory for men). The *Morung* is a social institution of Naga social life and to keep their unity among the villagers. The Morungs are common among Ao, Lotha, Konyak, and the Phom tribes of Naga.[94] From the *Morung*, the chief or the council of village elders assigned up to eight groups of men from each *khel* or ward from the concerned villages accompanied by *Mehmei* (literally meaning in Konyak dialect village elders/councilors) to go down to valley kingdom bearing gifts from the hills to Ahom Raja and to collect gifts from the Ahom villages.[95] The Konyak chiefs or Ao village elders when going down to the plains during the festivals or to collect annual grants they would dress up in traditional warrior attire, which are colourful and vibrant, different from the commoners accompanying them, this attire showed their status to the people of plains.[96] Another example, at Jaboka (Konyak village), the cases of theft such as fighting in the valley market (i.e., Haatnu in Chairadeo district), stealing paddy rice from the plain while going to collect grants, the case was settled in the concerned village and the culprit had to be compensated with pig which is to be partaken by all the members of the council. When the quantity stolen is large, the offender has to pay a fine of one silk cloth as well as a pig. In the olden days, if a person stole articles from a chief's house, he was detained and sold to another village for one elephant tusk and a gong, or three gongs and sixty beads. Thus, the Konyak maintained their political life through the help of the village council of elders, for whom the people still retained respect, and obey its order and decision.[97]

Imparting value and practical education to the youth was undoubtedly a major achievement of the *Morung*. The *Morung* sought to maintain a set of rules and regulations and prevent outsiders from interfering in its administrations. The members understandably come within the pale of the village authority and are liable to punishments, as any other ordinary villages, for breach of any traditional or customary laws.[98]

Panger Imchen in his book records the story of Immandangba of Khari village, Mokokchung, district, Nagaland who went through ritualised tests of manhood, he writes:

> The *Ariju* life was a life of military discipline. The elders of the *Ariju* taught us war tactics, such as throwing at us with husking poles, 'six to seven feet long' while we stood hiding behind the bamboo made shield and tested our courage by giving us difficult tasks. They used to send us to the most strategic jungles at night to collect fruits, flowers and *daos* they left behind. They use to threaten us by telling on our way through the jungle we might be attacked by wild animals or evil spirits.[99]

It was in the dormitories that the Nagas learnt the knack to perceive and live with order in the chaos and follow the law in the freedom. In the *Ariju*, codes of conduct and protocol were highly systematised and carefully inculcated in the younger generations.[100]

(I) The Ao

The Ao comes under the generic term '*Naga*' and they represent one of the major tribes of Nagaland. The Ao Nagas are found from the Doyang River almost to the great bend of the Dikkoo (Dikhow) River as it emerges from hills into plains, occupying the three ranges of hill faces between the latter river and the Assam valley.[101] The area inhabited by Ao Naga covers an area of 733 square miles[102] bounded by Assam Valley to the north, the Lotha area to the west, the Konyak area to its east and Sema to the south. The Ao*'s* are divided into three main languages groups- the '*Chungli,*' the '*Changki,*' and the '*Mongsen.*'[103] Each group has its specific dialects, its own set of clans, and its own customs. All the ranges in Ao villages have a parallel variation in their customary laws, folklore, myths, legends, folktales etc. When the British entered Ao country, they found most of the Ao villages had an alternate name given to it by the Ahom, for instance, the name Merankong as Naogaon, Mopongchuket as Molodubia etc.[104]

The following Ao groups mentioned in the *Buranjis* were

1. Hatigurias with 6 villages
2. Assyringias with 6 villages and
3. Dupdorias with 12 villages

According to the Ao tradition, their ancestor emerged from '*Longterok*' literary meaning "six stones" which are now in Chungliyimti, occupied by the Sangtam tribe of Tuensang district. These stones were again categorised individually into males, namely *Longphok, Tongpok, and Longjakep* and, females, namely *Longkakpokla, Yongmenala, and Elongse*. The legend of Lungterok states that the first three men who emerged out of the earth belonged to three distinct clans which are (i) Pongener (ii) Longkumer and (iii) Jamir. Even today these three clans can always trace their blood- ties to one of these main clans. This resulted from the various stages of the people's migration and settlement in different villages. The people did not lose their bearing nor forgot their affinities and continued to conduct their lives in the new village settlements according to the principle which governs the clan divisions.[105]

The Aos stayed at Chungliyimti for four *Aso* (generation), and from this historic village, they migrated to the rest of their settlement area. From their first settlement at Chungliyimti they migrated westward, and after crossing the Dikhu River, they settled at a place called Aunglenden, where Soyum village (now called Ungma) was founded. Later they shifted to Koridong. From there they scattered all over the six ranges of the present Ao settled area, establishing as many as 107 villages. These people who went ahead across the Dikhu River, leaving others behind, came to be known as Aor or Ao meaning, 'going' or 'gone' or 'those who went over.'[106]

Village and topography played a significant role in the formation of Ao society. When the Ao decide to establish a new village, it was formed with a combination of clans, i.e., where marital unions were possible among the members. The early Ao forefather looked for areas which were pleasant with sufficient area for cultivation, having good water sources, ample space for all the people to live in and it should also be in a strategic location as to be safe from enemy's attacks. The preference for strategic location on a hillock offered defense against any attack during the headhunting days.[107] In addition to the landscape suitability, before establishing the new village, the advice of soothsayer was imperative. A chosen person representing many clans of the village would go first to inspect the site.[108] To determine the fertility of the soil before deciding to settle in an area, they would dig a hole in the earth, take the soil out and put the same soil back from where it was dug. If the soil which has been taken out does not fill up the hole again the site is considered to be barren. Only when the soil filled the hole after it was taken out and put back, and it is considered to be good and fertile for settlement. It was only when an area met with all these requirements; it was deemed as an ideal site to set up a village.

Ariju: The learning Institution

After a village was founded, first the area for the Morung or '*Arju*' (bachelor hall); and '*Sungkong*' (log drum) was selected as it served an integral part of the village, the areas for cultivation and the burial and ritual ceremonies place were selected for the entire villagers.The '*Arju*' (meaning *Ar*-enemy, *Ju*- clash/fight/meet, where one meets or make a plan to fight with the enemy), is always constructed near the village gate at the entrance of the village so that it will protect the village in the olden days from any enemy attacks. On each end of the village there are gates, which were built with wooden door hewn out of a single piece of wood, designed with carved circles. These days, gates do not have doors and are made of bricks and cement, with the usages of wood in some villages just for decoration. The village was surrounded by a belt of bamboo clump and light jungles so that it can provide woods and other requirements to the inhabitants.[109]

Morung (the bachelor's dormitory) occupied a central place in the lives of the Aos. At a time when village boundaries were not fixed, it depended largely upon the strength of the village concerned[110] and when there were bitter feuds between villages; Morung played a significant role in maintaining the honour of the village. They were the life and force of the village, an ill- kept Morung meant a weak village and a well-kept Morung signified a strong prosperous village. A village was often known by its Morung. Besides, the Morung was also an institution of learning custom, culture, and recreation, which had been transmitted from generation to generation through folk-dance, music, folk-tales, oral history, wood carving etc., which was taught in the *Ariju*.[111]

The *Ariju* was classified into six batches of groups called *Zunger* and in each batch one had to spend three years before being promoted to the next higher batch. The work of each batch involved fetching water, collect firewood, lighting fire, etc. As, J.P. Mills noted, "A Morung is a microcosm of the village and has its own council, reminding one strongly again of a public school with its prefects."[112]

Society and Polity

The Ao society was exogamous, intermarriage within the village required different clans, each village comprised of numerous exogamic clans, with each clans combining of several lineages. The village served as a natural unit of organisation, self-contained, self-productive. Like all other Naga tribes, the real political unit of the tribe was the village. An Ao village is decidedly organised into unit in which every man of the village renders his services to the village.

All the villages are governed by the *Putu menden* (*Putu*-generation, *Menden*-seat). It is the highest authority organised by the village councils of elders (*putu menden*). The *putu menden* was managed by a council, whose method of election and tenure of position varied in different role. The whole village was divided into age-groups according to which the various communal duties were assigned to them. There was nothing corresponding to a hereditary chieftainship among the Ao's.[113] The *putu menden* is represented by all the clans in the village for the social and political organisation. It has the power to regulate law and order; it acts as the decision-making and organisational power in the village for the welfare of its people. This system of council of elders was first established by the Ao forefather at *Chulingyimti*. The *Chungli* and *Mongsen* system of *putu menden* is different. The *Mongsen* village political system is called *Samen Menchen* (literally meaning in *Mongsen* Ao dialect meat seat- the meat share entitled to every clan) and the *Chungli* village political system is called *putu menden* (meaning in Chungli Ao dialect *Generation seat*).

Role of ornaments in Ao society

Ornaments and clothing identified the status of men in Ao society. The difference between rich and poor in the society was identified by the kind of clothes, pattern of design and ornaments he/she wore. The Ao ornaments are hereditary honours which are treasured by the clans before passing it to the next generation. The ornamentation usually in blue and red shades varied from group in group or phratry to phratry. The body cloth for women is usually simple white or dark piece of cloth bound tightly round the body under the armpits. Until she is a mother, a woman may not expose her body. "*Aomelepu*" is one of the most decorative body cloths worn during the occasion of festivals.[114] One of the Ao oral narratives relates to the right of wearing certain ornaments worn by certain Ao clans Naga and in this the judgement was said to been made by an Ahom Raja.[115]

> The Ao oral tradition narrates that a quarrel broke out between the Pongen and Longkumer clan on their right to wear armlets and how this issue was taken over to the Ahom Raja to settle the matter. Pongen clan was represented by Rosangba and Longkumer clan by Mangyanger. It was said that Mangyanger was smart, good-looking and a great traveller who had many friends everywhere. Therefore, he attempted to take advantage of Rosang baby persuading him to go to the plains and present their case before the Chuba (Chuba-King, Ahom Raja). The Raja after hearing their case put the two into a

series of tests. The first test was, they were made to sit on a log of wood, in which Mangyanger chose the top end and Rosangba sat at the bottom end. The second test was to choose between a cock and an egg, Mangyanger suddenly picked up the cock even before Rosangba could utter a word. The third test was to carry a bag of earth and a bag of salt; Mangyanger without waiting for Rosangba to choose took the bag of salt.

Finally, they were asked to choose two drinking cups, one of a beautifully designed red clay and other of a grey metal. Mangyanger quickly grabbed the red cup and Rosangba was left with the metal cup. Afterwards the Raja told them to throw their cups on the ground, Mangyanger's clay cup broke on the ground, whereas Rosangba's metal did not. The Ahom Raja in his judgement stated that Mangyanger chose the top of the tree, but Rosangba sat at the root, from which all trees grow. Mangyanger chose the cock, while Rosangba took the egg from which all fowls are hatched. Mangyanger took the salt which is washed away by water but Rosangba took the earth which cannot be washed away. Lastly, Mangyanger took the clay cup while Rosangba took the cup that could not break. Hence, the Raja pronounced that Rosangba made a better choice, and that he and his descendants shall be superior to Mangyanger's descendants. The final decision over the wearing of the ornaments was that both the clans were permitted to wear ivory armlets on both arms, however, the spike metal armlets called *merangkhambang*, and the grooved metal armlets *kurakhambang* was given to Rosangba by the Ahom Raja. Both of them were given right to wear a certain trumpet-shaped brass ear ornament (*khiru*), to the women of both the clans he gave the right to wear heavily embroidered *mekhela* and to adorn their heads with brass rings (*yongmen*).[116]

Land ownership among the Ao

When the Ao founded a new village, the founding leaders reserved the best fertile land for themselves, it is known as *yimkumli*. The festival of the Aos-*Maotsu* and *Tsungremong*, involved God's blessing on sowing and good harvest denotes the prominence of land. Thus, economy and land was tied up in the early Ao society. The village land and boundaries were guarded and any encroachments, stealing or disputes related to land was strictly dealt with, and the offenders were sometimes excommunicated for generations.

The Ao Nagas practiced shifting cultivation, and each clan was allowed to cultivate the area they were allotted with during the formation of the village. A different area was cultivated every year so as to retain the fertility of the soil. It was distributed according to seniority of the clan members. The Ao divided the land into three types within a village, i.e., common land, clan land, and individual land. The land is demarcated when a village is founded under the guidance of the council of elders- a common land which can be converted into village ground for social gathering, the site for village, *Ariju* or *Morung,* log drum etc. along with the adjoining forest areas nearby the village, these sites are shared land. Clan lands are those which are divided amongst the founding clans of the village for cultivation, collecting of woods and other domestic uses. Individual lands are acquired through inheritance, exchanges and fines from others. The land can be used by the family as they wish and the head of the family owns it, on his death, the eldest son inherits. If a man dies leaving with no male heir, his nearest relative shall inherit his land. Otherwise it shall become the clans land. The villagers are free to hunt, fish on all the lands within the village. However, an outsider trespassing or hunting at the village is dealt with the customs or order of the villages.[117]

Domesticated animals

Most of the domestic animals are the same amongst the various Naga Hill tribes. *Gayal* or *mithun* or *bosfrontalis,* were usually kept under semi- feral conditions for sacrificial purposes. A sizeable number of goats were kept both for food and for the sake of their hair, which was extensively used in making ornaments. Wild pigs were reared in all the villages. The pig hair was in demand in the foothills *hats*. All the Nagas generally bred Naga dogs of two types (one for eating and other for hunting), pigs, fowls, and occasional cats, for the purposes of food as well as for sale and barter.[118]

Leather work

Animal skins were usually skinned before cut up; scraped, soaked and sewn up to make bags or shields. After drying stiff; a waterproof bag was made out of the skin of a goat*'s* testicles. The skin was soaked and shrunk on to the bamboo case and the top edge is caulked with *Ficussap.*[119]

Metal works

An oral narrative of the Ao states that *daos* (machetes) and other metals were mainly brought from Maibong (16th century Kachari capital in the North Cachar Hills), and from the Ahoms. An oral narrative of Merankong village mentions about the Ahoms coming and staying in the area from whom they learned how to make *daos* (machete). Nokpu village oral narratives also refer to the Aos getting the *daos* from the Ahoms. J.P. Mills writes that around 1706 when Rudra Singha (Ahom Raja) attacked the Kacharis at Maibong or it may have been a generation earlier,[120] or during Mir Jumla's expedition against the Ahom king this must have greatly disturbed the population of the Ahoms. A huge number of people went up from the plains and built villages on the hills. Later these people departed to the valley, leaving behind four men who settled in Kulingmen (Ao village), from there they went to different Ao villages and even performed the *mithun* sacrifice. These people assimilated into the Ao clan and then their descendants became smiths of the Ao country. Some of the blacksmiths settled at the roadside of Dodhar Ali (*Assiring khat*), latter they were known as *Alimenyinsem* (literally meaning in Ao dialects, *Alimen*- road side, *Yinsem*-blacksmiths). Later villages like Ungma learned the art and started making it.[121] These groups became experts in producing earring and bangles made out of ivory, stones, quartz and wood.[122]

Blades for axes, hoes, and sickles, articles were usually made by the Aos, and pipes of thick tin or sheet brass obtained from the plains were made at Chungtia village. Bracelets, women's head rings and heavy neck rings were cast from broken brass. The Ao man did not consider himself well-off unless he carried a spear ornamented with red goat hair. The daos were brought in for sale by men from Eastern Konyak and Phom villages for which they were famous. However, Phom and Konyak were less skilled in weaving complex patterns and designs and usually bartered their metals for a large number of cloths from Ao villages on the Langbangkong ranges.[123]

Basketry

All the Ao's made baskets and mats; this task was reserved exclusively for men and boys. Women were prohibited from making baskets. A temporary/rough basket was made of bamboos, while those for permanent use were usually made of cane. In the olden days, the only instrument used in basket making was a spike (*yipro/yipra* in Ao dialects) of cow, dog or monkey bone.[124] In carpentry, the Ao's possessed considerable skill and their wood carving particularly those of Changki group are as good as those of Konyak's. They were also good in cane and bamboo work.

Economic Resources

Ao's grew cotton in large quantity, and they exchanged with the Ahoms for salt, metal, iron, and later they introduced a metal currency called *Jabilis*.[125] Besides cotton, cane, honey a number of elephants were bartered by the Aos with the Ahoms for salt, dried fish, iron implements, tobacco. There was no salt well in the Ao region, so they had to barter it from Brahmaputra valley kingdom. The earthen pots were made at Changki, Chapvu, and Nancha, and sold in the plains.[126]

The Konyaks

The Konyaks (these include the Noctes and Wanchos), inhabiting the present areas of Mon district and Tirap and Changlang District in Arunachal Pradesh, a represent as one of the largest tribes in Nagaland. The district of Mon, where they reside, covers an area of 1786 sq. km, bounded on the north by the Sibsagar district of Assam, on the south by Tuensang district of Nagaland and Myanmar, on the east by Myanmar and on the west by the Ao*'s*. To the northeast lies the Tirap and Changlang district of Arunachal Pradesh. Mon is located between 26°45'N- 95°06'E and 26.75°N-95.1°E and has an average elevation of 655 meters. The Mon district except for foothills which are hilly with steep slopes, consisted of low-lying areas with undulating hills that characterise the home of the Konyak Nagas.[127]

The colonial ethnographers described the Konyaks as comprised of two groups- the '*thendu*' and the '*thenko,'*[128] The division was based on facial tattoos- the '*thendu*' group tattooed their faces. In contrast, the '*thenko*' group did not. This division roughly corresponds to today*'s* geographical division in the Mon district as Lower Konyak (mostly *thendu* meaning with tattoos on their faces) and Upper Konyak (mostly *thenko* meaning without tattoos on their face).[129] The Konyak-Wancho mainly dwell in the Northern region of present Nagaland. Today they are called Lower Konyak Naga, but the ones who inhabiting Tirap, Changlang, and Longding districts of Arunachal Pradesh are presently known as Wancho, Tangsa, Tutsa, and Nocte. Some Wancho Naga also dwell in Myanmar across the Patkai[130] mountain range of the north-western part of Saigaing provinces, Myanmar. During the Ahom days, the Nagas were given a name based on the area they visited the plains. These tribes were known by their clan names such as Namsangia, Banfera, Jabukas etc., during the pre-colonial period.[131]

The formal contact of the British with the Konyaks occurred around the end of the nineteenth century. As early as 1889, Tamlu, a village lying close to Ao and Phom area and towards Assam was taken over, along with a few other villages lying west of the Dikhu River, under the British administration.[132] A few decades earlier, Captain Vetch (in his tour diary dated 18 June 1842) toured around some prominent villages canvassing British over-lordship and has given an account of the

Konyak.[133] The Patkai hills in the south of Wancho area inhabit the tail end of Tirap District in Arunachal Pradesh, the area between Longding and Pongchau. Pongchau is just a few kilometres from the Burmese (present Myanmar) border. A network of rivers and stream drain the hillsides.[134] The offshoot of Konyak is now at Arunachal Pradesh and bifurcated into three districts- Changlang, Longding and Tirap district. The Tirap, Changlang, Londing district of present Arunachal Pradesh was a part of Eastern Naga Hills during British rule in India.

The whole group may be divided into two- Tangjan and Changjanon based on their migration. The Nocte, Wancho, and Lower Konyak are linguistically and culturally related. The area from Pongchau upto Nginu, Longkai and Wakka is occupied by Tangjans, and from Niausa to the border of Assam by the Changjans. The Wanchos occupy the western part beyond the Tista River in the erstwhile Tirap district. The Wancho predominantly inhabited in the areas of Kanubari, Pongchau, and Wakka circles of Longding district.[135] The Ahoms called this group of Konyak by different names such as:

1. Tablungias with 13 villages (now Wanching)
2. Jaktoongias with 8 villages (now Wakching)
3. Sangloias with 8 villages
4. Moolongs with 5 villages
5. Jabukas with 4 villages (now Yansa)
6. Banferas with 4 villages (now Yansa and Wancho)
7. Mutonsor with 4 villages
8. Bordwarias with 8 villages (now Nocte and Tutsa in Arunachal Pradesh)
9. Namsangias with 8 villages (now in Arunachal Pradesh)
10. Kolongs or Mutons with 4 villages.
11. Borgaon (now Pongkung)
12. Naugaon (now Oting)
13. Kailong (now Longkai)
14. Lakma (now Wangla)
15. Munigaon (now Lunglam).[136]

The Konyaks were called Taprongumi or Minyumo-Nagami by the Semas, Miri by the Aos and Chagk by the Changs.[137] At present about,

80% of the Wanchos are in Arunachal Pradesh, 12% as Lower Konyak in Mon areas of Nagaland and 8% in Burma of Saigaing provinces.[138]

Structure of Konyak Society and Economy

The Konyak society is divided into four social divisions: The *wangham*, *wangsa* (are considered to be the highest position), and *wangpen* and *wangsu* (commoner). There are many clans among the Konyaks, which are *wangnao*, Munham, *wangsu*, Hentokhu, Yanlam, Beham, Lwang, Longnok, etc. The members of clan were consanguineous kin. Bonds of loyalty and joint responsibility among the members of a clan are strong. Cooperation between the clan members also extended to the economic activities. A man building his house would get free voluntary labour from his clan's men. All individual considers themselves as equal to each other and *wangham/wangpa* (chief) were also treated in the same spirit. And in each group, they have *Paa,* which was headed by one member from *wangham* (chief) family. Preferably *wangham* sons are put in different *Paa* to give each of them a scope to get an experience of organising the villagers and also to have an idea to take care of his people.[139] The *Paa* and chiefs' houses are decorated with carvings of animals, birds, fishes and human which are associated with symbols of fertility.[140]

Only from the marriage of a great *Angh/Wangham* (chief) and a woman of great *Angh/Wangham* rank sprang sons entitled to succeed to their father's position. Ideally, they have to marry a man of the *wangham* (chief's) clan from other villages, who are unrelated to them. However, if an equal status spouse is not found, they are allowed to marry a man of *wangsa* clan from another village, as they believe she only inherits the sacred noble blood.

The children born of a *wangham* father and a *wangpen* mother are known as *wangsa*. Therefore, *wangsu* is the descendants of a *wangsa* father and *wangpen* mother. Regarding social hierarchy, the *wangham* occupy the top position, the *wangsa* occupy the second position and the *wangsu*. The *wangpen* group is considered the lowest in the hierarchy. As customary, a Konyak chief is entitled to take concubines from the commoner clans. The concubine's children's further give rise to two intermediate classes-*wangsa* and *wangsu*, however, they will not be eligible to inherit any property from their father. There is a hierarchical division of clan, and the most striking disparity between these clans is that the chiefly clan, as well as intermediate clan, keep their hair long. In contrast, all the commoner women, even those married to a paramount chief, have their heads shaved or hair closely cropped.

Among the *wangham* or chiefs' (i.e., Konyak-Wancho-Nocte) the process of redistribution, dependency and compulsory labour is common. The *wangham* also exercises autocratic power over the life of his subjects; and serves as the upholder of morals and customs of his people, with the help of a council of elders from each clan. Dormitories of the Konyak can be classified into two broad categories; one is made for the males, i.e., *paa* and another is made for females, i.e. *Ywo* (female dormitory). There are divisions of *paa* and *Ywo* based on the number of houses for easy management of intra- village activities. Each '*zongkam*'[141] (wards) has a *paa* and are controlled by the junior chief, under the *wanghampa* (deputy chief) of the village. The bigger village will have many '*zongkam*' (wards). For instance, Yansa village has eighteen wards. The population of each of these wards was divided between several clans of varying status.[142]

Agriculture was a prominent occupation for the Konyak society right from the early days.[143] C.V. Haimendorf remarked:

> The young people, at any rate, join groups and cultivate each other's fields in rotation. Even the small boys and girls are organised in groups, and all over the fields you can hear the songs and shout with which they accompany the work.[144]

The Konyaks practiced the jhum method of cultivation. They cultivated little rice; they grew varieties of crops and plants such as rice, millet, jobs tear, yam, sweet potato, ginger, garden- bugs, chillies, cotton, etc. After three years of cultivation, the field would be abandoned for about seven to ten years, apart from other factors (topography factor) which motivated the Konyak to practice jhuming. Throughout the headhunting days, it was always safer to cultivate in the same close area. At first, the *wangham* (chief) fields were cleared, and the entire village offered communal service to help the chief in clearing of jungles, construction of field huts. After each family completes the construction of their hut, the whole village builds the *wangham* house's which has ample cleared space in front of it. The clear spaced space was the village assembly spot, and it was here that one could see the sacrificial posts with heads taken in raids speared on to the posts. Opposite each house was a place of duty on which heads of all animals sacrificed, either on festivals or in cases of illness were tied. The Konyaks cultivated their own *kobar/ pai* (literally meaning cotton in Konyak-Wancho-Nocte dialects), and often sold in the foothills haat to supplement their economy; their chief stable crop is *yam* or *taro* (*kotchu* in Nagamese dialect).[145]

Besides, crop production, they also supplement their livelihood by rearing pig, mithun, goats, fowl, dogs, etc., and also had a custom of individual/community hunting and fishing. The *dao*, (spade) is generally used for cultivation, spear, a cross-bow, the arrows often poisoned with aconite were used for hunting animals.[146]

Domesticated Animals

R.G. Woodthorpe opined, 'The Nagas generally breed pig, goat, dogs, fowl, *mithun* for sale as well as for consumption.[147] The Konyaks domesticated cattle such as *mithun* and pigs, which were slaughtered for different important purposes. The Konyaks domesticated dogs for food, to keep a vigil at night and for *meijangkui* (hunting dogs), which they usually took along when they go for animal hunting.[148] In all the houses a herd of black pig were domesticated to consume during festivals, because a ceremonial feast without dishes of pork was quite unthinkable.

For the Konyak society, *mithun* were precious and valued animals, which were recognised as a medium of exchange. Besides, bride price, ransoms and fines were usually paid in *mithun*. No animal was considered worthy of sacrifice other than *mithun* for the chieftainship coronation ceremony. Though it can hardly be called a fully domesticated animal during the pre-colonial and early colonial era, it constituted the most valuable animal in the sense that *mithun* symbolised prestige, and power and for its economic and socio-religious activities revolved round it. While slaughtering of the *mithun* for feasts, a piece of cloth was tied round its eyes and the village priest who performed the ritual will have to ask for forgiveness for taking its life. Theft of *mithun* was seriously dealt with consequence, for instance the entire village united against the offender and his village, and they imposed repayment. The village most valuable items, i.e., biggest Burmese gongs (*Nyamnyu* in Konyak dialect) were oblige as compensation to the victim's village. It was just to convey the message to the villagers of the consequences of stealing the *mithun*. *Mithun* served as the negotiated settlement price when relating to inter-villages feuds and and elephants served as the political dispute settlement with the Ahoms.[149]

Crafts

J.H. Hutton remarked, 'Konyaks are great potters'.[150] Only women were allowed to do the pottery works. The pots were used for different purposes such as cooking, rice beer container, water reservoirs, storage of food grains in pots, storing ornaments etc. The Konyak also stored the skull in the pots, the skull pots were made of sandstone and intricate designs and marks were carved on them. With cane and bamboo, the

Konyak manufactured sleeping mats, baskets, etc. These were made to barter in the plain markets and for carrying stocks to the *haat*. Besides, small articles of personal adornment such as headgears, calf-lets, leg-lets, certain types of necklaces, small baskets to keep opium, betelnut, etc., were also made.

Konyaks were expert in blacksmithy, they were the first to make gun among the Nagas, the reputation of the Konyak blacksmith was known even in the plains of Assam.[151] During the early days Konyak blacksmith were also encouraged to manufacture various ornaments, such as brass replica of human head taken, headgear, bangles for women, earring. The ornaments had lot of significant identification and its role in the society. They also manufactured certain implements and tools like, dao, axe, hoe, scrapper, sickle and weapons like spear head, arrow head and musket. The extraction of salt and iron was largely in the hands of Eastern Nagas (Konyak-Wancho-Nocte-Tutsa).[152] Iron was found in plenty at the Upper and Lower Tiru and Yonhon which enabled the Konyaks to trade with the Ahoms.[153]

The Konyaks learnt the art of manufacturing muskets even before the arrival of Ahoms in the Brahmaputra valley; they turned iron in the form of narrow bore pipes into fairly serviceable muzzle loaders.[154] They called it *yanthow* (muskets) and for *khaat* (gun powder) and was used to protect and defend the villages from the wild animals and enemy attack.[155]

Community hunting and fishing

Hunting and fishing played a significant role for the Konyak society. Hunting was generally resorted to when they were free from their engagements in the cultivation of their fields. The *paa* (*morung*) which encompass several clans and households organised a community hunting. On that particular day, everyone was exempted from other duties, and everyone was expected to attend the *paa*. While the energetic young men went out for hunting, the older and children spend the day waiting for them by singing folk songs and fetching water and lightening up the *morung* to warm. Traditionally spears, bows and arrows, gun and various trapping methods were used as weapons The hunting strategy depended on the seasons, the location of the seasonal fruits and berries, and the species being hunted. Big animals like elephants, leopards, tiger, wild pigs, wild buffaloes, wild fowls, deer, bear, stags, porcupines, foxes, etc., and birds of all sizes was hunted.[156]

There are four types of community hunting firstly, during the coronations of chieftainship, secondly, marriages of chief's, thirdly, community feast (annually), and fourthly, to protect the crops, cattle and family's members from wild predators. The meat collected after the hunting was divided among all the *zongkam* (members of the *paa*), from oldest to youngest members. Lastly the heads of the animals and the bird's features were taken to *paa* for displaying their glory of hunting.[157]

Community fishing was also organised annually by the Konyak society, they make temporary shed at the banks of the river, then used poison leaves and fruits to intoxicate the fish, which they called as *zooh* and *taan*, for catching and trapping the fish. The fish collected by women can be kept for themselves; the fish caught by menfolk were gathered and from all the collected fish, the biggest one will be given to *wangham* (chiefs), followed by the village elder's who will get the biggest share.[158]

Deer and elephant were fairly plentiful in the Konyak areas, and there were large number of tiger or leopard found in the Dikhu valley of Konyak regions. Elephant hunting was common among the Konyak.[159] Often the clashes with the Ahoms happened because the Ahoms would trespass to the hills and hunt elephants without taking permission from the Konyak chief.[160] The Ahom would caught elephants from the Naga hills for their supply of ivory and sale in the markets at the Bengal market. Additionally, it was an imperative role for the Ahom army; the elephants were used for transportation, clearing jungles at remote areas and as a friend during their hunting expedition. For the Konyaks hunting of elephant was a means for survival during the times of famine and a source of mens' pride. The collection of skulls of the elephants, enemy, bear, tigers, wild pigs, boar, *mithun* was preserved at the chiefs' house as their important prize trophies.[161] Elephant, thus, was a very useful animal for the Ahom, Nagas, and even under the British India government.

Saline/Brine Water

The salt well referred as *Sum/Hum phong* were distributed in the Eastern Naga Hills, now located in erstwhile districts of Tirap and Changlang, in Arunachal Pradesh and Mon in Nagaland. Miles Bronson, the first Christian missionary to set his foot in the Naga hills and who had the opportunity of seeing a salt-well at Namsangia in operation gives the following vivid description of salt-making by the Nagas.

> ...at 10'clock reached one of the salt-springs worked by the Nagas. The water drawn from deep wells, by bucket of leaves, and poured into large wooden brought nearby, for the purpose of boiling. Their mode of boiling is rude, and to one who had not seen it, would appear to be perfectly impracticable. They build a long arch of stone

and clay. On the top, single joints of bamboos, cut thin, and spread open like a boat, are placed closely together. These hold from two to three quarts each. These boats are kept full of brine, and a large fire kept blazing under them, without injury to the bamboo. On this arch, I counted sixty boats, which they said would give, when boiled away, twenty or twenty- five boats of salt for the market. Thus, their ingenuity has made them quite independent of the expensive furniture required at our own salt-works. One man to attend to arch, one to bring the brine, and four to gather wood, are all that is necessary to complete the establishment.[162]

The brines were concentrated in and around the following areas now located in Arunachal Pradesh -Borduria, Tangsa, Khonsa, Namsang, Kalagaon, Yangkang, Tutnu, Nuauni, and several Wancho villages of Longding, Changlang, Pongchau, Wakka, and Laju circle and in several lower Konyak villages such as Yansa, Shangnu of Mon district in Nagaland.[163]

The Lothas

Called Lothas by other Naga and '*Mikhai*' by the Assamese[164] the Lothas are known as *Kyón* (meaning 'man'). The area inhabited by them is situated in the mid-west of Nagaland and adjoins the Jorhat and Golaghat sub-divisions of Sibsagar on the west, Mokokchung on the north, Zunheboto in the east and Kohima in the south. The Wokha district is intercepted at the heart by latitude 26° 8'N and longitude 94° 18'E.[165] It has an area of 1,628 square kilometres. The total population according to the 1981 census was 57,583 and the density of population per square kilometres is 35.[166] The Lotha area has three ranges which are known as Upper, Middle and Lower Ranges running almost parallel to each other, Doyang and Pangti Rivers dividing them. The Doyang (also known as *pofu*) originated in the Mao area and it flows into Dhansari River which further drains into the Brahmaputra River. The Lothas from the olden days carried on a barter trade with the Brahmaputra valley people mainly because of its adjoining the plains of Assam. The name given by the Ahom to Lothas Nagas were:

1. Panihatias consisting of ten villages
2. Torbatias and Doyangias with eleven villages.

Wokha, Sanis, Lakuti, Phiro, Saki, Lotsu, Yikhum, Longsa, Mangia, Pangti, Chedi and Kioyo were some important villages of the Lothas.[167]

The Lotha village was established after a proper survey by the founders of village elders which took into consideration the source of water near the village and strategic location in case of enemy attack. After picking a suitable place for the new village, they returned to their old village and checked the omen by interpreting the dream they saw that night. If the dream is good, they go to the selected site and the *pvüti* (village priest) will perform rituals. The enthusiasm of new village was done with the killing of human head (slave bought to cleanse the village). Similar traditions were followed to dedicate morung. If they failed to kill/buy a slave, the blood of *mithun* or dog was spread across the road of the village. After sacrificial of human for village dedication the entire villagers stayed inside the village for three days observing the taboos of village inauguration.

The Lotha village is divided into a number of *kithang* or *yankho* (i.e., colonies), each *kithang* consists of members from the same clan though in some villages it is a mixture of different clans. The political affairs and protection of the village was looked after by the *Tongti Chochang* while the religious affairs were looked after by the *pvuti*. The villages are crowded with pigs, dogs and cattle. The villagers planted several *erhingya* trees which they used to poison fish during the annually community fishing day.

Bundles of salt wrapped in leaves, cooking pots and spoons, baskets of yeast, traps, carrying baskets, etc., were kept over the fire, in a bamboo platform about five feet square. For cooking rice and meat all the Nagas made earthen pots which are used for heating '*madhu*' or rice beer.

Economic Resources

The main sources of livelihood of Lothas Nagas were rice and they grew varieties of crops besides rice, such as maize (*Tsunghundhro*), yam, millet (*Teni*), giant millet (*lichohuk*), chillies (*machi*) and cotton (*khungo*). These crops were grown alongside rice in the jhum field. The jhum or shifting cultivation remained the mainstay of the majority of Lotha villages. The tools used by the Lothas for cultivating were, spade, daos, axe, sickles, scraper, hoe, etc., these were obtained from the plains of Assam in exchange for cotton and other forest products. Lotha women like other Naga women played a major role in economic activities such as, agriculture, household chores, weaving, making clothes for the family and carrying firewood, fetching water, looking after the children. When not engaged in warfare, men did their part of clearing the jungle, felling trees, and preparing the ground for sowing by burning it, hunting games, they often accompanied women to the field not to work but to keep vigil. Lotha women like other Naga women made more contribution to the economy than the men in the pre-colonial economy of the Nagas. Naga society being patriarchal, though she had customary rights in certain areas, it did not make her equal as man.[168]

Lothas and Aos were known to export hill cotton into the plains, the tradition of Nagas bringing down-hill cotton to plains market were mentioned in many of the British official's expedition records on the Naga Hills. For instance, 1 kg of cotton was bartered for 5 *shorota* (literally meaning 5 kg salt in Lotha dialect), 1 kg black sesame was bartered for 3 *shorota* (3 kg salt) etc.[169]

Terrace cultivation was also practiced in the low lying areas. The Lothas learned wet rice cultivation from the Ahoms; the foothill Lotha areas like Merapani, Doyang valley, and Pangti valley were the first to practice wet rice cultivation. No other crops were grown besides paddy, and cultivation was usually carried out twice in a year and its yield was more than *jhum*. They took three meals in a day, once in the morning, at afternoon and in the evening. *Soko* (rice beer) was a popular drink; it was drunk during the special occasions like marriage, festival, and head- hunting feasts. Their diet included domesticated as well as wild birds and animals, fish, honey, wild worms and insects, dry fish, bamboo shoots (both wet and dry), vegetables and fruits.

The Lothas tamed animals for both meat and sacrifices and they also had certain tabooed food items. For instance, when a *mithun* calf is born the owner observes six days' "*genna*," during those days no stranger from another village can enter his house and he must not eat meat that was killed by tigers, or if a man cut off the tiger's head, he must not eat beef, pork, goat's flesh, jungle birds, *taro* (yam) etc. They believe that the consumption of the tabooed meats will bring bad luck to the eater and the belief is adhered to upto this day.[170] Most treasured animals for the Lothas were *mithun* and white goats (*nyanya*) with long hair which they reared in large numbers; the long hair is dyed red and sold it. The dyed goat's hair is used for all kinds of ornaments; *mithun* was also used as a medium of exchange.[171] Two types of dogs were reared, one is used for hunting and the other for consumption, the hunting dogs are never consumed, and when one dies it is wrapped in a cloth and given a decent burial outside the village. Wild pig (literally meaning *oni* or *lipung* in Lotha dialects), porcupines (*liso*), are occasionally hunted with hunting dogs.[172]

Manufactures and craft

Every Lotha women wove and was expected to weave the cloths of her husband and families. The Lothas reared cotton in large quantities like the Ao and Rengma, and they were known for high quality method of dyeing. They also reared silk-worm on the mulberry. Cotton was taken down to the plains of Assam to exchange for salt, agricultural implements, etc. In the pre-colonial period trade was usually carried on by barter system.[173] The Lothas also used *Jabilis/Chabilis*, similar to the one used by the Aos, however, it was limited in circulation. Among the Ao's and Lothas, one *Jabili* was equivalent to a day's work or 4 *annas*.[174]

For dyeing the clothes, they used three colours, red, dark blue and light blue for dyeing. Only women performed the dyeing, when they do the work, they must refrain from sexual intercourse, must not eat beef, goat's flesh, dog's meat, dried fish, fermented soya bean and stinking dal (*nyingtyingtsing*). Often red thread is bought either from the foothills *haat* or from an Ao village, because red dyeing is considered a risky occupation and likely to bring on dysentery and henceforth, the old women usually do this work, as they believed the old people will not have much contribution to the community. The root of *Rubiasikkimensis* (*karung*) and *ntawo* (leaf) is used to make the red dye. Dark blue dye is made from leaf of *Strobilanthes flaccidi-folius* (*tchemo*), this work was mainly carried only on a few Lothas villages such as Changsu and Okotso.[175]

For making light blue, the leaves which have been previously boiled are recycled for making dark blue dye, drained and dried, kept for a year. These are split into pieces and mixed with cold water and the white ash of burnt bark and left for a day or two. The thread is put in and allowed to soak for a day or two if the dye is not strong and then taken out and dried it.[176] After every migration search for food and shelter was the first priority once the Lothas began to live a settled life, they began to cultivate cotton plants.[177]

Pottery

Pottery making is one of the oldest traditions practiced by the Lothas. The Lothas made most of their own pots; the clay is obtained from the banks of small stream. Only women made the pots, they used two kinds of mud, grey (*linyikcho*) and red (*linyocho*), among these two the quality of grey is best, pots are made by hand without the use of a wheel or sometimes with the help of simple tools. Wares of different sizes and shapes are made. While making pots, she must refrain from eating food with strong smell and must not catch pigs or fowls. It was a belief if she does so, the pots will not be in proper shape and the pots will crack.

The occupation of blacksmith was considered as unfortunate, and it was constrained to certain family members. The Lothas believed that no blacksmith lived long after he stopped working, therefore only a few chose this profession. Besides, the foothill Lothas village bought their entire requirement from the foothill *hat*, or either from Rengmas reputed as great blacksmiths who supplied all the weapons and implements required by the Southern Lothas and Northern Lothas in a similar way depended on the Ao villages as well.[178]

Every man made his own household baskets, helmet (*kiven*), cane helmets, grain baskets, shields (*otsung*), cane seat, mat for sleeping and drying rice, etc., Women are not permissible to do any kinds of basket-work. *Vepvü* (meaning cane in Lotha dialect) is the most valuable item and was reserved only for articles which will last long. The baskets were required for the transport and storage of most of the material necessities even today in all the Naga villages. Any men setting out for work would carry appropriate types of baskets in which had to carry their things and tools. The baskets made of bamboo are used for heavy stuff like firewood, yam, to transport vegetables and forest products to barter in the plains *hat*. The baskets made of cane are used for carrying grains, shield (*otssüng*), valuable things and so on. The Lothas are experts in basket making, they sold varieties of baskets made of cane and bamboo to the foothill *haats* for rice, salt, utensil etc. Daos, knives were the tools used for making baskets. Fresh bamboos are used for rough baskets; each household produces the baskets and mats required, except for difficult ones which are left in the hands of the experts. The different kinds of baskets, the *okhyak* (a traditional basket) of the Lothas, which is big and v-shaped and it is used to carry grains. *Khungro* is an open square basket, used for carrying firewood; baskets are made either to stand in the house or to carry at the back and used for different purposes. *Loksa* (big size basket), was always kept in the Lotha households, the basket is used for keeping various articles, especially clothing's, *morow* (meaning flat or broad basket in Lotha dialect) for cleaning grains.

Bamboo and cane are two essential resources for the Lothas and it has a very significant place in the village economy and to many means of subsistence. Besides, bamboo is used in house construction, fencing, firewood, barricades, dried bamboo is burned as fuel, torches at night, young bamboo shoots for eating, bamboo pickles etc.

The Lothas were fond of carving wood works, in each household wooden shields are made, the posts of 'morungs' (*champo*) are carved with certain animals like hornbills, elephant, *mithun* head, tiger, monkey which embodied spirit of beliefs and luck. The work is done simple with dao. The Lothas sold *mithun*, ivory armlets and boar's tusk. They have faith that these articles are particularly liable to be infected with evil fortune, and it is considered as unlucky articles. Only an old man is hired as an intermediary (*lantse* or *thantsowe*), for the bargaining and settlement of the price. Any ill luck was believed to attach itself to him as nominal buyer, rather than to the real buyer, who paid him a commission of Re. 1 for a *mithun*, eight annas for ivory armlets, and four annas for a pairs of boar's tusks. If anything is closely associated with the person, such as a cloth or a dao be sold the seller retains a thread from the cloth or scrapes a tiny shaving off the handle of the dao, for were he to sell the whole of something which was almost part of himself the buyer might be able to exercise some magical influence over him[179] Most of the indigenous beads of the Nagas are little black beads (*eshe*), made of a species of wild plantain (*sheyu*) seeds, these beads are common among the Southern Lothas. The beads are used for necklaces.[180] Ornaments were usually made of metals, cowries, shell, wood, feathers and cane.

Land ownership

Traditionally land is the biggest asset of the Lothas villagers. Individual land ownership was common and community land owned by the clan was called *Motsüra*. Land ownership is hereditary from father to sons. In the Lotha custom, the youngest son gets the lion's share of the family's inheritance. If there are no sons and only female child in a family, then the inheritance would go the next male kin.[181] Marriage takes place between the different clans, intra clan marriage is not permissible as they are considered as incest. In some village marriage between certain clans are not legitimate because they live together as one family in that particular village. When a son reaches a marriageable age, the family looks out for a suitable girl and when they come across one, they make inquiries about the girls and her family. If they are satisfied, either the mother of the boy or the aunties go to the girl's house and if there is a positive response from the girl's side then the boy's family formally seeks for the girl's hand in marriage. Then engagement takes places, the boy and his family take rice beer to the girl's house after that the boy with the help of his age group collects firewood and keeps it outside the door of the girl's house to indicate that the girl is already engaged. For one whole year the boy works for the girl's family with his age group (*yingaten*) in the field.

Land was also allowed for cultivation to those people who were affected by famines or other natural calamities. Land boundaries amongst neigbouring villages was demarcated by river and huge trees, within village individual cultivated field and boundary was marked by lake, stone and the nature of field location.

Rice was the staple food of the Lothas, the dominant method of cultivation was 'jhuming.'The land is cultivated for two years, where they planted varieties of crops such as, rice, maize, millet, chillies, sweet potatoes, ginger, pumpkins, cotton, yam, etc. It was then allowed to lie fallow for about 10 to 15 years untill the soil regains its fertility.

Fishing

J.P. Mills noted that "Lothas are keen fishermen and expert swimmer; fishing rights over any particular stretch of water were governed by custom, being held by the village or villages who exercised them in the past." The Lothas practised community fishing and each village have the right to erect weirs in particular stretch to demarcate the water. The Lotha used *notsü* (root of a small plant) to poison the fishes. There were many ceremonial hunting and fishing expeditions. The expeditions being pre-planned, elaborate arrangements were made in advance as regards the distribution of work and other allied matters. The shares are distributed in accordance with the age and rank of the fishers or hunters.[182] There is a saying that fishes of hill-streams although smaller in size, however, it is considered to be tastier than those available from the plain *hat* market. Lothas caught fishes from the banks of Doyang river, dried and transacted on a small commercial basis.[183]

Summary

From the above it may surmised that the socio-economy and polity of the three major Naga tribes were relatively less stratified, depended on jhum cultivation, forest resources and undeveloped in terms of state formation as compared to the valley which was under the Ahom. The Ahom state in its developed form has been characterised as quasi-feudal and semi tribal.[184] In conventional historiography of the Ahoms the period of the eighteenth century has been depicted as the peak of its prosperity while for others the same period represented a period of crises.[185] The success of the state formation process under the Ahom has been attributed to the success of extension of wet rice cultivation, the systematisation of labour through the organisation of the *paik* system and its successful working. The emergence and growth of the neo-vaishnavite movement from the fifteenth century onwards, contact with the Mughals and weakening of the *paik* system and the outbreak of the Moamaria Rebellion have been seen as signs of weakening of the Ahom state.[186]

Hemmed in on all sides by the warlike hill tribes the Ahoms had to evolve a policy to maintain and strengthen their power and dominance in the region. The Ahoms as part of the larger Tai speaking people in southeast Asia and known as Shans in Upper Burma[187] carried on their cultural legacy of wet rice cultivation and polity formation to the Brahmaputra Valley which with suitable adaptations from the pan-Indian Brahmanical influences contributed to their state formation process.[188] By the 17th century the Ahoms had emerged as a stable and powerful kingdom with a stable ruling class, contributing to the consolidation of the concept of Assam, borrowing literary, cultural, linguistic, social, political and economic aspects from both Brahmanical and the tribe's cultures in the process of their state formation in medieval Assam.

Due to the geo-political, ecological and economic factors relations with the hill tribes including Nagas emerged to be of importance to the Ahoms. The Ahom rulers understood the situation of their valley kingdom being surrounded by hill tribes and they had to take measures in order to uphold stability in the region. For the hill tribes, to continue their way of life also required on their part to evolve tactics of survival and independence from being subjugated by the Ahom kingdom. The foothill Nagas bordering the plains were in regular contact through the foothill *haat.* The Nagas would offer hill products like cotton, betel leaves, craft product, forests resources, ginger, herbs, broom, salt etc., and in exchange take goods that were scarce in the hills. The self-sufficiency of the hill tribes was not absolute as they were dependent on the plains for scarce and prestige items. The Ahoms also sought to exercise their power to obtain a share of the resources generated from the hills such as salt, elephants, elephant ivory, cotton, honey, medicinal herbs etc. Furthermore, the Naga raids in the plains, the abduction and kidnapping of the Ahom subjects prompted the latter to send repeated expedition into the Naga hills.[189]

Notes

1. The *Buranjis* are one of the important corpuses of information on the Ahom history. Some of the popular *Buranjis* include Golap Chandra Barua (ed.), *Ahom Buranji from the Earliest Times To The End of Ahom Rule,* Spectrum Publication House, Guwahati, 1985;S.K. Bhuyan, (ed.), *Deodhai Assam Buranji*, Department of Historical and Antiquarian Studies, Guwahati, 1988; S.K. Bhuyan, (ed.), *Satsari Asam Buranji,* Guwahati University, Assam, 1960, (Reprint 1974); Assam Buranji, (Tr.) *A Chronicle Describing The Events of The Period From Suhungmung To Gadadhar Singha (1681- 1696*), No. 7, Vol. Pt.VII, DHAS, Guwahati; S.K. Bhuyan (ed.), *Tungkhungia Buranji,* 1681-1826 A.D. Oxford University Press, 1933.

2. At present in Arunachal Pradesh and Nagaland. The term Naga appears to be derived from *Noga* from root *nog* meaning 'folk' or people which were first given by the Ahoms while referring to a conglomerate group of tribes residing in the Patkai area and the hills bordering the erstwhile Sibsagar district of Assam. Refer to Edward Gait, *A History of Assam*, Lawyer's Book Stall, Gauhati, Assam, 1906, (Reprint 1984); Alexander Mackenzie, *The North- East Frontier of India*, Mittal Publications, New Delhi, 1884, (Reprint 1979); M. Alemchiba, *A Brief Historical Account of Nagaland*, Publisher Naga Institute of Culture Kohima, Nagaland, 1970; V.K. Anand, *Nagaland in Transition*, Associated Publishing House, New Delhi, 1969; Verrier Elwin, *The Nagas in the Nineteenth Century*, Oxford University Press, London, 1969; Christoph Von Furer Haimendorf, *The Konyak Nagas: An Indian Frontier Tribe*, Rinehart & Winston, New York, 1969; D.N. Majumdar, *Races and Cultures of India*, Asia Publishing House, Allahabad, 1944.
3. The Ahoms were a Tai speaking people who had entered Assam through the Patkai Pass during the thirteenth century from Burma. Sukhapha the founder of Ahom rule in Assam was given a resistance by the Patkai Nagas and he is said to have perpetrated such ghastly barbarity that other Nagas of the neighbourhood hastened to make their submission. Subsequently the Ahoms founded a monarchical state in the Brahmaputra Valley which ruled Assam till the British took over in 1838. The Ahom state was founded on an extensive wet rice economy, with an elaborate hierarchical administrative set up under the *paik* and *khel* system. Under the *paik* system, the whole male population between the age of fifteen and fifty with the exception of the nobility, slaves were liable to perform compulsory periodic service to the state. The *paiks* were further divided into *khels* depending on the nature of duty. The *paiks* were grouped into '*gots*' or '*squads*,' comprising three to four men. A levy of first man was known as *mel*, the second, as *dewal*; and the third as *tewal*. This type of service under the state could take the form of service to the Raja or to any officer of state to whom he might be assigned. In lieu of the service the state allowed to each *paik* in the '*got*' to hold two *purahs* or three acres of rice-land on a revenue free tenure. Thus, the *paiks* of Ahom kingdom functioned as the people militia and at the same time as peasant; Edward Gait, *A History of Assam, op.cit.*, p. 336. Most of the subsidiary needs of the family for crafts were satisfied within the household or village. The division of labour that prevailed was rudimentary; See Tejimala Gurung, "Social Formation in Eighteenth Century Assam," Department of History, NEHU, Shillong, 1990.
4. R.G. Woodthorpe, R.E., "Notes on Wild Tribes inhabiting the so-called Naga Hills, on our North East Frontier of India, Part.1, in *The Journal of the Anthropological Institute of Great Britain and Ireland*, published by the Anthropological institute of Great Britain and Ireland, London, 1882, p. 57.
5. S.K. Bhuyan (ed.), *Satsari Asam Buranji*, *op.cit*., pp. 17-21.
6. Lakshmi Devi, *Ahom-Tribal Relations: A Political Study*, Spectrum Publication, Gauhati, 1958, (Reprint 1969), pp. 15-42; Sajal Nag, *Contesting Marginality Ethnicity, Insurgency and Sub Nationalism in North-East India*, Manohar, New Delhi, 2002, p. 38.
7. It was these Eastern and Central Naga tribes such as the Wancho, Nocte, Konyak, Phom, the Ao, Lotha and Rengma who were in close contact with the Ahoms; L.A. Waddell, *Tribes of the Brahmaputra Valley*, Spectrum Publisher, Guwahati, 1994.
8. H.K. Barpujari, *The Comprehensive History of Assam*, Vol. I and II, Publication Board of Assam, Guwahati, 1990, p. 122.
9. B.K. Boruah, *Nagamese: The Language of Nagaland*, Mittal Publication, New Delhi, 1993.

10. Sajal Nag, "Contesting Exclusion, Resisting Inclusion: Contradictory Trends in Historical Research in North East India from the Nineteenth to the Twentieth Century," *op.cit.*, pp. 225-253.
11. The term tribe and its subsequent conceptualisation is as recent a phenomenon as colonialism.
12. Richard, M Dorson (ed.), *Folklore and Folklife: An Introduction,* University of Chicago Press, Chicago, 1972, p.1; Jan Vansina, *Oral Traditional As History*, The University of Wisconsin Press, 1985, p. 21.
13. Popular folklore is considered to be the historical remnant of an earlier stage of human history to understand the history of pre-literate hill tribes. See Mignonette Momin, "Contextualizing Origin Myths of Northeast India," in *Proceeding of North East India History Association, Twenty Second Session,* Darrang College, Tezpur, 2001, p. 30.
14. The term Konyak include for the present study, the various tribes earlier called as the Patkai or the Eastern Nagas.
15. S.K. Bhuyan, *Studies in the History of Assam,* Omsons Publication, 1965, (Reprint 1985); Padmeswar Gogoi, *The Tai and the Tai Kingdom*, Publication Board of Assam, Gauhati University, 1968; A.C. Sharma, *Tai-Ahom System of Government*, B.K. Publishing House, Delhi, 1986; S.K. Goswami, *A History of Revenue Administration of Assam*, Spectrum Publication, New Delhi, 1993; B.C. Kalita, *Military Activities in Medieval Assam*, Spectrum Publication, New Delhi, 1986.
16. For details see Tejimala Gurung, "The Concept of Social Formation: A Study in its Theory and Practice in India" in *NEHU Journal of Social Sciences and Humanities,* Vol. XI, No. 2, April-June 1993, pp. 13-23; Manorama Sharma, "Trends, Possibilities and Problems in History Writing in Pre-Colonial North East India Economy and Society," in F.A. Qadri (ed.), *Society and Economy in North-East India,* Vol. 2, Regency Publications, New Delhi. 2006; pp.1-21; *Idem*, 'Trends of History Writing in North East India Assessment of works on the Pre-Ahom-18th Century', in D.R. Syiemlieh and Manorama Sharma (eds.), *Society and Economy in North East India,* Vol. 3, Regency Publications, New Delhi, 2008, pp. 67-97; Sajal Nag, Contesting Exclusion, Resisting Inclusion Contradictory Trends in Historical Research in North East India (1800-1900), *op.cit.*, pp. 225-253.
17. See in review of literature.
18. Francis (Buchanan) Hamilton, *An Account of Assam With Some Notices on the Neighbouring Territories,* Annals of Oriental Literature, 1820; William Robinson, *A Descriptive Account of Assam*; R.P. Pemberton, *The Eastern Frontier of India*, Mittal Publication, New Delhi, 1835, (Reprint 1998); W.W. Hunter, *A Statistical Account of Assam*, Vol. I, Trubner and Co., London, 1897; Francis Jenkins, *Relations with the Hill Tribes on the Frontiers of Assam*, 1853; L.A. Waddell, *Tribes of the Brahmaputra Valley*, *op.cit.*; Christopher von Furer Haimendorf, *Return to the Naked Nagas*, Vikas Publishing House, New Delhi, 1976.
19. E.T. Dalton, *Descriptive Ethnology of Bengal*, Office of the Superintendent of Government Printing, Calcutta, 1872.
20. J.H. Hutton, *The Sema Nagas*, Oxford University Press, 1921, (Reprint 1968); *Idem*, *The Angami Nagas* Oxford University Press, 1921, (Reprint 1969); J.P. Mills, *The Rengma Nagas*, MacMillan, London, 1937; *Idem*, *The Ao Nagas,* Macmillan London, 1926; W.C. Smith, *The Ao Naga Tribe of Assam: A Study in Ethnology and Sociology*, Macmillan, London, 1925.
21. B.C. Allen, *Assam District Gazetteers, Summary of Government's Relations with Some Tribes of NEFA,* Lakhimpur, Shillong, 1906; *Idem*, *Gazetteer of Naga Hills and Manipur*, Mittal Publications, New Delhi, 1905, (Reprint 2002).

22. John Butler, *A Sketch of Assam: With Some Account of Hill Tribes*, Smith, Elder and Co., London, 1847, pp. 152.
23. Alexander Mackenzie, *The North East Frontier of India, op.cit.*, pp. 91-100.
24. Assam Secretariat Record Room, Government of Assam, 1933; The volume was borrowed in June 1933 from the Assam Secretariat Record Room with the permission of Mr. W.A. Cosgrave, then chief Secretary to the Government of Assam. A typewritten copy has been prepared for the Department.
25. G. Rengma, *Political History of Rengma Naga*, Innovation, Dimapur, 2006, (Reprint 2015).
26. Lila Gogoi, *The Buranjis,* 1986.
27. Surendra Kumar Goswami, *A History of Revenue Administration in Assam (1228-1826) (A Detailed History of the Revenue System of the Ahom Rulers),* 1986.
28. Shrutidev Goswami, "The Eastern Nagas and the Salt Trade of Upper Assam," in *Proceedings of NEIHA*, Fifth Session, Aizawl,1984, pp. 93-100; S.K. Barpujari, "Raja Purandar Singha's Management of Salt-wells in the Naga Hills," in J.B. Bhattacharjee (ed.), *Studies in the Economic History of North East India,* Har-Anand Publications, New Delhi, 1994, pp. 73-83.
29. S.K. Barpujari, *The Nagas: The Evolution of their History and Administration (1832-1839). A Documentary Study*, Spectrum Publication, Guwahati, 2003; S.K. Barpujari, "Raja Purandar Singha's Management of Salt-wells in the Naga hills," *op.cit.*, pp. 73-74.
30. Alexander Mackenzie, *op.cit.*, pp. 92-97.
31. L.W. Shakespear, *History of Upper Assam, Upper Burmah and North-Eastern Frontier*, MacMillan, London, 1914, (Reprint 2004), pp. 195-227.
32. Verrier Elwin, *Nagaland*, Research Department, Advisors, Shillong, 1969, p. 19.
33. Christopher von Furer Haimendorf, *Return to the Naked Nagas*, *op.cit.* pp. 24-25.
34. Hargovind Josh, *Nagaland Past and Present*, Akansha Publishing House, 2001.
35. H.K. Barpujari, *The Comprehensive History of Assam,* Vol. III, *op.cit.* pp. 121-131.
36. J.P. Mills, *The Ao Nagas, op.cit.*, pp. 102-103.
37. Edward Gait, *A History of Assam*, *op.cit.*, pp. 79, 80, 84, 90, 94, 117, 308.
38. Lakshmi Devi, *Ahom-Tribal Relations: A Political Study., op.cit.*
39. Uma Nath Gohain, *Assam Under the Ahoms*, Spectrum Publication, Gauhati, 1942; N.K. Basu, *Assam in the Ahom Age 1228-1826*, Sanskrit Pustak Bhandar, Calcutta, 1970; S.K. Bhuyan, *Studies in the History of Assam*, *op.cit*; H.K. Barpujari, *The Comprehensive History of Assam,* Vol, III, *op.cit*; N.N. Acharyya, *History of Medieval Assam (13th to 17th Centuries*), Omsons Publication, New Delhi,1984; S.L. Baruah, *A Comprehensive History of Assam,* Munshiram Manoharlal, New Delhi, 2007, (Reprint 2013); B.C. Bhuyan, *Political Development of the North East,* Vol. I, Omsons Publications, New Delhi, 1989.
40. M. Alemchiba, *A Brief Historical Account of Nagaland*, *op.cit*; M. Horam, *Naga Polity*, B.R. Publishing Corporation, New Delhi, 1975; Julian Jacobs, *Hill Peoples of Northeast India: The Nagas. Society, Culture and Colonial Encounter*, Thames and Hudson, London, 1990; Murkot Ramuny, *The World of Nagas*, Northern Book Centre, New Delhi, 1988.
41. M. Horam, *Social and Cultural Life of Nagas* (*The Tangkhul Nagas*) B.R. Corporation, Delhi, 1977.
42. L. Metjen Konyak, *The Socio-Cultural and Political Significance of the Monarchical System of the Konyak Nagas*, Indian Society for Promoting Christian Knowledge, New Delhi, 2003; A.Yanang Konyak, *From Darkness to Light*, Christian Literature Centre, Guwahati, 1986, pp.11-14; Chingang Konyak, *The Konyak Naga: Yesterday and Today*, Konyak Literature Committee, Dimapur, 2008; M. Mankang Walim,

History of the Konyak Baptist Church Association from 1950 to Present Time, Published by author, Mon Theological College, 2005.
43. S.C. Sardeshipande, *The Patkoi Nagas*, Daya Publishing House, Delhi, 1987.
44. Birendra Chandra Chakravorty, *British Relations with the Hill Tribes of Assam since* 1858, Firma K.L. Mukhopadhyay, 1964.
45. Rai, K.L. Barua and, B.L. Bahadur, *Early History of Kamarupa, From the Earliest Time to the End of the Sixteenth Century*, Published by Rai K.L. Barua Bahadur, Shillong, 1933, p. 135.
46. S.N. Bhattacharyya, *A History of Mughal North East Frontier Policy*, Calcutta, 1929, S.K. Bhuyan, *Tungkhungia Buranji*, *op.cit*., p. 54.
47. S.K. Bhuyan, *Lachit Barphukan And His Times,* Gauhati, 1947, p. 71.
48. John Bulter, *A Sketch of Assam*: *With some account of hill tribes, op.cit.,* p. 52.
49. Temsula Ao, *The Ao-Naga Oral Tradition,* Bhasha Publication, Baroda, 1999.
50. Tejimala Gurung, "Emergence of the Ahom Monarchy in Upper Assam (13th-15th Century)," F.A Qadri (ed.), in *Society and Economy, op.cit*., pp. 86-96.
51. L. Metjen Konyak, "Ahom-Konyak Naga Relation," *Indian Journal of Tai Studies*, Vol. IX, Moranhat, 2009, pp. 139-144; Nitul Kumar Gogoi, "History Through Folk-Narrative Understanding Ahom-Tribal Relation," in *Indian Journal of Tai Studies,* Vol. IX, Moranhat, 2009, pp. 132-138; F.A. Rohman, "Folk-Narratives and Social Reality in Northeast India," in *Proceedings of the National seminar on Oral Literature of Northeast India with special reference to Arunachal Pradesh*, Department of Tribal Studies, Itanagar, 1998.
52. C.L. Imchen, "Naga Myths of Origin and Historical Reconstruction," in Mignonette Momin and C.A. Mawlong (eds.), in *Society and Economy in North-East India*, Vol. 1, Regency Publications, New Delhi, 2004, pp. 118-164.
53. *Idem*, "History of the Relations between the Nagas and the Valley Kingdoms," in F.A. Qadri (ed.), *Society and Economy op. cit*., pp. 114-144.
54. B.B. Goswami, "The Tribes of Assam: A Few Comments on their Social and Cultural Ties with the Non-Tribes," in K. Suresh Singh (ed.), *Tribal Situation in India*, 1972, pp. 271-272.
55. Verrier Elwin, *Nagaland, op.cit.*
56. A. Grierson, "Linguistic Survey of India," part. I, Tibeto-Burman Family, Calcutta, 1847, p. 42.
57. B.B. Ghosh, *Nagaland District Gazetteers, Mokokchung District Gazetteer*, Government of Nagaland, 1979, p. 27.
58. W.C. Smith, *The Ao Naga tribe of Assam*, *op.cit*; J.P. Mills, *The Ao Nagas*, *op.cit*., pp. xii-xiii; Gazetteer of India: Nagaland, Kohima District, 1970, pp. 19-21.
59. R.W. Woodthorpe, "Notes on the Wild Tribes Inhabiting the So-called Naga Hills," *op.cit*., pp. 52-53.
60. A. Nshoga, *Traditional Naga Village System and its Transformation*, Maulana Abul Kalam Azad Institute of Asian Studies, Kolkata, 2009, p. 53.
61. A. Nshoga, *Traditional Naga Village System and its Transformation, op.cit*., p. 54.
62. L.A. Waddell, *op.cit*., p. 61.
63. L. A. Wadell, *Ibid.,* p. 6.
64. Panger Imchen, *Ancient Ao Naga Religion and Culture*, Har-Anand Publications, 1993, p. 13.
65. Jan Vansina, *Oral Traditions: A Study in Historical Methodology*, *op.cit.,* p. 27.
66. A. Nshoga has pointed out that the Nagas disperse to different places among whom the Lothas moved ahead of the other groups, erected monoliths and abandoned the village. The Semas taking the similar routes when encounterd with the abandoned

village with the monolith erected assumed that they were erected by the spirits and therefore named it as 'Terhouchiesemi' which meant 'spirit erected stone village'. See for more detail; A. Nshoga, 2009 *op.cit.*

67. These groups inhabit in the eastern part of present Nagaland except for the Aos who does not come under the ambit of Eastern Nagaland.
68. A. Nshoga, *Traditional Naga Village System and its Transformation*, *op.cit.*, p. 25.
69. Temsula Ao, *The Ao-Naga Oral Tradition, op.cit.*, p. 3.
70. Tiatoshi Jamir, "Late First Millennium BC to Second Millennium AD Agriculture in Nagaland: A Reconstruction based on Archaeo Botanical Evidence and Radiocarbon Dates" in *Current Science,* Vol. 104, No. 10, 25, May 2013, pp. 1341-1352.
71. T. C. Hodson, *The Naga Tribes of Manipur*, Forward Books, New Delhi 1911 (Reprint 2018), p. 8; Peihwang Wangsa, *Christianity and Social Change: A Case Study of Konyak,* Barkataki and Company Pvt. Ltd. Jorhat, Assam, 2000, p. 3.
72. T.C. Hodson, *The Naga Tribes of Manipur*, *op.cit.*, p. 13.
73. A. Nshoga, *Traditional Naga Village System and its Transformation*, *op.cit.,* p. 6.
74. W.C. Smith, *The Ao Naga Tribes of Assam*, *op.cit.,* p. 50.
75. Lorho Mary Maheo, *The Mao Naga Tribe of Manipur: A Demographic Anthropological Study*, Mittal Publications, New Delhi, 2004, pp. 21-22.
76. Foreign Department, Report on the Trans-Dikhu tour file no. 469, Government of Nagaland, 1913, pp. 9-10.
77. L.W. Shakespear, *History of Upper Assam, Upper Burmah and North-Eastern Frontier*, *op.cit.*, pp. 111.
78. Godwin Austen, "On the Rude Stone Monuments of Certain Naga Tribes, With Some Remarks on their Customs etc." *The Journal of the Anthropological Institute of Great Britain and Ireland,* Vol. 4, 1875, pp. 144-147.
79. W.C. Smith, *The Ao Naga Tribes of Assam*, Macmillan, London, 1925, p. 50.
80. Information recorded by author from Shri. Nyakwang Wangnao village Headman (Dobashi), Shangnyu village on 10.12.2018; K.S. Singh and C.L. Imchen, *People of India Nagaland,* Vol. XXXIV, Anthropological Survey of India, Calcutta, 1994, pp. 2-13.
81. John Butler, "Rough Notes in the Angami Nagas and their language," in *Journal of Asiatic Society of Bengal,* Vol. XLIV, Calcutta,1875, pp. 307-346.
82. Amba Jamir, "Understanding Local Self Governance in Nagaland-An essence of the Institutions and their activities," Republic an online community for the Nagas, India and the world, 10th October 2017.
83. Government of Nagaland, 25. Law and social changes, by Alemchiba Ao, File no. 94, Nagaland State Archive, p. 8.
84. J.T. Barnard, Report on a second expedition to the "Triangle" for the Liberation of slaves, season 1927-28, File No.144, Foreign Department, National Archives of India, New Delhi, 1928, p. 9.
85. Christoph von Furer-Haimendorf, *The Konyak Nagas, op.cit.*, p. 419.
86. Journal of Capt Jenkins, Borhath, dates 8th February 1839.
87. William Robinson, *A Descriptive Account of Assam*, pp. 380-398.
88. J. Butler, *Travels and Adventures in the Province of Assam: During a Residence of Fourteen Years*, Smith Elder & Co, London, 1855, p. 157
89. J. Hornell, The Chank shell cult of India, *Antiquity* 16:113-33, 1942, p.121; see, Aluk Kumar Kanungo, "Naga Ornaments and the Indian Ocean," in *Indo-Pacific Pre-History Association Bulletin* 26, 2006, p. 161.
90. Report of a visit by Captain Vetch to the Singphos and Naga Frontier of Luckhimpore, No. 05, 15th September 1841.
91. Foreign Departments, External A, Pros. No. 155-167, February, 1890, p. 5.

92. Information recorded by the author from Smt. Alih Wangcha (noblewoman) from Nokzang village, on 14.1.2020.
93. B.B. Kumar, *Introduction to the Naga Tribes*, Prakashan, Meerut, 1977, p. 53.
94. J.P. Mills, *The Ao Nagas, op.cit.*, pp. 179-181.
95. Census of India, Nagaland, series-14, part XII-B, District Census Handbook Mon, village and Town, wise Primary Census Abstract, Directorate of Census Operations Nagaland, 2011, pp. 8-13.
96. Verrier Elwin, *The Nagas in the 19th Century, op.cit.*, p. 409.
97. Verrier Elwin, *Democracy in NEFA,* Published by North-East Frontier Agency Shillong, 1965, pp. 181-182.
98. M. Horam, *The Naga polity.*, p. 69, notes, 3.
99. Panger Imchen, *Ancient Ao Nagas Religion and Culture,* Har Anand Publications, New Delhi, 1993, p. 99.
100. Tekatemjen, *Studies on Theology and Naga Culture,* C.T.C. Aolijen, Mokokchung, Nagaland, 1996, p. 13.
101. L.W. Shakespear, *History of Upper Assam, Upper Burmah and North-Eastern Frontier, op.cit.*, p. 201.
102. B.C. Allen, *Gazetteer of Bengal and North East India*, Mittal Publication, Delhi, (Reprint 1993), p. 480.
103. L. Shakespear, *History of Upper Burmah and North Eastern Frontier, op.cit.*, p. 202.
104. Robert Reid, *History of the Frontier Areas Bordering on Assam*, the Assam Government Press, Shillong, 1942, pp.109-110; B.B. Ghosh, *Nagaland District Gazetteer*, Mokokchung District, 1979, p. 53.
105. Temsula Ao, *The Ao-Naga Oral Tradition, op.cit.*, p. 30.
106. District Census Handbook, Mokokchung District Census, 1971.
107. Information recorded by the author from Shri. Pokyam Walling, 79-year-old members of *putu menden* elders of Nokpu village, 2016.
108. N. Venuh, *People, Heritage and Oral History of the Nagas*, Papyrus books & beyond, Panbazaar Guwahati, 2014, pp. 11-12.
109. Y.L. Roland Shimmim, *Comparative History of the Nagas, from Ancient Period till 1826*, Inter-India Publications, New Delhi, p. 132.
110. W.C. Smith, *The Ao Naga Tribes of Assam, op.cit.*, p. 32.
111. Mar Atsongchanger, *Christian Education and Social Change*, C.L.C. Guwahati, Assam, 1995, pp. 14-15.
112. J.P. Mills, *The Ao Nagas, op.cit.,* p. 180.
113. Y.L. Roland Shimmim, *Comparative History of the Nagas, from Ancient Period till 1826, op.cit.*, p. 132.
114. G.K. Ghosh, *Tribals and their Culture Manipur and Nagaland*, Vol. 3, Ashish Publishing House, New Delhi, 1992, p. 46.
115. J.P. Mills, *The Ao Nagas, op.cit.*, pp. 42-43.
116. Aokumla Walling, "Oral Traditions and Archaeological Reconstructing the Pre Colonial History of Ao Nagas with Special Reference to the Naga-Ahom Relationship," Ph.D. thesis, Department of Deccan College Post Graduate and Research Institute, 2016, pp. 46-47.
117. N Venuh, *People, Heritage and Oral History of the Nagas, op. cit.*, pp. 23-24.
118. J.H. Hutton, "The Mixed Culture of the Naga," in *The Journal of the Royal Anthropological Institute of Great Britian and Ireland,* Vol. 95, Jan-Jun, 1965, p. 29; R.G. Woodthorpe, R.E., "Notes on the wild tribes inhabiting the so-called Naga Hills, on our North East Frontier of India," *op.cit.,* pp. 63.
119. J.P. Mills, *Ibid.,* p. 97.
120. J.P. Mills, *Ibid.,* p. 97.

121. J.P. Mills, *Ibid.*, p. 98.
122. R.H. Rattan, *Moina of Ancient Ahom-Nokpu Naga Relation*, Shree Venkateswara Print, New Delhi, 2014, p. 56.
123. J.P. Mills, *The Ao Nagas*, *op.cit.*, 105-106.
124. J.P. Mills, *Ibid.*, pp. 99-100.
125. R.H. Rattan, *Moina of Ancient Ahom-Nokpu Naga Relation*, *op.cit.*, p. 56.
126. Foreign Proceedings, Report of a visit by Vetch to the Singphos and Naga Frontier of Luckhimpore, 1842.
127. Government of Nagaland, Department of Planning and Coordination, Mon District Human Development Report, 2011, p. 5.
128. The words *Thendu* and *Thenko* come from the dialect of Tamlu village. They were first used by John Henry Hutton, a British official and latter an anthropologist and professor.
129. The population is according to the government of Nagaland electoral Census 2011.
130. In the olden days the Patkai Hills were known as '*Daikarong*' meaning collection or composition of nine hills. (*Dai*- mountain, *Ka*- nine, Rong-meeting).
131. P.C. Dutt, *The Wancho*, Directorate of Research, Itanagar, 1990; A. Mackenzie, pp. 77-100; Alexander Mackenzie, *North East Frontier of India*, Mittal Publication, New Delhi, pp. 77-100.
132. F. Haimendorf, *The Naked Nagas*, *op.cit*, p. 5.
133. Robert Reid, *History of the Frontier Areas Bordering on Assam (1883-1941), op.cit.*, 1983.
134. Sokhep Kri, *Gazetteer of India, Arunachal Pradesh State Gazetteer*, Vol. I, Government of Arunachal Pradesh Gazetteers Department, 2010, p. 18.
135. P.C. Dutta, Cultural and Historical Background of the Wanchos of Arunachal Pradesh, 1990; P.C. Dutta, "The Wanchos-Their legendary beliefs regarding origin and migration in Rosarun," Vol. 3, No. 4. Oct. 1977.
136. 136 Foreign Department, Report on the Trans-Dikhu Tour, File No. 469, 1913, p. 1; Marrison Edward Geoffrey, "The classification of the Naga languages of North-East India," Ph.D. thesis, Department of Phonetic and Linguistic, School of Oriental and African Studies, University of London, 1967, p. 12.
137. Hutton, *The Sema Nagas, op.cit.*, p. 383.
138. P.C. Dutta and D.K. Duarah (eds.), *Aspects of Culture and Customs of Arunachal Pradesh,* Directorate of Research, Government of Arunachal Pradesh 1990.
139. The term *'Wang/Angh'* and *'Pen'* describe the social status of the clans, the *Wang* are the aristocrats and *Pen* are commoners
140. J.H. Hutton, "The Mixed Culture of the Naga Tribes," in *The Journal of the Royal Anthropological Institute of Great Britian and Ireland,* Vol. 95, Jan-Jun, 1965, pp. 26-27
141. The Morung is represented by *khel*, the *khel* is divided into clans or lineages in the village that resides Wards.
142. Information recorded by a author from Shri Nokpoh wangnao, 68-year-old former primary school teacher of Yansa (Jaboka) village, Mon district, on 03 03, 2018.
143. Based on field observation at Mon Town on 15.4.2016.
144. Christopher von Haimendorf, *Return to the Naked Nagas*, *op.cit.*, p. 75.
145. K. Dilip Lahiri and J. Bimal Dev, "Customs of a few Naga Tribes Some accounts derived from the old files," In *Folklore*, Vol, 24, No. 10, Whole No. 281, October, 1983, pp. 195-196.
146. J.H. Hutton, "The Mixed Culture of the Naga Tribes," *op.cit.*, p. 26.
147. R.G. Woodthrope, "Notes on the wild tribes inhabitating the so-called Naga Hills, on our North-East India Frontier of India," *op.cit.*, p. 63.

148. Chingang Konyak, *The Konyak Nagas: Yesterday and Today*, Konyak literature committee, Dimapur, 2008, p. 25.
149. Information recorded by the author from field studies at Mon district and Khonsa town (Tirap district, Arunachal Pradesh) from dated, 17.6.2018, to 23.6.2018.
150. J.P. Mills, "Certain Aspects of Naga Culture," in *The Journal of the Royal Anthropological Institute of Great Britain and Ireland*, 1926, p. 31.
151. G.K. Ghosh, *Tribals and their Culture Manipur and Nagaland*, Vol. III, Ashish Publishing House, New Delhi, 1992, p. 100.
152. Pratab Chandra Choudhury, *The History of Civilisation of the People of Assam for the Twelfth Century A.D.*, Spectrum Publications, Guwahati, (Reprint 2017), p. 348.
153. Lichumo Enie, "Trade Relationship Between Nagaland and Ahom," Unpublished Ph.D. thesis, Department of History and Archaelogy, Nagaland University, Kohima, Nagaland, 2016, p. 38.
154. J.H. Hutton, "The inventiveness of Savage," in Man, Vol. 44 (Sept. 1944), *Royal Anthropological Institute of Great Britian and Ireland, Stable*: URL: http: www.jstor.org/2792807, Access: 21.8.2020.
155. Chingang Konyak, *The Konyak Nagas: Yesterday and Today*, *op.cit.*, pp. 13-14.
156. *Ibid.*, p. 49-50.
157. *Ibid.*, p. 50.
158. Information collected by the author from field observation at Tizit town, Nagaland, 15.5.2017.
159. Foreign Proceedings, Report on the Trans-Dikhu Tour, Government of Nagaland, File No. 469, 1913, p. 10.
160. Foreign Proceedings, Report on the Trans-Dikhu Tour, Government of Nagaland, File No.469, 1913, p. 10.
161. Foreign Proceedings, Report of a visit by Captain Vetch to the Singpho and Naga Frontier of Luckhimpore, 1842, p. 262.
162. Foreign Political Proceedings, No. 83, 9 Nov, 1840.
163. S. Dutta Choudhary, *Gazetteer of India, Arunachal Pradesh Tirap District*, Publisher Directory of Information and Public Relatio Government of Arunachal Pradesh, Shillong, 1980, p. 9; P.C. Dutta and D.K. Duarah, (eds.) *Aspects of Culture and Customs of Arunachal Pradesh*, *op.cit*; P.C. Dutt, *The Wancho*, Directorate of Research, Itanagar, 1990.
164. L.A. Wandell, *The Tribes of the Brahmaputra Valley*, *op.cit.*, p. 53.
165. B.B. Ghosh, *Nagaland District Gazetteers,* Wokha District, 1979, p. 1.
166. Census of India, *District Census Handbook*, Wokha District, 1981, p. XV.
167. Kanwar Randip Singh, *The Nagas of Nagaland Desperadoes and Heroes of Peace,* Deep & Deep Publication, New Delhi, 1987, p. 46; J.P. Mills, *The Ao Nagas*, Macmillan, London, 1926, p. 71.
168. Adani Ngullie, *Christianisation and Empowerment of Lotha Naga Women in North East India*, Astra International Pvt. Ltd, Mittal Publication, 2014; Athungo Ovung, *Social Stratification in Naga Society*, Mittal Publication, New Delhi, 2012.
169. Lichumo Enie, Trade Relationship between Nagaland and Ahom, PhD thesis, Department of History and Archaeology, Nagaland University, Kohima Nagaland, 2016, p. 45.
170. J.P. Mills, *The Lhota Naga, op.cit.*, pp. 60 and 67.
171. M. Kikon, "Culture Change Among the Lotha Nagas- A Case Study of Wokha and Akuk Village in Nagaland," Unpublished Doctoral Dissertation, Department of Sociology, NEHU, Shillong, 2002.
172. J.P. Mills, *The Lhota Naga, op.cit.*, p. 65.
173. 173. *Ibid.*, p. 113.

174. B.B. Ghosh, *Nagaland District Gazetteer Wokha District*, Kohima Nagaland, 1976, p. 33.
175. J.P. Mills, *The Lhotas Nagas, op.cit.*, p.43; The Rising Naga *A Historical and Political Study*, Vivek Publishing House, New Delhi, 1974, p. 20.
176. Alemchiba, *The Arts and Crafts of Nagaland*, Naga Institute of Culture, Kohima, 1968, p. 8.
177. 177. *Ibid.*, p.10.
178. J.P. Mills, *The Lhotas Nagas*, *op.cit.*, p. 42.
179. J.P. Mills, *The Lhotas Nagas, op.cit.*, p. 44.
180. 180. *Ibid.*, p. 45.
181. N. Venuh, People, *Heritage and Oral History of the Nagas*, *op.cit.*, pp. 272-291.
182. H. Bareh, *Gazetteer of India Nagaland, Kohima District*, published by Government of Nagaland, May, 1970, p. 92.
183. 183. *Ibid.*, p. 92.
184. Tejimala Gurung, "Social Formation in Eighteenth Century Assam," Department of History, NEHU, Shillong, 1990, p. 192.
185. Tejimala Gurung , "Crisis of Sustenance and Decline of the Ahom State in Eighteenth Century" in *Early States in North East India,* Regency Publications, New Delhi, 2013, pp. 152-177
186. Ibid.
187. E R. Leach, *Political System of Highland Burma: A Study of Kachin Social Structure*, London School of Economics and Politics, University of London, G Bell and Sons, London, 1954, reprint 1964.
188. Tejimala Gurung, "Crisis of Sustenance and Decline of the Ahom State in Eighteenth Century" *op.cit, pp.* 151-177.
189. Sajal Nag, *Contesting Marginality, Ethnicity, Insurgent and Sub-nationalism in North-East Indian*, *op.cit.*, pp. 39- 41.

2

Early Contact and Political Relations

It was during the thirteenth century that the Nagas living on the slope of the Patkai hills, termed by the British as Eastern Nagas (viz. Tangsas,[1] Noctes, Singphos, Khamtis, Lajus, Tutsa and Wanchos of Tirap and Changlang District of present Eastern Arunachal Pradesh and Lower Konyak of Mon District, Nagaland), where the first to come into contact with the Ahoms.[2] The British use of diverse terms as Eastern Nagas, Nagas of Sibsagar, *Boree* Nagas (friendly), *Abori* Nagas, (unfriendly) Patkoi Nagas, etc., camouflaged the identities of the various tribes of now eastern Arunachal Pradesh and Mon in Nagaland.[3] This region lies on the great tri-junction of India, China, and Burma.[4]

The Ahom territory extended from the Patkai hills in the east to the Manas River in the west, approximately 800 kilometers in length; it enclosed both the north and south bank of the Brahmaputra valley. On the north, it touched the territories of the Bhutia, Aka, Dafla, Miri, Mishimi, and Singpho, whose habitation covered the area upto the foothills of the Himalayas bordering Tibet. To the south of Brahmaputra valley, the kingdom extended to the foothills of inhabitants of the Nagas, beyond which lay the kingdom of Manipur and Burma (Myanmar). Westward, on the southern border, were the principalities of Khasi and Garos and the kingdom of Cachar and Jantia. While Ahom rule was limited to the Brahmaputra valley, their supremacy in the entire region was acknowledged directly or indirectly.[5]

Under the Ahoms, the entire Brahmaputra valley, from Sadiya in the east to the eastern borders of Goalpara in the west, was under rice cultivation. According to Shihbuddin Talish, Assam in the mid-17th century was well cultivated, from Koliabar to the city of Garhgaon, then Ahom capital, and from Lakhugarh (near the western point of Majuli Island) to Garhgaon. Talish also states it was occupied by people who grew full of orchards, gardens, bamboos groves, and cultivation covered up to the foothills.[6] During the reign of Rudra Singha (1696-1714), he raised 4 lakhs people as a force to invade Bengal, out of this three and a half was to be native Ahom soldiers or *paik's* who could have cultivated at least 7 lakhs *puras* of lands at the rate of two *pura's* allotted to each of them.[7] Hamilton observes that about three-fourths of the total land area of Upper Assam was under cultivation prior to the Moamariya revolt,[8] which led to the decline of the Ahom kingdom.

The Ahom economy was based on agricultural production.[9] As stated by Guha, "the migrant Ahoms believed that they have a mission to introduce better cultivation" at Brahmaputra valley.[10] The Ahom rulers from the very beginning adopted the policy of extension of agriculture by opening new lands, elevating the fields, building embankments for protection of cultivated fields from floods, and above all, by collecting and engaging every adult male in agricultural pursuits. The Ahom introduced wet rice cultivation in the newly established region. The extension of wet rice cultivation had been the prime mover in the growth of the state's economy.[11] The economic stability made it possible for the political expansion of the Ahom kingdom from Upper Assam by sixteenth century and extension to Lower Assam during the seventeenth century.[12] This was accompanied by the growing acculturation of the population of diverse ethnic groups, professions, and cultures.

When the Ahoms led by their chief Sukapha left Maulung in 1228 A.D on their way to Assam, he was accompanied by seven noble families of Ahom, commonly known as *Satgharia* Ahoms or 'the Ahom of the Seven Houses.' The names of these families were Charingia, Namrupia, Tipamia, Tungkhungia, Dihingia, Samuguria and Parvati.[13] These families were generally named after the places where they were located or where their lands and establishments were situated. Initially, the *Satgharia* Ahoms were the direct descendants of Sukapha, Bura Gohain, Bar Gohain, Deodhai, Mohan, Bailung, and Chiring. The last four formed the Ahom priestly group and astrologer. The Gohains constituted the counsellors of Ahom rulers. In addition to the two existing offices, the Bura Gohain and the Bar Gohain, another office of Barpatra Gohain was created during the reign of Suhungmung or Dihingia Raja (1497-1539).[14] The office of Barpatra Gohain was created as a co-equal position to the other two offices of Gohains. The authority of the three Gohains was so considerable that they had virtually the power to depose and enthrone the king himself. Moreover, in the circumstances when the king had no direct successor, the Gohains could nominate any one from the princely lineages to be the successor.[15]

As noted above and according to the Ahom *Buranjis*, when the Ahoms first moved across the Patkai ranges,[16] where they were confronted by the Nagas, now represented by tribes and sub-tribes of Nocte, Tangsa, Tutsa, Lower Konyak, and Wancho.[17] It took Sukapha 13 years to bring the region from Hukawang Valley to the Patkai range into a 'fair order' before he could affect a toe-hold in the Brahmaputra valley, and keep the routes open. The Patkai ranges, having numerous strategic and trading routes, effectively connected the entire territory of Indian subcontinent to South Asia, China and the other countries of Far East.[18] *The Pangsao pass* was known as *Khyber pass* of the east or referred to as Patkai Pass.[19] The Bodo, Ahoms and most of the tribes occupying present day east Arunachal Pradesh, eastern Nagaland, and Assam migrated to the northeast region through the *Pangsao pass*. This highway had rendered this region as India's gateway to Southeast Asia, China and the Far East.[20] Thus, Tirap valley and Patkai hills constitute a tri-junction linking three great river valley civilisations of the world, Brahmaputra valley of India, Irrawaddy river valley of Burma, and Yangtse-kiang and Howang-Ho or Yellow river of China.[21]

Strategically the Patkai ranges of the north-east frontier served as a transit route for the Ahom and which they also used for interactions with their kith and kin in Burma; through this route, the Ahoms had migrated to the Brahmaputra valley.[22] The Shans or Naras (Burmese) addressed the Ahom rulers as *Bhaiti*-Raja (in Assamese language means junior brother king). The most significant challenge the Ahoms feared during the latter part of their rule was the expansion of the Imperial Burmese beyond the Patkai, who had their capital at Amarapura and Ava. So the Ahom rulers had to be ever vigilant on the frontier to avert any attack from them.[23] Thus the Ahom rulers right, from the beginning of their rule in Assam gave special attention towards the Nagas (eastern Arunachal Pradesh), for the purpose of maintaining security in this strategically important region. Interestingly, the Tirap-Patkai region was also used by the Burmese to organise military expeditions into Assam in 1817, 1819 and 1821 and later occupied the Brahmaputra valley. During the British colonial period, the Tirap-Patkai region witnessed a series of military expeditions conducted against the Singphos, the Burmese and other tribes of this region.[24]

John M'Cosh, referred to five prominent routes from Sadiya, the frontier station of the Brahmaputra Valley into Tibet (China).[25] These were (i) passes of the Dihong, (ii) the Mishmi route, (iii) the Phungan pass to Munchee and China, (iv) the route by Manipur to the Irrawaddy, and (v) the Patkai pass to Bhamo on the Irrawaddy. The most important and easy route was the Patkai pass to the upper district of Burma into the Chinese provinces of Yunnan. Through this route, the Shans entered into the Brahmaputra valley of India, the Irrawaddy River valley of Burma, Yangtse-kiang and Howang-Ho or Yellow River of China.[26] The route of Nonyang Lake lies at the southern foot of the Patkai and from where various forms of economic transactions, i.e., salt production, trans-polity barter and control trade-routes lay.

Ancient Trade Route from South & Southwest China to Northeast India and beyond, through Northern Myanmar (Burma) and Northern Assam's Patkai Range

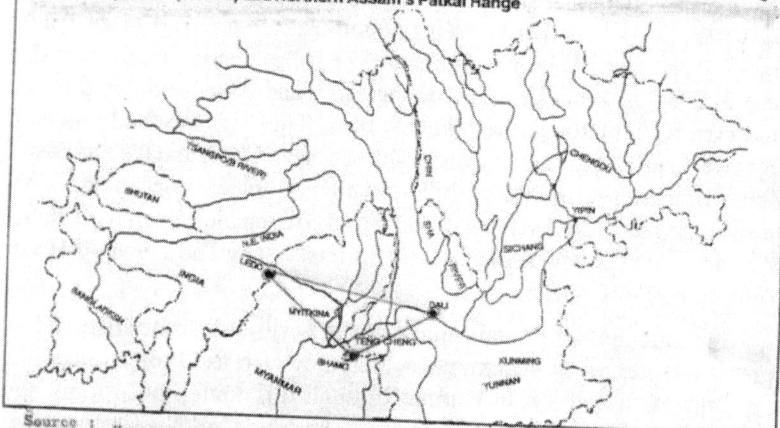

Source : Haraprasad Ray , Trade & Trade Routes Between India & China, Kolkata,2003 p.330

Figure - 1

Strategically and economically, maintaining relations with the Nagas were important to the Ahoms, as the areas inhabited by the Nagas served as transit routes to Burma and beyond for the Ahoms. Besides, the period of foreign wars against the Koch and Mughals during the sixteenth seventeenth centuries demanded active help and cooperation and, in any case, the neutrality of the neighbouring tribes and chiefs.[27] Any unwanted attack from the east was through this route, the Ahom rulers, therefore, had to be on constant guard on this frontier in order to avert any attacks. This route became a geo-strategic hotspot during the Second World War. When Japanese troops advance closed off in March 1942, the Patkai Ranges became the last hope of reaching India. Thousands of men, women and children with very little to eat or clothe themselves travelled through the Chindwin and reached Patkai pass to arrive in Upper Assam. A few went up the northern route via the Lohit valley.[28] Furthermore, the eastern Naga salt-well was another imperative economic consideration for the Ahom.

The Ahoms sought to maintain a cordial relationship with the Nagas for practical, political, and strategic reasons.

Early Ahom relation with the Nagas

Sukapha is said to have left Maulung about the year 1215 AD from his homeland with a following of eight nobles, 9,000 infantries, three thousand cavalries, two elephants and 300 horses.[29] The Ahoms entered Assam from North Myanmar through *pangchau pass* 'lake of no return' over the Patkai hills, they had to fight their way through the land inhabited by the Wancho, Konyak, Tangsa, Noctes (then referred to as Bordurias, Paniduarias, Namsangia, Tablungias).[30] For 13 years the Ahoms wandered on the Patkai Range, making occasional raids on the Nagas villages, who inhabited the region extending from the Hukong valley to the Patkai range. Sukapha reached Brahmaputra Valley in 1228 AD and established the first kingdom at Charaideo in 1253. He laid the foundation of Ahom rule in Assam, for almost three decades after his arrival, he came as the head of an agricultural folk in search of suitable land for wet-rice cultivation.[31]

The early history of Sukapha's contact with the Nagas refers to the harsh methods adopted by him against the Nagas. Gait has stated that as the Nagas had exasperated him with their resistance, he further terrorised the Nagas by 'killing them and roasted and even compelled their relatives to eat their flesh.'[32] This quietened the Nagas for some time and thus Sukapha and his group had a safe passage to Assam.[33] However, the brutal action of Sukapha, only infuriated the Nagas. The first Naga villages who fought against the Ahom and then brought under Ahom control were Khrarukhung, Pungkkong, Tikhand, Binglang, Latoma, Lanpak, Taru, Tapa, Tapu, Luknam, Lukna, Papukia, Tangtingia, Jakhrangia, Khamtengia, Khunkhatia, Khuntungua (at present termed as Lower Konyak, in Mon district Nagaland; and Upper Nocte, Tutsas, Wanchos, Tangsa, in Arunachal Pradesh). These tribes were earlier termed by the British as Eastern Nagas, they lived between the Dikhow and the Buri-Dihing.[34] The Nagas retaliated with guerilla ambush on the Ahom villages. The Ahom Raja posted an officer called Kang Jang Mung in the region to look after the welfare in their new capital at Khamjang (Sibsagar).[35]

When the Nagas raided the Ahom villages, the Ahom chief took prompt action every time, even though fighting in the hills against the inhabitants was a difficult proposition and very little war booty was available.[36] The memory of the Ahoms wandering along the valley of the Dihing River is still preserved in the various local names and traditions.[37] Thereafter, Sukapha followed the courses of the rivers Namruk (Assamese variant Namruk), Buri Dihing, Brahmaputra and Dikhow, establishing an outpost at every vital strategic location, finally came to Che-Rai-Doi (Charaideo or the Bird-God, first capital of Ahom kingdom). After settling at the bank of the Dikhow, he sent an embassy to Mong Mao to inform Siu-Ka-Pha thus: "We are now at this place."[38] Gifts of gold, silver water jars, and numerous varieties of cloth were sent. The establishment of a new kingdom in the Brahmaputra valley by Siu-Ka-Pha was a virtual extension of the suzerainty of Mong Mao. Thus even after the death of Siu-Ka-Pha in 1268, his successor maintained allegiance with letters and presents to the ruler of Mong Mao.[39] The Ahom maintained consistent communication with Mong Mao until the fourth Ahom king Siu-Khang-Pha who came to the throne in 1293 started to discontinue this relationship. The transit path however had to be clear inorder to maintain proper channel of interaction with their kith and kin from Burma.

The Konyak, Ao, and Lotha Nagas differed in their political organisation. There were the autocratic *Angh* or chief (known as *Khunbaos* in the Assamese *Buranjis*), among the Konyak, Nocte, Tutsa, Lotha, and Wancho who possessed the authority to control the subordinate villages. Among the Konyak each village had five to six deputy chiefs, and the eldest son took over the role during his father's lifetime should the latter become infirm; the practical affairs of the tribe were settled by a council of aged chiefs and warriors, they also received a leg of every animal killed for a feast, and the assistance of the village in his cultivation.[40] The Ao had a council of village elders (*tatar*), who conferred on matters of public importance, and who administered punishment for crime.[41]

The Ahom *Buranjis* give comprehensive evidence of the tribal communities and clan system with whom the Ahoms came into contact during 1226-1805. Clan, as well as village-wise details, are given in the *Buranjis*. The *Buranjis* also give a chronology of various events and military expeditions into the Tirap and Changlang districts; Jaboka, Khamjang, Tabhlung, Shangnyu, Moolung, in present Mon district (Patkai hills). To name a few, in 1487- 1488, the Tangsa Nagas revolted against Suhenpha after his succession in 1498; In 1504 the Aitonia Nagas of Khanjang (Patkai) who were vassal to the Ahoms since the time of Sukapha. They once again rebelled; In 1559, the Banfera Nagas appealed for help from the Ahom king against their enemy Banchangia

Nagas; In 1576, the Aitonia Nagas were invaded by the Ahom; In 1661-1662 AD, when Mir Jumla attacked the Ahom Kingdom, the Ao, Lotha, and Konyak fought alongside Ahom; From 1679 to 1681 Gadadhar took refuge at the Naga hills when there was turmoil in the Ahom capital. Later after establishing the *Tungkhungia* dynasty in 1681 AD, he married a Konyak chief's daughter Watlong; In 1701, Nagas raided the Ahom fortress at Borhat. In the battle 60 Nagas were killed; In 1702, Rudra Singha sent an expedition under Basang Phukan against the Nagas who were severely defeated in the battle; In 1807 AD an expedition was sent to suppress the rebellion of Nagas to Borhat and Tiru *duar* and the Nagas were defeated, etc.[42]

The policy of Ahom rulers towards the Patkai Naga varied from time to time according to the exigencies of the political situation.[43]

To keep the foothill tribes in check, frontier officials designated as Salal Gohain, Marangi Khowa and Sadiya Khowa Gohain were stationed at Sala, Marung and Sadiya.[44]

Prelude to Negotiation with the Nagas

The prelude of negotiation started when the Ahoms first encountered the Eastern Nagas (Nocte, Konyak, Wanchos, Tangsa, Tutsa), of Patkai mountain living near the plains.[45] The intense love of independence of the hillmen, and resentment at the subordinate status which the Ahoms tried to impose on them, forced them to stand up against the Ahom intruders. Sporadic fighting often broke out followed by reconciliation.

As the valley was surrounded by hill tribes, the Ahoms had to evolve a policy to maintain the security of their state and to keep the channels of communication open towards the east. During times of turmoil the hills provided a haven for the persecuted. In the later period of their rule the Ahom grew conscious of the Burmese, far beyond the Patkai, who had their capital at Amarapura and later at Ava. The Ahom rulers had to be watchful on the frontier to avert any attack from them.[46] The Ahom Raja felt that the only practical means would be to negotiate with the various hill tribes, including the Nagas.

Hence, the Ahom rulers clearly understood the strategic prominence of the Nagas for the security of their kingdom against invasion from Burma and also from the hills which surrounded the Brahmaputra Valley inhabited by different warlike ethnic groups.[47] To establish their supremacy in the Brahmaputra valley, the Ahom Raja needed to establish stability relations with the Nagas. In a nutshell, the Naga-Ahom relationship was characterised by practical and political expediency.

In 1439, Susenpha ascended the throne; he was the son of Suphakpha by a Tipam chief's daughter (Tipam Fakial village, now located in Dibrugarh district, the nearest town is Nagarkatia). During that period, the Tangsu Nagas raided the Ahom kingdom. The Ahom troops led by king Susenpha confronted the Tangsu Nagas but were defeated in the clash, out of it, the Nagas killed one hundred and forty Ahoms. Subsequently, some other Nagas like, Akhampa, the enemies of Tangsu Nagas, as the tradition indicates, exchanged gifts, including swords, with the Ahom Raja as a token of their friendship and allegiance to his authority. They even sought help from Raja against the Tangsa Nagas, who were giving them trouble and later defeated the Tangsa.[48] However, the Tangsa Nagas, inspite of their defeat, did not conclude peace with the Ahoms.[49]

During the reign of Susenpha (1439-1488), the successor of Suphakpha (1422-1439), while commanding an expedition against Tangsa Nagas (now in Changlang and Longding districts of Arunachal Pradesh), in retaliation to a raid committed by Nagas the Ahoms were again defeated by them. The Ahoms regrouped their army, retaliated against the Nagas under Bura Gohain and defeated the Tangsa Nagas. During that time, some Naga children, spears and other things, along with the three Tangsu/Tangsa families, were taken as booty by the Ahom. These Tangsu Nagas were the people living in the erstwhile Tirap Division of NEFA on the Assam-Burma border.[50]

Susenpha died in 1488, and his successor son Suhenpha (1488-1493) renewed war with the Tangsa Nagas. In the battle, the Nagas again defeated the Ahoms and in which the supreme commander Bar Gohain was killed in the battle. Eventually, the Nagas were defeated by the Ahoms and the Tangsa Naga sought peace with the Ahom Rajas. The peace settlement failed due to turmoil in the kingdom. The Ahom Raja Suhenpha was assassinated in 1493 in a palace conspiracy by the new Bura Gohain. The king's successor Supimpha (1493-1497), who ruled for four years, attempted ineffectively to punish his father's assassin. The other memorable event of Supimpha was that he gave away one of his wives to a Naga chief who had come to the Ahom kingdom to pay homage.[51]

This event is also remembered in a Banfera (Wancho-Konyak) folklore. According to this, a Naga Khunbao (chief) named Karengpa had developed a close friendship with king Supimpha (1493-1497). One day when Karengpa came to the valley kingdom to pay his tribute to king Supimpha, one of Supimpha's wives belonging from the *Chamua* clan, (these clans were below the nobility and above the rank of *kanri paik*), saw the Banfera *Khunbao* (chief) from inside the palace. When the king went inside the chamber, the queen became captivated by Karengpa, and constantly glancing, praised him in the presence of the Ahom Raja. The Ahom Raja was infuriated with his wife and sent her to the chief's village. She was already pregnant at that time. She gave birth to a son named Senglung. Supimpha was succeeded in 1497, by Suhungmung (Dihingia Raja 1497-1539). On one occasion Suhungmung met the boy who had accompanied the foster Naga chief when he visited the Ahom kingdom. The Ahom Raja was intriqued by the boy 's high-bred appearance.

After a long conversation with the Naga *Khunbao* (chief) he learned that the boy's mother was already pregnant before his father Supimpha sent her to the Naga Khunbao. The chief had adopted the boy and brought him back to the Ahom kingdom. As he was not the son of a queen of a higher rank so, Suhungmung (Dihingia Raja 1497-1539) created a new post of Barpatra Gohain, which he made equivalent to Bar Gohain and the Bura Gohain.[52] He gave an Ahom name to the boy as Kangcheng Barpatra. Nevertheless, the measure was opposed by officials; secondly, they refused to give up any of the men under their control. Ultimately, the king overcame this difficult decision by giving the title Barpatra Gohain. The Barahis, Chutiyas and Morans, who had not been placed under either of the other Gohains were put under the new official. He then called a council of all the leading nobles, gave Senglung a seat between the Bar Gohain and the Burha Gohain, publicly announced him with a new appointment and declared his rank equal to the other two. Later, Suhungmung converted to Hinduism, assumed the title, Svarga Narayan (Dihingia Raja) made his capital at Bakata on the Dihingia and successfully repulsed three Mohammedan invasions.[53]

The above folklore indicates a tradition of close friendship with the Ahom king that was established by the Banfera Nagas."[54] As Kangcheng Barpatra was born and raised in the Naga village, his family came to be known as 'Naga Barpatra's ghar' (house of Naga).

Suhungmung was ambitious and wanted to expand his territory and subdue the neighbouring independent hill tribes. In 1504, a revolt of Aitonia Nagas[55] took place. The Bar Gohain and Bura Gohain were placed in charge of an expedition against the Aitonia Nagas.[56] The Aitonia Nagas were defeated, who then renounced to the Ahom king, to whom they sent a daughter of their chief for matrimonial alliance and gifts four elephants as amity offering; they also agreed to pay a yearly tribute of axes, gongs and amber. Indeed, clashes between the Ahom and the Naga were a matter of usual episode throughout the entire period of the Ahom rule in Assam.[57]

One of the Ahom *Buranjis* also narrates the story of a childless Borahi, who adopted a son of a Banfera Naga[58] and brought him up as his son. The Ahom king admired the handsome looking Naga boy and so adopted him, making him Barphukan (Viceroy of Gauhati in place of Langi Barphukan), who later became one of the ministers in the Ahom kingdom.

The Nagas occasionally ransacked Ahom villages. Most of these groups of communities who do looting came from the Konyak, Wanchos, Tangsa, Tutsa, and Noctes. The Ahoms, in return, dispatched punitive expeditions in retaliation. Once the Ahom kingdom was formally established, they adopted a policy of mutual settlement with the Nagas primarily due to the farsightedness of King Pratap Singha (1603-1641). Often the Nagas invited the Ahom rulers to help them in their internal disputes; for example, a Banfera chief seek Pratap Singha help when they disagreed with the Abor Nagas of Bangang to resolved the matter.[59]

Economic Importance of the Naga Hills to the Ahoms

The hills occupied by the Patkai Nagas were important due to the existence of salt springs. Salt during the medieval period in Assam was a scarce commodity. Most of the inhabitants of Assam used a substitute made of burnt plantain called *khar*. Salt was also a precious commodity for other Nagas living in the interior who had to procure it from the salt spring owning Nagas. Early colonial sources refer to the presence of the salt well and conflict emerging due to the attempt to control these wells by both parties. People in the plains of Assam and even Sinphos, Kachin (Myanmar) depended upon the supply of salt extracted from different salt-wells located in the land of Eastern Nagas.

The British records of 1840, indicated that the low hills of Tirap and Changlang, close to the plains of Sibsagar and Lakhimpur were of economic importance to the Ahom rulers. There were several salts well in the region inhabited by the Nocte, the Namsang, the Paniduar and Borduaria who lived chiefly by manufacturing salt and its trade.[60] The area is blessed with plenty of natural resources such as oil, salt, coal, timber, elephant, honey, evergreen forest, rivers, streams, and fountains. This area was found economically valuable by the Ahoms and eventually by the British too.[61]

Behind the raids and counter-raids of the Nagas and Ahoms the economic interests were thus paramount. The Ahom king had to fight the Nagas in order to access the salt wells of the Eastern Naga. The economic interest of the Ahoms compelled them to fight against the Nagas presently living in Tirap, Longding, Changlang districts of Arunachal Pradesh, and Mon district Nagaland.[62] With the rising power of the Ahoms, the Nagas subsequently agreed to share some of these salt wells with great reluctance. Until the westward expansion of the Ahom kingdom to Lower Assam made it possible to open up trade relations with Bengal and large qualities of salt began to be imported annually (about 10,00,000 maunds),[63] scarcity of salt in the Ahom kingdom made the Ahoms depend on the local Eastern Naga salt, and brines of Sadiya.[64]

Salt was therefore one of the main causes for several military encounters between the Ahoms and Eastern Nagas (Nocte, Wancho, Tutsa, Konyak, and the Muklom), who lived in the Patkai ranges, close to the plains of Sibsagar and adjoining areas. Initially, the Ahom rulers attempted to annex the Naga territories either to control the salt wells or as punitive measures. The Nagas, who were extremely sensitive about their freedom, had repulsed the attacks Ahom villages with guerilla warfare, raiding, and frequently captured the Ahom subjects.

Besides, the route to Burma lay via the Patkai Pass under the trans-Patkai Nagas. So conciliations were also made from time to time during the entire period of the Ahom rule in Assam. It was the same Patkai route Captain Jenkins travelled to China between 1869-70 smuggling opium.[65] According to the *Buranjis,* the Ahoms followed a policy of conciliation, sometimes backed by display or might right toward the Nagas. Besides, the Ahom Raja wanted peace on the Eastern Nagas borders as during the 17th century the kingdom was threatened by the Mughals on the west.[66]

Politics of Salt

Salt was thus an important factor in the politics of Naga-Ahom relations. The Moamariyas, the Ahom, the Burmese and even the British initially were interested in the region either to occupy Mohong area (now part of Dibrugarh district of Assam), and present day Tirap-Changlang districts of Arunachal Pradesh and to ensure a regular supply of salt, to earn more profit out of the flourishing salt trade.[67] The salt wells started from "Borhat" and extended along the Naga-Patkai foothills up to Namphai reserve forest which includes part of Naga hills.[68]

The Ahoms obtained exclusive control over some salt wells in the region of Eastern Nagas (Noctes, Tutsa, and the Muklom), by defeating the local tribal chiefs. The tribal chieftains strongly opposed the advance of Ahom army and did not agree to share the salt with them.[69] Frequent retaliation and raids were organised against the Ahom military contingents to drive away the Ahom officials in charge of the salt-wells.[70]

To maintain political control over the salt-producing areas of Tirap valley and Patkai hills, the Ahom Raja Susenpha (1439-1488) dispatched a military expedition against the Nocte, Tangsa, and Tutsa chief in 1487. During this operation, the Ahom lost 140 soldiers. The conflict with the Ahoms continued even during the reign of Sehenpha (1488-1493), and Borgohain Chaokanbanruk died while fighting in one of such battles.[71] In 1536, the Ahom occupied two regions of the Nocte-Borduaria and Paniduarias (known as Mohongias). Mohong was one of the major salt producing area located in the heart of Nocte land. The Nocte Lungwang (chief)[72] of Namsang also confronted the Ahoms several times. Such confrontations testify to the fact that the Ahoms were interested in having access to procure salt which was a scarce commodity in Assam.[73] In 1563, during the reign of Sukhampha 1552-1603 (Khora Raja), he was defeated by Koch Raja Narayan. The Raja fled to Namsang, a major salt producing area, and stayed in Tirap for about six months. From January to July 1563 CE, the Ahom Raja acquired first-hand report on salt production, its distribution system, and the eco-strategic importance of the areas. Subsequently, the Ahoms organised a series of military expeditions further to tighten their military control over salt producing areas and systematically exploit the salt-wells located in the regions.[74]

The Noctes of the salt producing area again rose in rebellion against the Ahom. An armed attack on salt-wells held by the Ahoms was organised in 1692 near Borduaria and twenty-three persons were killed. The Ahom ruler dispatched strong body of troops under the command of Tamcheng Chinghat Phukan and Laling Phukan, and the army succeeded in defeating the Noctes, and the Nocte Lowang (chief) was put to death in Longkei village.[75] Again in 1701 C.E., when salt traders killed sixty Noctes, the Noctes retaliated by forcibly entering into the Ahom garrison at Borhat, killing a large number of Ahom soldiers guarding salt-wells in the area. They looted and devastated several Ahom villages, the Ahom army organised an expedition upon Borhat and compelled the Noctes to maintain peace in the area and refrain from organising further raids on salt producing areas in the hills. The Ahom-Nocte conflict which started in 1536 CE continued upto 1811. The Ahoms were not able to secure any permanent hold over the salt producing areas throughout the period from 1215 to 1811 C.E.76 Though some salt-wells producing areas came under the possession of the Ahom, the salt was shared mutually. The Ahoms sought to maintain a cordial relationship with the Eastern Naga living in villages of the Mohong area now in Tirap.[77]

Oral traditions of Naga-Ahom conflict

An oral tradition of Tutsa village,[78] narrates how during the 17*th* century, the Ahom Lungwang (Raja), with a strong contingent of soldiers, passed through Tutsa village and came to know about the salt-wells. The Ahoms claimed that the salt wells belonged to them but the Tutsa firmly opposed them and did not accept their argument. After heated negotiation it was decided to resolve this dispute through a display of skill-anyone who cut the stone slab meant for sharpening the edge of a *dao* (dagger) in one stroke will be the master of the salt-wells. First the Ahom Lungwang tried his luck and gave a blow on the stone slab but failed to cut it into two pieces. After him the Muttock Moran Lungwang tried with his utmost strength to cut the stone slab but failed. Finally, the Tutsa Lungwang (chief) took a *dao* into his hands and made a forceful strike on the slab, the slab was cut into two pieces. However, the Ahom *Lungwang* (Raja), did not accept his defeat and suggested another round of tests that anyone who pulled down the bamboo, will have the right to control the salt producing areas. Both Ahom and Muttock Lungwang failed in this bet and the Tutsa Lungwang once again was prosperous. The Ahom Lungwang did not accept the right of the Tutsa over the salt-wells this time too and insinuated that the dispute should be referred to Lekhophang (a type of grass), to give its judgment that the salt well belongs to whom- the Tutsa, Muttock, or the Ahom. The Muttock and Ahom Lungwang both in turn, asked three times each to the grass as to whom the salt well belongs. The grass did not reply. However, when the Tutsa chief asked whether the salt well belonged to him, instantly there was a reply. "Yes, salt-well belongs to Tutsa or Tutnu Lungwang." This way, the right of Tutsa over the salt wells was confirmed. The Ahom Lungwang became very angry and ordered them to burn the Lekhopbang grass completely and return to his kingdom. The soul of the grass assumed the form of a bird called 'Tutnu Jongsun wo,' this bird is noticed even today in Tutsa areas. The Tutsa say that even now if Lekhopbang grass is cut, it secretes some red colour liquid which is believed to be blood by the Tutsa. This folklore indicates how hard the Muttock and the Ahoms had tried to occupy the salt-wells.

Another oral narrative of Tutsa village refers to the conflicts which took place during the 18th century between the Tutsas, the Ahoms and Moamariyas. The elders of Jongpho hate and Yankang villages (Changlang district, Arunachal Pradesh) narrate the presence of a Muttock Moran who visited Tutsa areas to occupy the salt-wells, as there was an acute shortage of salt in the Ahom territory. This incident reportedly occurred in the 18th century when the Ahom kingdom was on the periphery of declining and accordingly, political instability prevailed in the region. The Moamariya rebellion that began in 1769 continued upto 1804 CE. The Burmese rulers organised a series of military expeditions to conquer the Brahmaputra valley. At this critical juncture, it was necessary for the Ahoms to adopt friendly attitude towards the tribes of Patkai ranges. And that means not placating everone but rather play to strengths and have other hill tribes cancel each other out whenever they can. The Tutsas were wise enough to take advantage of this situation. They tightened their control over the region and acquired more villages and land under their sphere of influence. Despite the Ahom ruler's concerted efforts to acquire control of salt-wells in the Tutsa villages, the firm determination and spirit of resistance of the Tutsa prevented the Ahoms from establishing their (political) hegemonic control over salt producing areas of the region.

The Ahom Lungwang visited Tirap valley time and again to stake his claim to the salt producing areas. The conflict between Ahom and the Nagas (Tirap) continued. By the close of 18th century, the Tutsa and Nocte (Eastern Nagas) took advantage of the political crisis in the Ahom state and shoved the Ahom as well as the Moamariyas out of the Tirap-Patkai region. With the decline of Ahom kingdom and the annexation of Assam by the British East India Company, the Ahom control over Tirap-Patkai region came to an end (the tribes of Tirap valley regained their control over all the salt-wells). After the Ahoms lost power to the British, as well as the control of Eastern Naga salt wells (Nocte and other tribes) passed to British. Though, they did not show any intention to occupy the salt-wells; instead a duty of 20 percent on the salt brought to markets and fairs in the plains was imposed.[79] From the colonial period the importance of these salt wells declined. By the late nineteenth century barely any salt was extracted, only a few people from Joypore, Namsang, Paniduar, Borduar in Mohong areas and Changlang extracted for medicinal purpose.[80]

The constant conflicts between the Nagas and Ahoms happened over control over the salt-wells. It resulted in conflict between the Naga chiefs and the Ahom rulers. The Ahom occupied the salt-wells of Mohong and Borhat during the 16th century from the Nagas i.e. Nocte, Tutsa, and Tangsa of the Tirap region. However, none of the parties could permanently establish their control over the salt-wells. Thus, the scarcity of salt and quests of Ahom and Naga chief to retain control over salt-wells dominated the politics of Naga-Ahom relations for 600 years. The great demand for salt in the Ahom Kingdom is corroborated by British official records such as in Captain Welsh's Report on Assam, 1794 submitted to the then Governor General of East India Company in which it was mentioned that if law and order is restored in Assam, then the Company could sell 1,00,000 *maunds* of salt every year in Assam.[81]

Konyak-Ahom Relations in Oral Traditions

According to an oral narrative of Konyak myths of origin (as narrated to the scholar by a Gaonbura (village headman) Shri Nyakwang Goanbura (Shangnu village, in Mon), the Ahom king Chaoppha (Sukapha) and the Konyak chief Teinok were brothers.

> One day their mother tied the boys with ropes before going to the fields; she used a cane rope to tie the older son and the younger son with a tender creeper, both of them were tied to a tree. The younger son shortly got free and followed his mother. He grabbed her feet and rolled to the ground out of excitement. The area where the younger son rolled turns into valley. The elder brother accomplished to untie the cane rope a few days later and started looking for his mother and brother. However, he was unsuccessful in tracking them. He was overwhelmed by the loss of his family, and he hit the ground with a stick out of frustration with anguish. The area he struck with a stick developed into rivers, cliffs, and hills. A year later, the elder brother received information from one of the villagers who had gone to the plain to barter his commodities. He mentioned that his mother and brother were settled in the valley, so he searched for his missing family.

When he reached his younger brother's Chaopha's (Sukapha) house, he saw him wearing clothes, plentiful gold, silver, enormous stock of salt, and rice granaries. For a moment, the luxury and lavish life of the plains attracted the elder brother, but he did not find inner peace in his heart. Teinok missed his home in the hills and decided to return home. He kept turning around to look at the plains; he was unhappy after parting with his brother and mother, missed them. When he reached his home in the hills, he discovered that his livestock had escaped into the forest and become wild animals. The goat had turned into a deer, the pig a wild boar, and the pony into a wild horse. Even the vegetables in his garden became wild. The betel nuts in his garden became bitter, and his vegetables turned into inedible plants. Since then, the inedible vegetables and plants belonged to the elder brother who lived in the hills, while the edible plants and good clothing belonged to the younger brother in the plains.[82] Since then the Ahom Raja Chaopha (Sukapha) paid respect to his older Konyak brother by gifting him in kind.[83] This story shed light on a broken relationship of brotherhood and that was narrated to reconcile the warring groups.

The origin myths about the brother are not about reiterating a hill- valley framework. It narrated to designate accounts of getaway, friendship, refuge, and tranquility and how people altered local legends to establish social and political alliances and to require restoration of kinship ties. It is not possible to pinpoint with any great accuracy the actual events or even the probability of the existence of the legends, such narratives broadly delineate certain landmarks in the political scenario of that time of history and memory overlap with communities and landscape- such accounts take us beyond the binary of the hill-valley distinction.

Posa System

The Ahom state surrounded on all sides by the hills had to evolve tactics to deal with the continuance for the steadiness of its kingdom. Special officers were appointed by them to keep close contact with each hill tribe and also to regulate the relations between the tribesmen and the villagers living in the plains along the foot hills belt.[84] When the Ahom developed acquaintance with the hill tribes like Nagas, Nyishi, Aka, Monpa, Sherdukpen, etc., they found out the tribes had the habit of coming down to the valley and took away whatever they found before them. Occasionally, they raided the valley people and ransacked all their essential commodities.

After each raid, the Ahom kings sent the military to punish the offenders, but they failed to trace the offenders. Ultimately, the Ahom kings realised the ineffectiveness of retaliatory military expeditions and having hostile relationships with the tribal people only cost a lot to its kingdom and so settled for arriving at a solution.

King Pratap Singha (1603-41) was the first to introduce a policy of reconciling with certain hill tribes living along the frontier of their kingdom through what came to be known as the *posa*. *Posa*[85] was a kind of deal or settlement between the Ahom and the tribal chiefs.[86] The hill tribes from the north would descend annually to the plains to receive payments in kind. For certain border villages the subscriptions raised by a village to meet the customary demands of the hillmen were paid in kind. The quantities demanded from each village were fixed and well known to both parties and as no inhabitant of a plains village was liable for any particular article the whole amount was raised collectively as village payment (*posa*). One of the important factors to be noted in connection with revenue was that the Akas, Miris, Nagas, Nyishi, and the Bhutias enjoyed the privilege of '*posa*' i.e., the right to levy tribute from certain villages in the plains set apart for that purpose by the Ahom Raja Pratap Singha. The Nagas reciprocated by offering gifts to the Ahom Raja.[87] Different strategies were adopted by the Ahom in order to administer the diverse hill tribes as per circumstances and location, in return the hill tribes were anticipated to uphold peace and good relation with the Ahom kings and also cease from raiding the Ahom villages.[88]

Hutton, the British Indian civil servant, had remarked that the Konyak chief and village elders used to collect *posa* through Bhitar Namsang *duar* (pass). The *duar's* situated in Konyak areas were broadly divided into two divisions namely: Sangnyu and Jaboka, where there used to be independent Assamese village paying revenue to the Nagas.[89] This village was taken by the British Government by swearing to compensated to the Nagas in perpetuity a sum of Rs 79 *khat* money. In 1841-42, when Brodie visited the villages of Banfera, Jaboka, Mulung, Jaktong and Changno (these people are now known as Konyak, Mon district) he made an agreement with the chiefs of these villages that they will be allowed to use those *khat's* in lieu of payment of a trifling tribute. In 1873-74, the Government resumed some of the *khat's* of Namsangia and Borduria chiefs, which were previously associated with the tea garden, for annual payment in cash. By 1920-21, all the *khat's* were under the control of the administration.[90]

Table No. 1: Details of resumption of certain Naga *khats* and Payment to the Naga owners of fixed allowance (Malikana).

Sl. No.	*Description of khat*	*No.*	*Amount to be paid annually*
1.	Hatigrah Duar, Samsa Borduria Goya	No. 6	Rs. 63
2.	Hatigarhia Duar, Bordubi Mariani Goya	No. 8	Rs. 83
3.	Asring Naga *khat*, Charingdhar Khampong, Lachu, Asring, Nagoya Benagoya, Mudchung, Khari letia chung	…..	Rs. 70
4.	Charigoya	No. 9	Rs. 100
5.	Ditto	No. 10	Rs. 133
6.	Malachi Naga Chang	No. 11	Rs. 180
7.	Tarfat Duar, Akuk Naga	Rs. 18	Rs. 80
8.	Harho's Duar, Janpang Chang	Rs. 12	Rs. 85
9.	Mikilai khat, Chereli Duar, Mikilai Naga	Rs. 12	Rs. 90
10.	Borgoya Duar, Chang Naga	Rs. 14	Rs. 90
11.	Borgoya Naga *khat*, Tarfat Duar, Borgoya chang	….	…..
12.	Lungtang Duar, Lungsang Chang, Lungrang Naga	No. 16	Rs. 80
13.	Ditto. Ditto. Ditto	No. 16	Rs. 40

14.	Siligoya Naga Khat, Taraft Duar, Siligoya chang	No. 19	Rs. 60
15.	Chanigoya Khat, Tarafat Duar, Khurgram Chang Charigoya	No. 10	Rs. 55
16.	Nichang Naga Khat, Tarfat Duar Nichang Naga	....	Rs. 70
17.	Tarfat Duar, Bhedari Chang	No. 22	Rs. 110
18.	Nagoya Khat, Tarfat Duar, Nagoya	No. 23	Rs. 80
19.	Khabun Khat, Tarfat Duar, Khabang Goya	No. 24	Rs. 60
20.	Geleki Duar, Tablungia chang	No. 5	Rs. 140
21.	Geleki Duar, Tablungia chang	No. 5	Rs. 25
22.	Has been identified within Tiruduar Borgoya Khat in the Deputy Commissioner, Sibsagars list possibly incorrectly. It appears in a later list as at Khapan, Pathar, Ogiriyan.	No. 4	Rs. 50

Letter No. 899T, Dated 24th Oct, 1921, pp. 7-8.[91]

The *posa* system continued with certain modifications even after British occupied Assam following the First Anglo-Burmese War.[92] Later, the British fixed a suitable amount to be paid in cash. Subsequently, the British government closed the labour service (*paik's)* which was offered to the Nagas by the Ahom.[93] For instance, reference is made to 84 *bighas* of Naga *khat* or land in the plains, granted revenue free to Nagas. This area represented by *Paniduaria khat* (now in Changlang, district), *Sangnyu* and *Jaboka* (presently Mon, district).[94] 88 *kotokie's* were assigned to look after Nagas in Seebsagor and a total revenue remission on account of Naga (*kotokie's*) was Rs 797.[95] The main objective of the British to continue this system was to establish peaceful relations with the Nagas and try to have commercial and geo-strategic control over the region inhabited by the Eastern Nagas. They also sought to have commercial control over the region with flows of the British manufactured goods; intention being to make them habituated to British goods.[96]

The following excerpts from the colonial report of Jenkins provide imperative facts of the Ahom policy and Naga-Ahom relations during the Ahom period. According to Major Francis Jenkins,[97] in the year 1842, he had gone to Tabloong, a Naga village lying a few miles to the west of Jaktoong. The chief there mentioned that one of the Assam kings had made him a grant of a certain number of *pyke's,* and that he formerly held three *khat*'s or farms in Dhopabur. The *pyke's,* it would appear, had fled during the trouble with the Moamarias, and the *khat*'s had gone to waste since the period. He also laid claim to three *bheel*'s, but it appears that one of these has been washed away by the Brahmaputra and the remaining two were filled up and could no longer be fished in. Under these circumstances, Jenkins told him that he have at authorization to take up any quantity of land he might desire to cultivate at the foot of the hills to the extent of the three *khat's* he formerly held; that he would use all the influence he possessed to induce the return of his *pyke*'s, if they could be found, and were not disinclined to remove from their present locations; and that at any rate he would prohibit the fiscal officers from detaining any *pyke*'s who wished to settle on the land the chief took up. He told him he could not pledge to the grant of any new *bheel*'s, but that if he was desirous of such a grant, would recommend it being made if not open to any serious objections. This communication was perfectly satisfactory; and chief, came down with Jenkins to Jaktoong and there entered into the engagements, which were subsequently given in by every chief of any note along the line of the route to the Buri Dihing.

The substance of these engagements was to abstain from raids in the plains; to be responsible for the surrender of offenders within its limits of their *duar's*; to discontinue hostilities with other tribes leaving the British Government to punish any attack made upon themselves; and finally, abstain from importing Naga children as slaves into the British territories, a practice that was of daily occurrence under the rule of Raja Poorunder Singha, which Jenkins had reason to think had been carried on since to some limited extent.

Lotha-Ahom Relations

The existence of *khat* system was evident, especially in the area between Doyang and the Dikhow where there were no salt wells. The Ahom government granted the Nagas (Lotha, Ao, Phom, Rengma) land and *paik*'s. A.J. Moffatt Mills, observed many villages' even possessed gifts of land in the plains, given by the Ahom Rajas.[98] This agreement was reliably maintained. The grants given to Lotha *Pvuti* (meaning chief in Lotha dialect) by the Ahom Rajas, was on the understanding that the Lothas in return for the land, would refrain from taking Assamese heads. Thus, the agreement was loyally kept, and villages such as Khoro, who had no hostile Naga neighbours whom they could raid, used to content themselves with waylaying and killing an occasional Mikir on his way to or from market in the plains. There is no record of any fighting between Lothas and Assamese, save a raid in 1685 on some villages of the plains near the Doyang by Lhotas Nagas.[99]

The policy of giving grants of *khat's* and *bheel's* to Nagas to stop raiding in the plains began with the reign of King Jayadhvaj Singha (1648- 1663 AD). This continued till the beginning of 19th century when the Ahom power was on its decline. So long as the Ahom government was strong enough to maintain their suzerainty by controlling conflicts within the kingdom and resisting foreign invasions, the Nagas tribes remained cordial with the Ahom rulers and annually visited the Ahom kingdom.[100] The same policy applied to other tribes such as Kachari, Khasi, Jantia, and Boro; wherein the elements of mutual exchange prevailed in their traditions. Each side acquired what each needed. The Ahoms remained satisfied with receiving allegiance annually from the hill tribe's. The flow of mutual goods and exchange between the foothill Naga villages and the Brahmaputra Valley continued until the last days of Ahom rule. Many valley people preferred the produce that arrived from upland Naga villages. For instance, Shri. Girin Phukon, a local Ahom historian from Moranhat, Upper Assam, describes how the people of Ahom liked the Nagas products from the Naga hills, such as *paan*, areca nut, yam, pumpkin, banana, Naga chillies, (*raja mircha*) etc. The hill products are sweeter and better and he even describes the vegetables from the plains as bitter and tasteless. The households from Ahom villages loved and preferred any Naga products and are drawn toward it. The flow of goods between the upland Naga villages and the Brahmaputra valley has continued.

Much of the Ahoms households consumed large quantities of areca nuts with lime and *paan* (betel leaf). Even though areca nuts and betel leave grew abundantly in the plains of the Assam, the Ahom villages preferred the ones that arrived from the upland Naga villages.[101]

The Solitude of the Naga tribes

Even though the Nagas have lived for centuries in their habitat, they have preserved a way of life that distinguishes them from their valley neighbours Assam (Hindu culture) and Burma (Buddhist culture). Their villages usually are built on hill tops whose slopes are covered with thick jungle and are separated by deep ravines and river valley from the surrounding country where they maintained their cultural tradition and way of life. Furthermore, they maintain communications with their neighbour the Ahoms for their political and economic purposes.[102]

From the beginning of 16th century the process of expansion of the Ahom kingdom in the Brahmaputra valley by subjugating the tribes who had held significant portions of the plains territory was slow and a steady process. The existence and independence of Ahom state depended on the measure of success attained in maintaining a policy of coercion and friendship. However, it was attended with much blood-shed. As their kingdom expanded the Ahoms were burdened with the additional responsibility of protecting their expanding kingdom from the inroads of the hill-tribes who inhabited on the frontier of Assam on all three sides.[103]

The Ahoms never attempted to completely subjugate or annex Naga territory- instead they were left to continue with their autonomy in their homeland. The Ahoms upheld political alliance; the reason may be that the Ahoms did so because they saw in the Nagas a warlike people who loved their independence, to remain a free spirit without being subjugated to control and rigour of a state regime. The Nagas are hospitable by nature, brave, and they respect even a guest, honour, and protect them.[104] A 70-year-old Hazarika, a trader from Charaideo (Sonari) described his late Konyak friend (*mita*). He stated that the Nagas were good, but the plains people like us ruined them. We taught them all bad things. He believed the Nagas do not often shower, but what they said from their mouth was clean-their minds are innocent.[105] However, "they are somewhat sensitive, inclined to be independent in their attitude and resentful against injustice, whether real or imaginary."[106]

In *Tarik-i-Asam* during Mir Jumla's invasion of Assam the hill tribes are referred to as fierce and capable of holding their own despite living isolated from the touch of civilisation, so the Ahom king came to know the crucial values of Nagas for their kingdom.[107] Shihabuddin Talish also mentions the encounter in one of their expeditions during Mir Jumla's invasion. Mention is made of the Nagas using guerilla tactics, though the Mughal army was better equipped with comparatively advance weapons like matchlock and guns as against the primitive weapons of the tribesmen, yet there was little scope to utilise them, as the hillmen resorting to guerrilla and ambuscade methods of warfare conducted their operations from unexpected woods and defiles. The difficulties of a hill campaign, particularly in connection with communication and transport, can be best understood from these explanations. Besides, many Mughal soldiers died of blood-dysentery and food provisions also failed. There was no provision supply and the Nagas did not allow passage, they used to roll down stones from the hill tops and kill the men by that method. The soldiers proceeded one month's journey by clearing the jungle, but could not find any clue whatsoever.[108] Captain St. John F. Michel also state in one of his 'Report on the North-East Frontier, 1883' says, 'The Assamese army appears at this time 1660 to have been largely recruited from the Nagas and the Miri, and it is evident that they were quite able to hold their own against the well-trained armies of Hindustan.'[109] During the Moamaria revolt despite repeated appeals from the Ahom king Kamaleswar Singha (1795-1810 AD), the Kachari King Krishnachandra Narayan did not try to discourage his subjects from allying themselves with the rebellious Moamarias who had taken up arms against the Ahom government.[110] However, in the case of the Nagas according to the oral traditions of the Ao and the Konyak the Nagas remained faithful to the Ahom rulers during the Moamaria rebellion. However, in the area where salt mines lay, the villages like Borduaria, and Nocte villages like Yangkang took advantage to regain their control. Whereas Ao, Lotha villages and Konyak villages like Jaboka, Tablung, Moohung aided to help the Ahoms by given them shelter and fought alongside with the Ahoms.

Role of *Katakis* as moderator in Naga-Ahom relations

The Ahom state appointed officials such as *chautong* and *kataki's* for the maintenance of regular political and commercial relations with the independent hill tribes. Under the Ahoms there were three categories of *Katakis* – the *Barkataki*, the *Majukataki*, and the *Sarukataki*. They had to be present in the court meeting held by the king or the Barphukan. They served under the Majindar Barua and were dependent on him. On occasion when an envoy had to be sent to the Emperor of Gaur or the Emperor of Delhi or to the Nawab of Lucknow, a good, intelligent *Barkataki* was selected and sent for the job.[111]

The Ahom kings needed to deal with the circumstances that arose out of frequent raiding by the Nagas and the prospect of Mughal invasion. The *kataki's* had an essential role to play in achieving its territorial integrity and maintaining harmony with various objectives, such as trade, etc. The Ahom Raja Susenpha (Burha Raja or Pratap Singha 1603-1641) after consulting the Naga chiefs appointed the *kataki's* and *Doloi's* as an envoy. The recruited candidate had to be gifted with persuasive character and intelligence, who were familiar with the Naga customary laws and cultures and could deal with them. Pratap Singha*'s* gave detailed instructions to the *kataki's* relating the manner in which the *kataki's* had to start on his mission. The *kataki's* enjoyed immunity from violence and insult.

Katakis did not hold his position for life; he often wished to relinquish the post for some reason such as old age. The usual procedure was to suggest a successor to the Nagas and hand over charge to him with their approval. Position of *kataki's* was doubtless a lucrative one. It was only to be expected that the *kataki's* should suggest one of his relations as successor, but the position was not hereditary. However, it tended to remain in one family since the Nagas having no means of selecting suitable candidates themselves, were almost bound to accept the suggestion of the retiring *kataki's*. For instance, when the Naga chiefs went down to the valley kingdom to collect grants, he wouldn't go empty handed. He will be bringing gifts to the Ahom Raja, such gifts consisted of a tube of salt, *daos*, spear head, elephant tusks, reed cane, birds feather, honey, mithun, etc. The gifts were reciprocated by the Ahoms, by arranging food and accommodations when they come down to plains during their annually visit. For instance, when the representative of Jaboka villagers (Konyak) went to collect grants in the plains, headed by a *wangsa* (small chief), a *mehmei* (an adult man) of the village, a *kataki* had to arrange all the necessities for the chief's and his attendants.[112] However, they would not allow Nagas to enter their house saying the Nagas smelled and so they were offered huts near the cowshed or outside granary house to take shelter for a night, often the Nagas slept under the rice straw to warm their body. The Nagas often went down during the winter season after finishing their *jhum* works, when the Nagas would come down to the plains through their prescribed paths or gateways under the escort of the *kataki's* to catch the fish from the *bheel* in Sibsagar, Geleky, Dibrugarh, Borhat, Jorhat, Simulguri, Nagagaon (upper Assam). They caught fish, dried the same and prepared powder of dried fish to preserve, which was called *Sukati mass*. Putting it in bamboo barrels, which they carried the same to the hills.

Details from British archival sources regarding Naga *khat's* and *kataki's*[113] are given below to have an idea of their work and payment received by the Nagas during the Ahom period.

Lonogoham (Hilligaon located in Sibsagar)- The *kataki's* at Lonogoham used to pay Rs 20 a year. When the boundaries of the *khat* was defined, apparently at the resettlement of Sibsagar, this was raised to Rs 30. The *mauzadar* now paid this amount.

Impang- This *khat* consisted of 2 plots of 12 and 3 *puras* respectively on either bank of the Mekrang. A definite arrangement was made with a former *kataki* called "*polai*" that the Nagas were not satisfied and as a result of the arrangement that they should get half the rent, this payment was raised to Rs 30 and various articles of essential commodities were added. *Polai's* successor paid Rs 52 and since then payments have risen through the stages of Rs 80 and Rs 83 to Rs 89-11 which was paid by the mauzadar.

Akuk- There were two *khats in Akuk duar*; Separate *kataki's* were appointed when the land was granted by the Raja. In both cases the arrangement was that the *kataki's* should realise the rent on behalf of the Nagas, and pay 2/3, keeping 1/3 as commission. The *kataki's* were also to feast them when they went to the valley. The Nagas often went down to help the *kataki* to realise the rent, and also induced him to pay up their share.

(a) One *khat* was in Golaghat elaka, run by the mauzadar, the payment by *kataki's* rose as follows: Rs 9 and gifts in kind, Rs 20, Rs 33.-7-6.

The jump from Rs 9 to Rs 20 took place about 16 or 17 years ago when the Nagas saw the *mandal* lay the boundaries and realised how badly they had been cheated. The *khat* is now managed by the mauzadar who paid them Rs 63 a year and they might get as much as Rs 100 next year. He asked them to accept a flat rate, but the Nagas refused and continued to stick to their demand for 2/3 share. This was fixed by the mauzadar at Rs 63. It was clear that the *kataki* was cheating them badly. He offered to pay them much more than Rs 33, if they would affix their thump impressions to a petition asking that the *khat* be handed over to the mauzadar. These demands were sensibly refused.

(b) The other *khat* was in Jorhat sadar ilaka, belonging to Lhota village called Mirasi, which has now merged with Akuk. The present *kataki*, was Beparem, who was appointed in place of his father-in-law, Kepiya a most unlikely arrangement. If any hereditary right existed payments have been as follows. Rs 40, Rs 20, Rs 63, Rs 85 was paid that year. There was a dispute on that year in about March, and the *katakis* had agreed to pay Rs 47 more in addition to the Rs 85 already paid. The *kataki* submitted rough accounts to the Nagas showing the names of tenants, rents, etc.

Lakhuti

(a) One *khat* belonged to Lakhuti village, formerly the Nagas used to go down and collect the rent themselves, the *kataki* going round to the various houses and giving the necessary information. The Nagas kept half and gave half as commission to the *kataki*. Later the Nagas ceased going down and entrusted *kataki* to give their share. They were paid Rs 14-10 *annas* annually. After some years they suspected that more land has been opened out and that their payments ought to have been increased. They put pressure on the *kataki* and payments were increased. The next year they received Rs 66-10 from the mauzadar, and following year Rs 67-15.

(b) The other *khat* was still held in the name of Lungtem village, though this is combined with Lakhuti. For convenience sake there was one *kataki* for both the *khat's*. The Nagas used to receive Rs 10 and a feast every year. But they had the land measured up and put pressure on the *kataki*, who increased the payments. They were still far from satisfied and were very glad when the management was taken over by the mauzadar. The *kataki* was far from being (pleased and offered them Rs 40 and Rs 5 worth of liquor for their thump impression on a petition protesting against the change. Last year they received Rs 22-7 from mauzadar and this year Rs 33-31.

Bhandari- This village had two *khat's* with separate *kataki's*. The agreement was that the *kataki's* collect the rent and get half as commission. Bhandari could have handed their *khat's* over to the mauzadar; but the *kataki's* and pleader got round them and persuaded them to put their thump impression to a petition which they did not understand, by a promise to raise the payments. One cash payments have been raised from Rs 60 to Rs 72 and in the other from Rs 80 to Rs 100.

Sanis- There were two *kataki's* for this *khat*, one representing Sanis and one Sanglap and Yansucho. The earliest payments were Rs 10 and a feast by each *kataki*; and later Rs 20 by each *katakis* and no feast. That year the mauzadar paid Rs 50-56, to be divided equally between Sanis, Yansucho and Sanglap.

Miri Nokpu- This village managed its *khat* through a *kataki* but some years later gave up the practice and now go down and collect the rent every year and they get about Rs 70.

Changki and Semsa- (a) From a *khat* near Mariani each village gets Rs 18 per year, and has done so for a long time. (b) From a *khat* near Kokilamukh, Changki gets Rs 10-8 and Semsa Rs 10-8. There are separate *katakis* for the two villages for these *khats*.

Tsori- In this *khat* the Nagas got about Rs 60.

Mon- Wakching, Jaboka, Shangnyu, Punkung, and Namsang received their rent from Assam Company through the officers. Neither the *khat* of Kongang, nor that of Wanching were managed by *katakis*.

Resumption of Certain Naga *khats* in the Sibsagar District and Payment of fixed allowances to the Naga owners in final Settlement of their claims 1922.

Resumption of Certain Naga Khats in the Sibsagar District and Payment of fixed allowances to the Naga owners in final Settlement of their claims 1922.[1]

List of Naga *khats* Borne in the Register of Sibsagar. Table 2.

Name of Naga khats	***Total area of khat***	***Total cultivable area of khat***	***Amount of revenue payable on the settled production of the khat or ordinary rate***	***Amount received by the Naga khat khatdars in the past (as reported by the D.C. Naga Hills) In cash***	***In kind.***	***Right of katakis if any***	***Price nature of profits obtained by the katakis (excluding the local rate and the amount paid to the khatdars)***	***Amount recommended for payment in perpetuity to the Naga khatadars in extension of all rights on the khat land by***		***Compensation recommended to katakis***	***Remarks***
1	2	3	4	5	6	7	8	D.C Naga Hills 9	D.C Sibsagar 10	11	12
1. Samsa Bardubia khat	B.K.I 60.2.10	B.K.L 60.2.10	Rs.a.p. 69.2.0	Rs.a.p. 22.8.0	Rs.a.p 22	There are two katakis holding katakiship for three generations the present katakis claims for settlement of the khatland with them in the ordinary way.	Rs.a.p 37	Rs 75	Rs 45	Rs 30 A year or settlement.	Rate for sub- letting is Rs 1-9 per bigha. If we adopt recommendation of D.C Naga Hills for compensation Govt. will lose considerably by taking over the khat

1. Revenue Department, Resumption of Certain Naga Khats in the Sibsagar District and Payment of fixed allowances to the Naga owned in final settlement of their claims, Government of Nagaland, Archive 1922.

2. Hatigatia Bardubia khat.	25-0-17	25-0-17	27-.14.0	36.00	47. (according to the katakis Rs 30 only)	The present katakis has worked for 6 years and is the son-in-law of the previous kataki	18. (taking the amount paid in kind Rs,30 only)	86.	66.	Nill or settlement.	Rental value of the lands being Rs 3-8 per bigha, total income to the katakis amount to Rs 87-8 out of which Rs 66 paid to the Nagas and Rs 35 is the profit intercepted by the katakis. According to the katakis Rs 30 is paid in kind. But the D.C. Naga hills says, that Rs 47 was paid in kind by subscriptions by other villagers who do not possess khat lands.
3. Asing Naga khat	57.1 6	57.1 6	54.7.0	77.0.0	-------	No katakis for this. It is administered by the Naga themselves	-------	75	75	Nill	Rental value Rs 1-12 per bigha
4. Charigaon khat	52.2.6	52.2 6	49.9.0	100.0.0	-------	Ditto	-------	100	100	Nill	Rental value Rs 3 per bigha
5. Charigaon khat	70.0.[illegible]4	70.0.[illegible]4	43.9.0	130.0.0	3.0.0	3.0.0 Holding katakiship for 3 generations	[illegible]1. and enjoys	135	133	Com-pensation	Rental value Rs 5

6. Jangpang khat	95.2.11	95.2.11	91.7.0	80.0.0	5.0.0	Japora Kachari is the present kataki. It is reported tht this khat has been managed by this family from the beginning.	85	100	85	85 a year	The rental of value of the land is Rs 2 per bigha
7. Mikilai khat	92.3.8	92.3.8	101.0.8	85.0.0	5.0.0	Kataki for three generations. The name of the present kataki is Rangai	80	116	90	Rs.80 a year	The rental value Rs 2 per bigha
8. Bagaya khat (Bargaya Duar)	52.0.17	52.0.17	69.14.0	-----	-----	-----	-----	-----	-----	-----	Rental value is Rs 2 per bigha. 44 bighas are under cultivation.
9.Bargaya khat (Darfat Duar)	59.0.16	59.0.16	77.0.6	89.11.0	Srijut Rahdhanath Borbora, ex-mauzadar of Gilladhai, has been appointed kataki from 1915 by the S.D.O. Mokokchung.	68.	100	90 for both the khats.	Nill	Rental value is Rs 1-8 per bigha 59 bighas are under cultivation.	Mr.Mill's note shows that formerly the Nagas received only Rs 10 a year for these two khats and these payment have risen by successive stages to Rs 89-11 less half the local rates the local rates. I see no sufficient reason for raising the payment to Rs 100 except that it is a convenient round sum for division J.E.W.

10. Lakhuti Naga khat	87.2.8	37.2.8	81.0.0	79.11.0	-----	Ditto	34	90	80	Nill	Rental value is Rs 1-8 per bigha.83 bighas under cultivation
11. Siligaya	112.1.8	112.1.8	73.13.0	59.9.0	-----	Srijut Radhanath Borbors, ex-mauzadar of Ghilladhari is the kataki from 1915	55	70	60	Nill	Rental value of Rs 1-8 per bighas are under cultivation.
12. Changaya khat (Kheseni khat)	94.3.16	94.3 16	54.5.0	-----	Ditto	Ditto	75	68	55	Nill	Rental value
13. Nichang Naga khat	88.1.14	88.1.14	109.0.0	55.0.0	15.0.0	Kataki for 3 generations	30	75	70	Rs. 30 a year	Rental value is Rs 1-8 per bigha 76 bigha a.e. under cultivation
14. Bhandari khat	129.4.0 (according to the khat register) 144.4.15 (reported by the sub-Deputy collector)	Entire area	175.9.0	101.0.0	78.8.0	Kataki for 3 generations. The present kataki cultivates 13 bighas of land himself	85	120	189	Rs. 85	Rental value Rs 1-3 per bighas 144 bigha i.e. under cultivation
15. Nagaya khat	104.4.5	104.4.5	117.0.0	70.0.0	7.8.0	Kataki for 3 generations	45	65	78	Rs. 45 a year	The rate of sub-letting is Rs 1-8 per bigha. 92 bighas are under cultivation.

16. Khabung khat	69.2.6 Shown as 89-2-6 by the D.C Naga Hills.	69.2.6	101.0.0	40.0.0	20.0.0	The present kataki lives solely on the khat land. Holding katakiship from his forefather's time.	39	65	60	Rs.40 a year	Rental value per bigha is Rs 2-6. 45 bighas are under cultivation
17. Akuk Naga khat (sl. No.7 in the D.C Naga Hills.)	81.2.6	81.2.6	66.13.0	63.0.0	-----	Srijut Radhanath Bordora, ex-mauzadar, is the kataki from the year 1915	50	80	63	Nil	Rental value per bigha is Rs 1-8, entire area is under cultivation.
18. Tablungia khat	(i) 55.0.15 (ii) 11.3.4	56.0.15 11.3.4	59.5.0 6.2.0	140.0.0 20.0.0	4-4	No kataki	-----	145 25	145 20	Nil	Khat land of i) has been sub-let to Mr.L.Aahfield of Bihubar Tea Estate in 1917-16 who pays annually a rent of Rs. 144-4.
19. Kongan khat (This khat is also known as Tirupura Borgoya khat and Owgurijan Khepon pathar) Nos. 22 and 23)	Previous area 63b-2k Area ascertained by Kessrs. Thomas and Hills in excess of the area shown above.	63.2.0	30.1.0 159.6.0	38.12.0 -----	----- -----	No kataki No kataki	Nil Nil	50	50	Nil	-----

20. Bitas Nam-chang (Owner Brochang Changai) in Abhopur mauza of Sibsagar Sub-division.	560.0.12	Lying waste No culti-vation	Rs. 315 (c-alculated at the pound rate of annas 9 per bighas, sanctioned for unserved areas of this districts)	No kataki	-----	-----	Not suggested)	Rs. 79. i.e. 25 per cent of the present annual value	-----		This khat is situated beyond the Ladaigar off Namtola tea garden near Towkak. People say that during the days of the Assam Rajas the kacharis and the mahuts whose descendants are now inhabitants of the Nokobari and Lekomage and other adjacent village of this khat. This khat has long been abandoned and now exists only in name. There is no cultivation, it belongs to the Changnoi Nagas.
21. Panduria khat (owner: - Panicura chang) in Abhoypur mauza of Sibsagar sub-division.	84.0.0	84.0.0	83..8.0	Not known	No kataki	No kataki	Not suggested			Rs.63 (i.e 75 percent of the annual value.)	The khat is situated in Siloni Naga village in Abhoypur nauza. The khat has been demarcated. It belongs to the Panduria Nagas and now stands in the name of Yangchai Nagas one of the Pandiduria Nagas. there are about 17 families of the Nagas who live close

											to the khat and cultivate the khat land. No land is sub-let to Assam of other people. The local rate of Rs 10-4 due on this khat is collected by Yangchai from the Nagas who cultivate the land. It is not known what profits the Nagas who receive in the past. According to the statement of Nirmal Gaonbura, the sub-Deputy Collector, Nazira, reports

Raids and Trade

According to *Buranjis*, raids and retaliations were part and parcel of Naga-Ahom relations, sometimes the Nagas would accept the Ahom suzerainty, and frequently they will come down to raid in the plains.[115] Fierce clashes followed, with killing or capturing a large number of hill peoples. More often, the Ahom army would find the hostile villages completed abandoned, as its inhabitants, not keen on confronting the Ahom forces, had already taken shelter in the jungle or moved to higher altitudes. Infrequently, the Ahom army would recapture some of the stolen belongings, and took retaliation by razing down and burning the abandoned villages. However, the hill peoples reorganised speedily and their thatched houses were rebuilt; it was only a matter of time before they gained sufficient strength to raid the plains again.[116]

In order to ensure the peace and security of the Ahom kingdom from the Naga raids the frontier had to be kept under control. Subsequently, the Ahoms came to develop various policies in the frontier in order to avert any attack.[117] A significant aspect of this was institutionalised in the form of *duar* (pass or gate) by the Ahoms. The foothill Nagas frequently exchanged and interacted with the plains through these *duar*'s (each *duar* has a markets or *haat* attached to it).[118] The Ahoms felt the need to protect and guard whatever areas they managed to bring under their control by establishing hats at the foothills. The Eastern Naga salt wells were another area where the Nagas-Ahom often clashed. However, it was settled amicably. In order to maintain peace and tranquility the Ahom king appointed an official called Khamjang Gohain to look after the salt brine.[119]

However, pre-colonial Naga raids and feuds were conducted within the purview of certain framework or inter village/regional councils/leagues (i.e., pertaining to law of warfare). When a warrior/village captured/ killed men/women without justifiable reasons, or violated codes of conduct in warfare, the village or the individual warrior would be punished as per its 'laws of warfare.' All these for long acted as court of justice concerning crimes, wars/raids, and other issues within their respective jurisdictions. The councils/leagues were endowed with the power to demarcate "safe zones" and "war zones," and also to decide upon "warring season" and "off seasons". When the first European (Lieutenant H. Brigge), set foot on Naga soil in 1841[120] he observed, the Lotha Nagas raiding in the late 18th and early 19th centuries had a league of villages (formed for purposes of war) in existence.[121] Such leagues were headed by the more powerful villages, like Pangti and Tsingaki (Lotha villages), which respectively headed two different leagues, formed for wars against the Aos and Semas. J.P. Mills also observed that wars between Lotha villages were rare and a Lotha taking another Lotha's head was "absolute forbidden".[122] That suggests the prevalence of a consciousness among the Lotha Nagas of their collective identity despite the absence of any socio-political organisations comprising the entire 'tribe'. Thus, the existence of regional or inter-village leagues/ councils, the prevalence of different types of war/raids, practices pertaining to warfare, capturing enemies and taking heads of slain enemies, invalidate the portrayal of the Naga society as lawless and unruly/anarchic society.[123]

There were frequent disputes between the Nagas-Ahoms, often the Nagas launched raids upon the Ahom villages to take vengeance for assaulting Nagas during their visit to valley for trade or to collect revenue and they also plundered when refused to pay '*posa*' to them. The initial contacts were marred by a strong feeling of hostility on both sides, which never resulted in the subjugation of either one by the other. Geographical proximity and economic exigencies made them inevitably dependent on each other.[124]

Also, raiding was done not for the sake of procuring heads as generally stated by colonial authorities and ethnographers. It appears that 'heads' were merely outcomes, not the cause of the raids. The raids in pre-colonial Naga society were driven by eschatological reasons, socio-economic necessities, and political considerations and ideas of justice and honour/ revenge. Apart from raiding, it appeared that the Nagas did not seem to have any interest in extending their territories.

The Ahom king Sukhampha alias Khora Raja (1552-1603) is said to have stated, one of the main reasons for the Naga raids was the economic inadequacy in the hills.[125] However, the census of 1921 on the Nagas cited: the economic condition of the tribes was good and there was no shortages of land or food and the Nagas (Lotha, Ao and Konyak) was unequalled as a cultivator of *jhum* field. Cotton, oranges, and yam was grown for export. In character the Nagas (Lotha, Ao) were honest, a lover of soil, the river, and the jungles. Crimes of serious nature was practically non-existent.[126]

The Nagas believed that they had rights in the foothill areas and had the right to claim their rightful shares. If the Ahoms didn't share the dues on time they went down to raid the plains to claim it. In order to stop Nagas from raiding, and in recognition of the services rendered by Nagas living by the side of river Dikhow, he granted several *bheel's* (fishing water areas) to name a few in Geleky, Songtok, Jorhat, and Maurani etc., to the Nagas (Konyak-Wancho, Lotha, and Ao).[127] The king also allocated fishermen to the Nagas, in this way they reciprocated each other until the British arrival.

Raja Pratap Singha also granted revenue-free land (Naga *khat*) along with retainers (*Bahatias*) supervised by Assamese agents (Naga *kataki's*) to the Naga chiefs. He also constructed many roads and tanks, built up the great Dopgarh embankment as a protection against Naga inroads, and developed backward tracts. He built the forts at Samdhara, Safrai, Sila, and several stone bridges during his reign.[128]

Elwin referred to twenty-two Naga *khat*'s, of which three villages came under erstwhile Mokokchung district in Naga Hills, namely, Changki, Longsemdang and Nokpu villages. The payment was given to Ao Naga of those areas to prevent them from raiding into the plains.[129]

In an Ao village called Changki (Mokokchung District, two-and-a-half-hour journey from Mariani in Assam) according to Changki village tradition, members of the village council made annual trips to foothill Ahom village areas to collect 'taxes' in the form of livestock, ducks, chickens, rice, salt, betel nuts, etc.[130] The *khats* were subsequently taken over by the British in return for a fixed payment. A letter written by B.C. Allen in 1921, stated:

> a fixed payment was made to the Nagas through the Deputy Commissioner of the Naga hills so that the Naga *khat*'s as such should be taken under their reign. A settlement would be made ordinarily with the persons now in possession. The land now lying waste would be dealt with just as if it was ordinary Government way.[131]

The British arranged by paying a lump sum in a year to the Nagas after the downfall of Ahom kingdom. These *khat's* were practically abolished after 1967.[132]

Table 3. Statement of *kataki's* remission to Nagas of Sibsagar District in 1844

SI. No.	Names of Dwars	No.of Kataki's	Remission for Kataki's land	Remission for Naga khats	Total amount of Remission
1.	Mohong Bor Dwariya	2	6-0-0	0-0-0	6-0-0
2.	Namsang	3	9-0-0	0-0-0	9-0-0
3.	Moothoon	2	6-0-0	0-0-0	6-0-0
4.	Bheetur Namsang	3	9-0-0	16-6-8	25-6-8
5.	Teeree	3	9-0-0	15-13-7	24-13-7
6.	Dobdhor	7	21-0-0	16-0-0	36-0-0
7.	Assiringia	2	6-0-0	35-5-9	41-5-9
8.	Hatteeghur Dyung Dwar	2	6-0-0	24-6-10	30-6-10

9.	Chareegaih	2	6-0-0	10-0-0	16-0-0
10.	Jungpang	3	9-0-0	24-2-0	35-2-0
11.	Lakoteeah	8	24-0-0	45-12-2	69-12-2
12.	Saneegaon and Kergaon	2	6-0-0	23-13-4	29-13-4
13.	Borgaon	3	9-0-0	34-8-7	43-8-7
14.	Hilleegaon	3	9-0-0	40-7-10	49-7-10
15.	Nowgong	2	6-0-0	26-8-0	32-8-0
16.	Akook	3	9-0-0	20-11-3	29-11-3
17.	Oorboong	0	0-0-0	12-0-0	12-0-0
	Total	88	264-0-0	533-4-0	797-4-9

Source: FC, 19 October 1844, No. 124.[133]

Another example of the Ahom political diplomatic relations with the chief of Konyak-Wanchos can be given. The Yansa/Jaboka village (in Mon district) also has a tradition of annual trips to the Ahom kingdom referred to as '*sei sai*' or '*Attahatam*' meaning collect shares or gifts for the Konyak chief. A *sei sai* (literally in Konyak dialect meaning collect gifts for the chief) is an article of a specified homage paid to the chief in kinds. In each feud, detailed lists of these articles are furnished by the chiefs or elders deciding the feuds. Recognised *sei sai* from former times were:[134]

(a) Gong-there are several types of gong, and in each case, a specific type was mentioned.
(b) Silver bullion.
(c) Slaves
(d) A dao
(e) Spear head
(f) Opium

In return, the Naga chief gave a standard-sized bunch of *taro*, or one of the ordinary baskets of *tao* (yams), honey, bamboo, mat, elephant tusk, pig hair, bamboo, comb, cane, and baskets to the Ahoms. The element of trust entered into this relation when the Ahom gave gifts in kind and things to the Nagas. Initial rules were that the other parties could not refuse gifts given to someone. The recipient must reciprocate as equal to the giver. All these elements show the existence of mutual reciprocity and the obligation of accepting a social partnership that the Naga-Ahom inhabitants developed.[135]

Paiks granted to Nagas

In 1510 A.D., state census for the adult male population known as *paik* was conducted by the Ahom ruler. The *paik* system served as an effective weapon to dissolve tribal communities and to free the kingdom from the likely danger of tribal mutinies.[136] Starting from the reign of Pratap Singha (1603-1641), through the instrumentality of his minister, Momai Tamuli Barbarua, the feudal *paik* system became rationalised and mobilised. Under this system, except nobles, priests, and persons of high caste and their slaves, all the Ahom community were liable to render necessary services to the state on a rotational basis.[137] A levy of the first man was known as *mel*, second as *dewal* and the third as *tewal*.[138] This type of service under the state could take the form of service to the Raja or to any officer of state to whom he might be assigned. Lachit Barphukan fixed the quota of *paik's* attached to watch and checked by the immediate supervisors, 'Bora' 'Saikia,' 'Hazarika.'[139] Phukan was the highest title, and his contingent numbered 6,000 who had twenty men or *paik's* in his charge at a time. On occasions when the Bora found it challenging to take charge of them, his immediate supervisor Saikia would take up the role of supervising.[140] Some *paik*'s in the foothill areas near the hill tribes were assigned to give a certain amount of their products to the hill tribes so that the rage of the hill tribes could be mitigated.[141] These *paik*'s were known as *bahatiyas*[142] who had to carry on the commands of both the Nagas and the valley kingdom officers. The *khaiyas* also carry the commands and supply rations to the Nagas. Thus the overall burden of taxes and imposts on the *bahatiya paik*'s was heavier than those of the other category of *paik*'s.[143]

S.L. Baruah observed that the under the Ahom *posa* system the *bahatiyas* were made authorised victims of exploitation by the tribal people.[144] The lives, properties and crops of the *bahatiyas* were at the mercy of the hillmen. Despite this, they had to pay certain revenue to the Ahom government and proceeded to the battlefield when called upon. These *paik*'s were thus to serve two masters- the tribal chiefs and the Ahom monarch at the same time and were thus exploited by both. Always looking skeptical at both the masters, they were prone to be on the side of the stronger, the Ahoms. However, as the Ahom subjects elsewhere raised their standard of rebellion and fought for freedom from bondage, they soon joined hands with them. During the last years of Ahom rule, some hills chiefs found their allies among the *bahatiyas,* and together they proceeded to help the rebels to overthrow the Ahom government.

Geleky Bheel

Geleky is a small foothill town (between Sibsagar and Chariado district), a venue of meeting place, and its boundary with the Longleng, Mon and Mokokchung districts. The inhabitants from Konyak, Phom, Ao, Chang, and Ahom gathered and held feast. Mr Thorton, Assistant Surveyor, stated that when he visited Jaktoong (Konyak village), the chief mentioned that Ahom kings offered certain grants and that he formerly held three *bheels* in Dhoparbur. In return, the Nagas offered help and allegiance in exchange for assistance against any intrusion from foreign invasions.[145]

The Ahom Raja granted *bheels* in the border areas on lease to the hill tribes.[146] The Nagas too received from the Ahom government in the shape of land and fishing waters called *bheel* along with the retainer.[147] Ahom king Sukhampha, Khora Raja (1552-1603) rewarded the Tablungia Nagas (Konyak tribes living by the side of the Dikhow) with a *bheel* (fishing well) on the plains in recognition of some valuable services rendered by them to the Ahom king. Along with the *bheels* they were also assigned fishermen *paiks* (*Dom-bahatia*) to supply with them dried fish from the *bheels* assigned to them.[148]

Pratap Singha (1603-41) constructed an embankment called "*Nagagarh*" and an embankment called Naga Ali raised as a protection against their incursions or as a line of defence on the borders of Sibsagar and Lakhimpur.[149] The Naga had to be accompanied by *Chaotang* (interpreter) to pass the rampart.[150] The rampart through which the Nagas came down were Namsangia, Tiru, Jaboka, Tablungia, Assiringia pass (*duar*), etc.[151] The construction of numerous embankments and spurs on the Brahmaputra Valley and its tributaries was a device to extend cultivable land, connecting network, and to separate the valley kingdom. For instance, the city of Garhgaon was full of a network of roads, which were built connecting parts of the kingdom. The roads were known as Borpatra-Ali, Taimur- Ali, Chatai-Ali, Dhudar-Ali, Bor-Ali, Haripara-Ali, Meteka-Ali, Naga-Ali, Taimur-Ali, Salaguri-Ali, Sukati-Ali, Garhgaon -Ali and Kareng-Ali etc.[152] These embankments served as the main traffic to use by the pedestrians when all the rest of the valley was submerged by water.

The longest road constructed by Gadadhar Singha was called Dhodar Ali. It starts from Garhgaon till Naharkatiya in the east, touching the places of Simaluguri, Charaideo, Sonari and extended to Kamargaon in the west, bringing in fringe places like Nazira, Namti, Amguri, Marioni, Titabar, Golaghat, and others where it joined the Cheuni Ali. The distance of Dhodar Ali is almost 211 k.m.[153] Shihabuddin Talish mentions that one of such embankments was constructed from Lakhugarh to Garhgaon. Another long embankment, which extended from Koch Behar to Sadiya, existed till 1826, under thick jungle cover.[154] This policy was also introduced to expand their territory and protect themselves from intruders. Here are some of the important roads connecting the Naga hill.

Naga Ali: The Naga *Ali* was an important *Ali* for communication to Charing near the Namdang Silar Saku and the Naga hills. It was constructed by the Swargadeo Raja from the Namdang Silar Saku via Charing to Amguri in the district of Sibsagar. In the Morajar Mouza there was a Moidam of the Deoraja by the side of the Naga *Ali*. Chuleng himself constructed the Maidam, after his defeat in the battle with Chilarai the younger brother of Narayana (Naranarayan) the powerful king of Koch state.

Na-Ali: During the last part, the Ahom period of Swargadeo Kamaleshwara Singha made an *Ali* from the capital Jorhat to Titabar known as *Na-Ali* and excavated the river Bhugdoi near the capital Jorhat. The king constructed a few roads as the Kamarbandha *Ali* from the capital Jorhat to Kacharihat, the Rahabahar *Ali* from Titabor to the Bacha Pather and the Mohnandha *Ali* which is situated at a distance of 16 km, western side of the capital Jorhat, towards the north-south direction.

Borbarua Ali: The Swargadeo Gadadhar Singha made the important road called Borbarua Ali, under the supervision of Dihingia Alum Borbarua, who was an important minister of King Gadadhar Singha*'s*. The road started from Sibsagar to Dibrugarh via Dimove, Moran, Khowang and merged with the historical Haripara *Ali* from Dimow to Kutuha.

The relation with the Kacharis and the Nagas were under the vigilance of Marangikhowa Gohain, who governed a small district called Morung, on the west bank of the Dhansiri valley with headquarter at Marangi.[155] He had a thousand men under his command, and to him was entrusted the protection of the frontier from the incursions of the hill tribes. The Solal Gohain governed another small territory, including the east end of the island between the Brahmaputra and the Kullung rivers. He also managed about a fourth part of the territory of Chardwar, collected the royal revenues, and administered justice. His force, stationed at Kaliabar, and in Noaduwar, had to check the conducting act of the Bhutias, Miris, Nagas, and Dalflas, when these hill tribes came down to levy on the districts of Choudwar, Noadwar, and Chardwar.[156]

Chatal Ali: An important road was made by the Swargadeo Pratap Singha known as Chatai *Ali*, from Haripara *Ali* by the side in Sibsagar,

Kheloa to Ladoigorh via Hahchara, Mechagorh, Maduri and Mejenga. During the reign of Swargadeo Pratap Singha many communication network was built up.

Dhudar Ali: The Swargadeo Gadadhar Singha made an important road known as the Dhudar *Ali* from Kamargaon to Joypur in the district of Dibrugarh. The length of the road is 288 km, connecting the places as Kamargaon, Golaghat, Kamarbandha, Mariani, Titabar, Nakachari Debdrpara in the district of Jorhat; Simaluguri, Nazira, Garhgaon, Namti, Sonari in the district of Sibsagar Namrup, Naharkatia and Joypur in the district of Dibrugarh, Assam.[157]

Summary

The politico-economic links between the Ahoms and Nagas stretched over a period of nearly 600 years. The Ahoms never subjugated the Nagas and as the land inhabited by them was strategically located so the Ahoms had to make a political alliance with the Nagas so that the transit route to their kith and kin in Burma lay open. Besides, the political and economic interest of the Ahoms led the Ahoms to adopt a policy of conciliation and to enable them to focus against 'external' threats such as the Mughal invasion. The Naga-Ahom political relationship was however, not without hostilities. Furthermore, the perpetual Naga raids in the plains, the abduction and kidnapping of the Ahom subjects prompted the latter to send repeated expeditions into the Naga hills.[158] The Naga-Ahom political relationship was facilitated through the *duar*'s in which the Nagas were granted special rights. Through these several *duar*'s the Naga came down to the plains to collect their dues from *khat, bheel, paik*'s. The Aos and the Lothas were known as small groups, while the Konyak-Wancho-Noctes were known by the dominions of their respective *Wangham/Lowang* (chiefs)

The political expansion of the Ahoms began from the time they settled down in Upper Assam until the close of the 17th century. The Ahoms migrated with limited numbered, approximately nine hundred males according to one version of the Ahom Buranjis and nine thousand, according to another. Initially the Ahom tried coercive by sending punitive expeditions against the Nagas to destroy them. The Ahom armies was confronted with great trouble when fighting with the hill tribes, of which the Nagas have distinctly defeared the mighy well equip soldiers with guerilla tactics. Often the Nagas, when they were defeated, fled from the battleground and concealed themselves in the interior parts of the forest, thus making it impossible for the Ahom army to pursue them. The Ahoms thus came to adopt and pursue a tactful policy towards the surrounding hill tribes. Annexation of such heterogeneous hill tribes would mean additional problems to the Ahom rulers, as the tribes, with their diverse social setup, would hardly regulate themselves to the Ahom *paik* system of administration.[159]

The political dynamics of the Ahom state were many a times decided by the state of their control over the salt producing wells. The Ahoms negotiated decisively, with the Nagas. The Ahoms considered it enough to receive the submission of the Nagas and to allow them to enjoy their tribal autonomy so long as the Nagas, living near the plains, who were granted revenue-free lands and fishing waters along with retainers in the plains, did not raid Ahom territories and the Nagas on the Indo-Burma frontier did not ally themselves with the rivals of the Ahoms beyond the Patkai range to jeopardise the kingdom so, the Ahom king settled to conciliate the rebellious Nagas.

Friendly relations developed between the Ahom rulers and the Banfera Nagas in the 16th and 17th centuries. The Naga chiefs often visited the Ahom capital to strengthen the friendship, to reciprocate and established relations by offering presents and agreeing to pay annual tributes, though of course, they often flouted their agreements.[160] The Ahom rulers, for their part, regarded the Naga peoples living in the peripheries of their realms as being in a different category from their lowland peasant subjects. This analysis can also be applied to the highland peoples of northeastern India.[161]

A significant aspect of their relations was the political kinship that was articulated between Ahom and the Konyak ruling chief. One of the well-known Konyak oral tradition narrates that the Ahom king Chaopha (Sukapha) and the Konyak chief Teinok were brothers. This story links the Konyak with the Ahoms. During the last years of Ahom rule some Naga hill chiefs proceeded to help the Ahoms against the Mughals, Singphos and Burmese. The policy of allowing the tribes to enjoy their autonomy was initially followed by the British. However, they soon adopted a radically different policy towards the tribes as a whole.

Notes

1. See Political Department, Expedition from the Upper Chindwin District into Unadministered Naga territory, (Branch Political), File No. XXII-6/26, Serial No. 20(A), 1926, Muklom Tangsas is now one of the major sub-tribe which resides in Changlang, Namtok and Miao circle of Nao Dihing and Buri Dihing rivers, which originate in the Patkai hill and joins the Brahmaputra. The district has about 20 Tangsa villages at present; S. Dutta Choudhary (ed.), *Gazetteer of India, Arunachal Pradesh,* Tirap District Shillong, 1980, pp. 1-25.

2. Edward Gait, *A History of Assam*, Lawyer's Book Stall, Gauhati Assam, 1906, (Reprint 1984), p. 336; Alexander Mackenzie, *North East Frontier of India*, Mittal Publications, New Delhi, (Reprint 2010), pp. 77-100.
3. Alexander Mackenzie, *North East Frontier of India, Ibid.*, pp. 77-100.
4. Narayan Singh Rao, *The Tutsa Tribe of North East India Origin, Migration and History,* parts II, Mittal Publications, New Delhi, 2010, p. 1.
5. John M'Cosh, *Topography of Assam*, G.H. Huttmann, Calcutta, 1837, p. 82.
6. Edward Gait, *A History of Assam, op.cit.*, pp. 298-302; Jahnabi Nath Gogoi, "Agrarian System of Medieval Assam," Ph.D. Dissertation, Department of History, Dibrugarh University, Assam 1993, pp. 87-88.
7. Jahnabi Nath Gogoi, "Agrarian System of Medieval Assam," *Ibid.*, pp. 87-88.
8. Francis Buchanan Hamilton, *An Account of Assam, With Some Other Notices Concerning the Neighbouring Territories, first compiled in 1807-1814,* DHAS, 1940, p. 26; The first Moamaria Revolt occurred in 1769-1770.
9. Jahnabi Nath Gogoi, *Agrarian System of Medieval Assam*, Concept Publishing Company, New Delhi, 2002.
10. Amalendu Guha, *Medieval and Early Colonial Assam: Society, Polity, Economy*, Publisher South Asia Books, New Delhi, 1991, p. 63.
11. N.N. Acharyya, *The History of Medieval Assam (13th to 17th Centuries),* First edition Guwahati, 1966, (Reprint 1984).
12. Tejimala Gurung, "Emergence of the Ahom Monarchy in Upper Assam (13th-15th Century), in Fozail Ahmad Qadri (ed.), *Society and Economy in North-East India*, Vol.2, Regency Publication, New Delhi, 2006, pp. 86-96.
13. S.K. Bhuyan (ed.), *Assam Buranji or A History of Assam from the Commencement of the Ahom Rule to the British Occupation of Assam in 1826 A.D., Being an Enlarged Version of the Chronicle of Kasinath Tamuli- Phukan*, (tr.), Sanjeev Nath, DHAS, 2010, p. 15.
14. S.K. Bhuyan, *Atan Buragohain and His Times*, p. 26.
15. The Ahom had the traditions that a ruler should not be a mutilated person or have disability on any part of their body.
16. In the olden times, the Patkai hills were known as '*Daikarong*,' meaning collection or composition of nine hills. Scholars believe that the term Daikarong is a Bodo term (*Dai*-mountain, *Kao*-nine, *Rang*-meeting), prior to the advent of Tangsa, Tutsa, Wancho-Nocte-Konyak, etc; Hem Barua, *The Red River and the Blue Hill*, New Delhi (Reprint, 1991), pp. 1-7.
17. V. Elwin, *India's North-Eastern in the Nineteenth Century*, Oxford University Press, London, 1959, p. 34.
18. Narayan Singh Rao, "A Note on the History of the Longchang Tangsas of Arunachal Pradesh," in *North East India History Association Proceedings, 27th session,* Mizoram University Aizawl, 2006, pp. 128-129; Hem Barua, *The Red River and the Blue Hill*, New Delhi, (Reprint 1991), pp. 1-13.
19. Lakshmi Devi, *Ahom Tribal Relations*, *op.cit.*, p. 25.
20. Hem Barua, *The Red River, op.cit.*, pp. 1-12.
21. S.N. Barua, *Tribes of Indo-Burma Border,* New Delhi, 1991, pp. 37-97.
22. Lakshmi Devi, *Ahom-Tribal Relations, op.cit.,* p. 21.
23. S.L. Baruah, Munshiram Manoharlal Publishers, New Delhi, 2013, p. 377; U.N. Gohain, *Assam Under the Ahoms*, Jorhat, 1942, p. 139; S.L. Baruah, *A Comprehensive History of Assam*, *op.cit.*, p. 139.
24. S. Dutta Choudhary (ed.), *Gazetteer of India, Arunachal Pradesh, Tirap District*, 1980, pp. 1-25.

25. John M'Cosh, "On the various lines of overland communication between India and China," P.R.G.S., London, Vol. 1860-61, pp. 47-54.
26. S.K. Chatterji, *The Place of Assam in the History of the Civilisation of India*, Department of Publication, University of Gauhati, 1970, pp. 15-16; The groups especially the Nocte, Tangsa, Konyak and Wancho enjoy the various forms of economic transactions, i.e., salt production, trans-polity barter and control trade-routes. They could then sustain advanced polities like the *Anghdom* (chieftainship); S.N. Barua, *Tribes of Indo-Burma Border*, Mittal Publications, New Delhi, 1991, pp. 37-97.
27. H.K. Barpujari, *The Comprehensive History of Assam, From Thirteen Century A.D. to the Treaty of Yandabo, 1826, Medieval Period: Political*, Vol. II, Publication Board Assam, Guwahati, 1992, p. 266.
28. Hugh Tinker, "A Forgotten Long March: The Indian Exodus from Burma, 1942", in *Journal of Southeast Asian Studies* 6:1, 1975, pp. 1-15.
29. Edward Gait, *A History of Assam*, *op.cit.*, p. 78.
30. R.N. Bagchi, *Gazetteer of India, Arunachal Pradesh, Tirap District,* 1980, pp. 26-31. Rusa were called as Khulun or Khuluniya.
31. Alexander Mackenzie, *North-East Frontier of India, op.cit.*, p. 93; S.L. Baruah, *op.cit*, p. 222.
32. Gait, *A History of Assam, op.cit.*, p.77; G. Barua, *Ahom Buranji*, p. 45.
33. Edward Gait, *A History of Assam,* pp. 78-79.
34. Mashewar Neog, *The Nocte*' an article incorporated in "Asamar Janajati" (ed.), P.C. Bhattacharya, pp. 245-46; Elwin Verrier, *A Philosophy for N.E.F.A.*, pp. 4-5; P.C. Bhattacharya, "A Few Elements of the Indo-Mongoloid Boro Culture," in *The Journal of the Assam Research Society*, Vol. XVI, 1964.
35. S.K. Bhuyan, *Deodhai Asam Buranji, op.cit.*, p. 8.
36. Alexander Mackenzie, *North-East Frontier of India, op.cit.*, p. 19.
37. Y.L. Roland Shimmi, *Comparative History of the Nagas from Ancient Period till 1826, op.cit.,* p. 147.
38. S.K. Bhuyan (ed.), *Deodhai Assam Buranji, op.cit.*, 1962, p. 9.
39. *Ibid.*, p. 102.
40. Gertrude M. Godden, "Naga and Other Frontier Tribes of North-East India," in *The Journal of the Anthropological Institute of Great Britain and Ireland,* Vol. 26, 1897, p. 168.
41. *Ibid.*, p. 172.
42. V.R. Trivedi (ed.), *Important events of Assam*, Omsons publications, New Delhi, 1997, pp. 8-29.
43. H.K. Barpujari, *The Comprehensive History of Assam, from Thirteen Century A.D. to the Treaty of Yandabo, 1826, Medieval period: Political*, Vol. II, Publication Board Assam, Guwahati, 1992, p. 266.
44. Golap Chandra Barua, *Ahom-Buranji from The Earliest Time to The End of Ahom Rule*. With Parallel English Translation, Spectrum publication, Guwahati, 1985, pp. 95-96.
45. Lakshmi Devi, *Ahom-Tribulus Relations, op.cit.*, p. 31.
46. S.L. Baruah, *A Comprehensive History of Assam*, *op.cit.*, p. 377.
47. S.K. Bhuyan, *Studies in the History of Assam, op.cit.*, pp. 150-161.
48. Y.L. Roland Shimmi, *Comparative History of the Nagas from Ancient period till 1826, op.cit.*, p. 148; Golap Chandra Barua, *Ahom Buranji from the Earliest Time to the End of Ahom Rule, op.cit.*, p. 52
49. Lakshmi Devi., *Ahom-Tribal Relations, op.cit.*, p. 17.

50. Hemchandra Goswami, *Purani Assam Buranji.*, p. 50; S.K. Bhuyan, *Assam Buranji*, p. 8; L. Devi, *Ahom- Tribal Relations, op.cit.*, p. 25.
51. Rai Saheb Golap Chandra Baruah, *Ahom Buranji from the Earliest Time to the End of Ahom Rule, op.cit.*, pp. 53-54.
52. The Bar Gohain and Bura Gohain served as a noble /ministers in the Ahom court.
53. J. Butler, *A Sketch of Assam, op.cit.,* p. 152.
54. Gazetteer of India, *Arunachal Pradesh, Tirap District, Government of Arunachal Pradesh*, Itanagar, 1980, pp. 28-29.
55. The Aitonias Nagas are now included under Khamtis, they have converted into Buddhism; E.H. Pakyntein, *Census of India 1961,* Vol. III, part V-A, *Scheduled Tribes and Scheduled Castes Assam*, printed in India by the Manager, Government of India Press, Faridabad, Delhi, 1964.
56. At present regarded as a sub-branch of Ahoms, living in Dibrugarh and east Arunachal Pradesh.
57. Golap Chandra Barua, *Ahom-Buranji from the Earliest Time to the End of Ahom Rule, op.cit.*, p. 52.
58. Banfera (now Zunu in Changlang district of Arunachal Pradesh) is a Wancho-Konyak village close to Charaideo district and Kanubari in Sivasagar district, Assam.The subordinate villages under Banfera were as follows: Banfera, Oanoogaon, Nokrang, Nuagaon.
59. Lakshmi Devi, *Ahom-Tribal Relations, op.cit.*, p. 43.
60. In 1536, the Ahom *Buranjis* first mentioned trouble with the wild hill tribes who inhabited the surrounding hills of Upper Assam, which were then known as the Khamjang, Namsang and Tablung Nagas (now Wancho, Nocte, Tangsa, and Konyak tribes); Alexander Mackenzie, *North-East Frontier of India, op.cit.,* p. 92. Also, Golap Chandra Barua, *Ahom Buranji from the Earliest Timee, op.cit.*, p. 45; S.K. Bhuyan, *Deodhai Assam Buranji, op.cit.*, pp. 6-7.
61. T. Pertin and N.S. Rao, "The impact of Salt Economy on Ahom Tribal Relations," unpublished paper presented in ICHR Seminar at Changlang, February 1998.
62. Lakshmi Devi, *Ahom-Tribal Relations, op.cit.*, pp. 19-59.
63. S.K. Bhuyan, *Anglo-Assamese Relations, 1771-1826: A History of the Relations of Assam with the East India Company from 1771 to 1826*, Department of Historical and Antiquarian Studies in Assam, Guwahati, 1949, p. 53.
64. S.K. Bhuyan, *Deodhai Assam Buranji, op.cit.*, pp. 5-6.
65. H.L. Jenkins, "Notes on the Burmese Route from Assam to the Hookoong Valley," in *Hill Tracts Between Assam and Burma,* Selections of Paper, Vivek Publishing Company, Delhi, 1979.
66. S.K. Bose, "The Ao Nagas and their Medium of Exchange," in Fozail Ahmad Qadri (ed.), *Society and Economy in North-East India,* 2006, p. 149.
67. Information recorded by the author from Shri Wangju Kungkho Lungwang a village elders of Yangkang village, Changlang district, Arunachal Pradesh, on 17.8. 2016.
68. Foreign Political Proceedings, 9 November, No.82, 1840; Raktim Ranjan Saikia and Nurul Amin, "A Study on the Salt Production of Ancient Assam," in *IJHS*, Vol. 54.4, December, 2019, p. 486.
69. Information recorded by the scholar from Shri Wangju Kungkho Lungwang village elders of Yangkang village, Changlang district Arunachal Pradesh, on 17.8. 2016.
70. Lakshmi Devi, *Ahom Tribal Relations, op.cit.*, pp. 19-58.
71. Golab Chandra Barua (ed.), *Ahom Buranji, op.cit.*, pp. 52-53.
72. These are the name address to their respective chief's the *Wang* (Konyak), *Lungwang* (Nocte), *Wang* (Wancho).

73. Golab Chandra Barua (ed.), *Ahom Buranji, op.cit.*, Guwahati, 1985, pp. 74-75.
74. Golab Chandra Barua (ed.), *Ibid.*, p. 87.
75. S.K. Bhuyan (ed.), *Tungkhungia Buranji,* pp. 26-27.
76. Lakshmi Devi, *Ahom Tribal Relations, op.cit.,* pp. 36-56.
77. S.N. Barua, *Tribes of Indo-Myanmar Border: A Socio-Cultural History,* New Delhi, 1991, p. 104.
78. Information recorded by the author from Tutsa (Changlang district, Arunachal Pradesh), village elders Shri. Wangju Kungkho, Tesam Pongte, Wangjit Konglom, Hangkap Songthing, Nokjam pongte, Samangak on 14th-15th April, 2016.
79. Narayan Singh Rao, "Salt, Economy and Politics in East Arunachal Pradesh during c.1200-1945," in Proceedings of *NEIHA,* Twenty Second Session, Tezpur, 2002, pp. 139-151.
80. Alexander Mackenzie, *The North-East Frontier of India*, *op.cit.*, p. 92.
81. *Ibid.,* pp. 413-544.
82. Information recorded by the author from Shri Nyakwang Wangnao, a 75-year-old Dobashi (headman) of Shangnyu village, on 23.01.2018.
83. Information recorded by the author from Shri Nyakwang Wangnao, a 75-year-old Dobashi (headman) of Shangnyu village, on 23.01.2018.
84. Sokhep Kri, *State Gazetteer of Arunachal Pradesh* Vol.I, Government of Arunachal Pradesh Gazetteer Department, 2010, p. 134.
85. A. Ramachandran, "A Survey of Nyishi British Relations (1825-1947)," in NEIHA, Twelfth Session, Jagiroad Shillong, 1991, p. 259; according to Ramachandra, the term *posa* means '*pacha*' which is probably connected with the word *panch* (five) in Assamese language. The *Boheteahs* of Assam used to pay five rupees to Nyishi. The Nagas has commonly used the term *Posa* as *Pencha* or *Pomcha* which mean 'tribute or ownership allowance' to meet their customary demand.
86. I.S. Muntaza*'s,* "Posa: Was it a Black-mail," in *Proceeding of North East India History Association,* 14th session, Jorhat, 1993, Shillong, p. 147; Revenue Department, Naga khats in Sibsagar, Nos. 592, Government of Nagaland, 1928.
87. Alexander Mackenzie, *The North-East Frontier of India, op.cit.,* pp. 7-8.
88. Lakshmi Devi, *Ahom-Tribal Relations, op.cit.,* p. 199.
89. Appointment and Political Department, Political A, "Amendment of the Eastern Boundary of the Naga Hills Districts by inclusion of the Bhitar Namsang Area, Nos. 1424, File No. 453 Government of Nagaland, 1936. The inhabitants of Namsang, Borduria and Paniduaria were also called Mohongias, being residents of lands that was earlier called Mohong. It was famous for rock salt. Mohong in Kachari means salt wells and the land was earlier occupied by the Kacharis.
90. Political Proceedings, 19th October, 1844, Nos, 128-126; A. Mackenzie, *The North-East Frontier of India*, *op.cit.*, p. 94.
91. Resumption of certain Naga *khats* in the Sibsagar District and Payment of fixed allowances to the Naga owners in final settlement of their claims, Government of Nagaland Revenue Department, 1922, p. 20.
92. A. Mackenzie, *The North-East Frontier of India*, *op.cit.*, p. 21.
93. Braj Narain Jha, "Politics of Posa: A Case Study of Pre and Post-independence scenario in Arunachal Pradesh and Assam," in *Proceedings of the Indian History Congress*, Vol. 57, 1996, p. 452.
94. Revenue Department, No. 780 R. DY REV/55, Government of Nagaland, Dated 3.2.1921-1922.
95. Political Proceeding, Nos. 58-61, 18th January 1845.
96. Political Proceeding, Nos, 14 to 18, 15th May, 1847.

97. Revenue Department, Resumption of certain Naga *khat's* in the Sibsagar District and payment of fixed allowance to the Naga owners in final settlement of their claims,' File No. 580, Government of Nagaland, 1922.
98. J.P. Mills, *The Lhota Nagas*, *op.cit*., p. 1; Also see A. J. Moffatt. Mills, *Report on the provinces of Assam*, Thos. Jones, Calcutta Gazette Office, 1854, p. 11.
99. E.A. Gaits, *A History of Assam*, *op.cit*., p. 162; J.P. Mills, *The Lhotas Nagas*, *op.cit*., p. 1.
100. Lakshmi Devi, *Ahom Tribal Relations, op.cit.,* p. 45.
101. Information recorded by the author from Shri Girin Phukon, Director of Tai Research institute Moran, Assam, who has worked on Ahom dietary history of Ahom, 10.01. 2017.
102. S.K. Bhuyan, *Bulletin II* of the Department of History and Antiquarian Studies in Assam, p. 1.
103. Lakshmi Devi, *Ahom Tribal Relations*, *op.cit.,* p. 6.
104. P.D. Stracey, *Nagaland Nightmare,* Allied Publishers Private Limited, New Delhi, 1968, p. 12; Mills also mentions in one of his writing "Nagas never lie" Stracey has also mentioned "Naga had a great reputation for truthfulness and honesty" a simple tribe who in turn was always a good fellow to his master, particularly compared to the tricky plainsman.
105. Information recorded by author from Shri Hazarika, 80-year-old trader of Sonari, Charaideo District on October 2019.
106. P.D. Stracey, *Nagaland Nightmare, op.cit*., p. 15.
107. Lakshmi Devi, *op.cit.,* p. 37.
108. S.K. Bhuyan (ed.), *Tungkhungia Buranji 1681-1826 A.D*, Oxford University, Press, 1933, pp. 54f.
109. S.K. Bhuyan, *Anglo-Assamese Relations*, *op.cit*., p. 47.
110. Lakshmi Devi, *op.cit.,* p. 100.
111. S.K. Bhuyan (ed.), *Assam Buranji*, *op.cit*., p. 328.
112. Information recorded by the author from Shri Panwang Wangham (chief) of Borduria Arunachal Pradesh, on August 2019.
113. Foreign Department, India, to Assam, No. 1046 E.B., 18 May 1900: A.F.P.., August 1900, No. 9.
114. Revenue Department, Resumption of Certain Naga *khats* in the Sibsagar District and Payment of fixed allowances to the Naga owned in final settlement of their claims, Government of Nagaland, Archive 1922.
115. H.K. Barpujari, *Problems of the Hills tribes- Northeast Frontie*r, Lawyer's Book Stall, Guwahati, 1970 (Reprint 1992), p. 127.
116. L. Devi, *op.cit.*
117. *Ibid*., p. 21.
118. Alexander Mackenzie, *The North-East Frontier of India*, *op.cit*., p. 97.
119. S.K. Bhuyan, *Studies in the History of Assam*, *op.cit*., p. 50.
120. J.P. Mills, *The Lhotas Nagas*, *op.cit.,* p. 2.
121. 121. *Ibid*., p. 96.
122. J.P. Mills, *The Lhotas Nagas, op.cit.,* p. 96.
123. Rammathot Khongreiwo, "Raids, Customary Laws and Slavery: Re-interpreting pre-colonial Naga warfare" in *NMML Occasional Paper History and Society, New Series*, Vol. 39, Nehru Memorial Museum and Library, 2013, pp. 23-24.
124. S.K. Bhuyan, *Studies in the History of Assam*, *op.cit*., p. 50.
125. N. N, Acharyya, *History of Medieval Assam (13th to 17th Centuries*), Omsons Publication, New Delhi, 1966 (Reprint 1984).

126. Government of Nagaland, Appointment & Political Department, Proposal for the Formation of a Tribal Authority Among the Lhotas in the Naga Hills District, File No.424, No. 110, 1929, p. 9.
127. S.K. Bose, "The Ao Nagas and their Medium of Exchange," in Fozail Ahmad Qadri (ed.), *Society and Economy in North-East India,* 2006, p. 149.
128. L.W. Shakespear, *History of Upper Assam, Upper Burmah and North Eastern Frontier, op.cit.*, p. 39.
129. Verrier Elwin, *Nagaland, op.cit*., p. 22.
130. Temsula Ao, *The Ao-Naga Oral Tradition, op.cit*., p. 11.
131. Revenue Department, Resumption of certain Naga *khat's* in the Sibsagar District and payment of fixed allowance to the Naga owners in final settlement of their claims, Government of Nagaland, 1922.
132. Letter No. LR-8/71-72/1996 dated July 1972 by S.C. Dey, Commissioner of Nagaland, Kohima, Chief secretary of Nagaland, Kohima; Letter No. 1149-R dated 20th April 1921 Guwahati from B. C Allen Esquire B.A(ICS) Commissioner of the Assam Valley District Division to the Deputy Commissioner of Sibsagar Guwahati, Letter No. 1149, 19th January 1921, regarding *khat's* report on the measurement of the *khat* area/ payment of compensation to the Naga *kataki's* and the Naga *khat* owner's payment of annual Revenue already paid to Naga *khat* owners; Letter No. 4400-R dated Shillong, the 5th December 1921 from the Chief Secretariat of the Government of Assam to Commissioner of Surma Valley and Hill division in response to Letter No. 899-T dated 24th October 1921 regarding resumption of certain Naga *khats* and payment of revenue to *khat* owners including Assiring *khat* and the financial year 1922-23 to the following *khat* owners with the cop to the Deputy Commissioner of Naga Hills; Letter No. LR-9-73-74/1046 dated Mokokchung the 26th March 1974 sanction of Rs 1823 for Payment of Revenue to Naga *khat* owners Notified by L. Toshi Ao. Deputy Commissioner of Nagaland and Account Branch of D.C. office for release of payment of *khat* revenue; Letter No. LR-6/63-6/723-26 dated Mokokchung the 25th March 1964. Notified by M.L. Kampani, Deputy Commissioner of Mokokchung. Copy marked to the Chief Secretary of Nagaland, Shillong and Bill Section in duplicate/ sanction and release of payment of Revenue of *khats*.
133. Ved Prakash, *Encyclopedia of North-East India,* Vol. 5, Atlantic Publishers and distributors Ltd., Delhi, p. 1907; Also see B.B. Ghosh, *History of Nagaland*, S. Chand, New Delhi, 1982, p. 79.
134. In Jaboka and Shangnu villages of Mon district Nagaland, had the tradition of collecting *seih sai* from the Ahom villages. However, after the British intervention into Naga hills, the privileges enjoyed by the Nagas gradually declined.
135. Information received by the author from Shri Chuiwang wangham (chief), a 62-year-old, of Nokzang village, on 1st-10th April, 2018.
136. S.L. Baruah, *A Comprehensive History of Assam, op.cit.,* p. 370.
137. Sanjeep Kakoty, "Agrarian Dynamics and Technology in the Ahom State," in Fozail Ahmad Qadri (eds.), *Society and Economy in North-East India,* Vol. 2, Regency Publication, New Delhi, 2006, p. 100.
138. S.K. Bhuyan, *Atan Burangohain and His Times*, Lawyer's Book Stall, Gauhati, 1975, p. 16.
139. S.K. Bhuyan, *Lachit Barphukan And His Times*, DHAS, Gauhati, 1947, p. 18.
140. S.K. Bhuyan, *Atan Burangohain And His Times, op.cit.*, pp. 17-18.
141. The *Bahatiyas* in the northern hill sides were constantly under the domination of the Daflas, used to imitate Dafla dress and ways of living in subsequent periods. There was very little that made them different from their tribal master. These *Bahatiyas* were the peasant-paiks residing in the foot-hill areas of Assam. They were allotted to

the hill tribes by the Ahom rulers for rendering service or to pay a stipulated tribute in kind called *Posa* to their hill masters; see S.K. Bhuyan, *Rajeswar Singha, op.cit.*, p. 238.

142. See, for the class hierarchy and their behaviour pattern, A.B.H.B, p. 95ff; Jahnabi Gogoi, *Agrarian System of Medieval Assam*, Concept Publishing Company, New Delhi, 2002, p. 124.
143. Lila Gogoi, *The Buranjis Historical Literature of Assam (A Critical Survey),* New Delhi, p. 179.
144. S.L. Baruah, *A Comprehensive History of Assam, op.cit.*, p. 384.
145. Jahnabi Gogoi, *Agrarian System of Medieval Assam, op.cit.*, p. 38.
146. *Ibid.*, p. 38.
147. Lakshmi Devi, *Ahom-Tribal Relations, op.cit.*, p. 45.
148. *Ibid.*, p. 34.
149. L.W. Shakespear, *History of Upper Assam, Upper Burmah and North-Eastern Frontier, op.cit.*, p. 211.
150. Edward Gait, *op.cit.,* p.122; A.C. Sarma, *Tai Ahom System of Government*, B.K. Publishing House, Delhi, 1986, p. 259.
151. A.C. Sarma, *Tai Ahom System of Government, Ibid.*, p. 365.
152. Chow Lao Tze, *Architecture of the Tai Ahom Period,* Krantika Prakashan, Assam, 2016, pp. 150-175.
153. Government of Bengal, R.D. Nathal to D.C. Sibsagar, 8th March, 1863, pp. 11-12; L.W. Shakespear, *History of Assam Rifles,* MacMillan, London, 1929, pp. 272-273.
154. Walter Hamilton, *The East-India Gazetteer*, Vol. I, B.R. Publishing Corporation, Delhi, Reprint 1984 (1828), p. 70.
155. William Robinson, *A Descriptive Account of Assam, op.cit.,* p. 194.
156. 156. *Ibid.,* p. 194.
157. Chow Lao Tze, *Architecture of The Tai Ahom Period,* Krantika Prakashan, Nagaon, 1999, pp. 10-70.
158. Sajal Nag, *Contesting Marginality, Ethnicity, Insurgent and Sub-nationalism in North-East India, op.cit.*, pp. 39-41.
159. S.K. Bhuyan, *Studies in the History of Assam, op.cit.*, pp. 150-161.
160. For details see Chapter IV.
161. Edmund Leach, *Political Systems of Highland Burma A Study of Kachin Social Structure*, Fletcher and Son Ltd, Norwich, first published 1954 (Reprint 1964), pp. 21-22.

3

Economic Relations

The economic relations of the Nagas with the Ahoms mainly developed in the context of trade carried out in the foothill markets established for the purpose and for the control of salt springs located in the foothills. Trade is commonly defined as a commercial transaction between people and places involving an exchange of commodities. It can easily be identified with certain durable objects found on archaeological sites, such as imported and exported commodities. 'Exchange' is a closely connected term that refers to the reciprocal process in which people give and receive something in place of another. That something can be almost anything, ranging from ideas, food, livestock, raw materials, manufactured goods, services, etc. Interaction is related to how people established economic and social relations with each other in the past, as traders and travellers engaged in a long-distance network of contacts, supply, and redistribution. Gradually trade has become an essential factor in the study of complex social formations all over the world.[1]

The relationship between the Ahom valley kingdom and the inhabitants of the surrounding hills has been, in many ways, associated with intimidations, raids, and retaliation which occurred frequently. People living in the tracts between the foothills and the plains often felt the brunt of the raids of the hill tribes like Noctes,[2] Wanchos,[3] Tangsa, Ao, Lotha, etc., yet there were more to valley-hill relations than hostilities. A lively barter trade flourished between the Naga-Ahom foothill areas.[4] Traditionally barter trade between the hill and valley has a deep connection with the beliefs and practices of the tribal communities.[5] The boundaries of the valley and tribal territory are, in general, clearly distinct. The forest, river, lake, mountain, or watershed provides a landmark. Sometimes, some objects marked a line of separation, such as an upright stone. Even in the primitive period, artificial boundaries were recognised. The foothill regions were fertile and produced a profusion of rice, cotton, and other staples treasured by the neighbouring tribes, hence; the Ahom rulers aspired to keep it under their control and mechanism.[6] Economically, the Nagas also specialised in different products depending on their environment where they lived.

There were fourteen *duars*/dwars (passes) between the valley and foothills, covering Wancho, Konyak, Phom, Ao, and Lotha segments. These were known, each according to the physical features of the areas from which the tribes descended through the passes to trade with the plains, while the Konyaks, Wanchos and Noctes were known by the dominions of their respective *Lowang/Wang* (chiefs).[7] The *duars*' between Dikho and Desang rivers were Kapam, Tero, Bhetur, Namsang, Jaboka, Banphira, and Koolem Motoniya, etc.[8] Several Nagas who inhabited the hills between the Dikho and Booree Dihing Rivers[9] were engaged in exchange even during the rule of the Kachari rulers. The Nagas mainly lived on the hill slopes bordering the erstwhile Nowgong, Dibrugarh, Sibsagar, and Lakhimpur districts of Upper Assam.[10] In the pre-colonial period, the northern Nagas, i.e., Konyak,[11] Phom, Ao, and Lotha of now Nagaland, and Nocte and Wancho tribes of present-day Tirap and Changlang districts of Arunachal Pradesh, were living alongside the Kacharis.[12] On the other hand, the northern mountains towards the west were occupied by the Abors, Mishmis, and Miris towards the north easts who were also involved in trade with the Ahoms. The Abor, Miri, and Mishmis brought down silver, copper, tin and Manjeet (madder). The Abor and Miri also brought down pepper, ginger and wax. The Mishmi mainly brought down swords, spears, little musk, and ivory, which they obtained from Tibet and a considerable quantity of vegetable poison used in poisoning arrows. These they exchange for cloths, salt, money and glass beads, of which they were very fond of clothes, salt and money.[13]

There are indications that the Eastern Nagas (i.e., Nocte, Konyak, Wanchos, Tangsa, Ao, Lotha, Khiamniungans, etc., in the early period were living alongside the Kacharis. S.L. Baruah also refers to a *Buranji* source that speaks of Sukapha encountering a large number of Kacharis in then Naga hills (present Tirap and Changlang districts of Arunachal Pradesh). It was either Sukapha (1228-1268) or Supimpha (1281-1293) who pushed out the Kachari Raja Dersongpha to the hills. The Kacharis were then removed to the south bank of river Dikhu by the Dihingia Raja. An Ao Naga tradition also talks about the existence of Kachari settlements in the lower ranges of their hills).[14] Some of these groups are now called Nagas of Burma in Sagaing division; they also exchanged their produce for their cultural necessities from Tibet and Burma. The now Lower Konyak-Wancho-Upper Nocte-Tangsa are the Trans-Dikhu villages.[15] They were active trader's in the Sagaing province in present-day north-west Burma (Myanmar). These tribes were intermediaries in the Naga-Burmese trade; they visited each other's villages carrying their goods to barter. However, only the known villages and powerful villages travelled for long distance trade because there was a question of life and death as headhunting was widespread among the Nagas. The Naga traders often travelled on the hilly bridle paths carrying heavy loads for two to three days as far as Amguri in the Brahmaputra valley and to Zingkaling Khamti in Burma, despite having to traverse hostile regions in between. There was no medium of exchange between the Burmese-Naga traders.[16]

On the Tibet side, the Monpas, Mishmis, and Khamtis had direct access to Tibet, and this contact was linked up with the Angami traders for internal circulation among the Nagas.[17] However, the coming of the Shans (Ahoms) from Upper Burma changed the trading scenario of the Nagas. The entry of the Shans into northern Assam brought about a change in the Naga traditional links with the Tibetan trade, which were upheld through the inhabitants of present Arunachal Pradesh.[18] The change became marked when the Ahoms under Sukrungpha or Rudra Singha (1696-1717) monopolised the Tibetan trade for the transaction of goods.[19] As the Naga contact with the plains became more frequent; subsequently, their demands increased. Trading became a necessity as the Nagas became accustomed to consumption new products, which were beyond their ability to produce. Trade by way of barter between the Naga-Ahom was mostly happen during winter seasons as this region receives high rainfall during the summer, which hindered their trading activities. Trading activities were highest between harvesting annually crop and cleaning land for the next year's planting.

The Ahom rulers encouraged local markets and also permitted long- distance trade. However, no outside traders were allowed to prolong their stay at Assam. The kings built their capital in such places, which had acquired prominence owing to strategic locations, trade and commerce, religious, and political activities.[20] Permanent markets, as well as periodical *haat* and annual trading fairs, were carried out in these frontier markets.[21]

Foothill and Valley Markets

The Ahom monarchs not only granted certain rights to foothill tribes in the adjoining plains but also set up *hat* and fairs for the exchange of commodities at convenient places.[22] To carry on trade with the hill tribes, markets were established at the foothills by the Ahoms. Internal trade markets were established at Dihing, Bakata, Kacharihat, Barhat, Namsang, Abhaypur, Borduwaria (further sub-divided into different weekly *haats*), etc., Varieties of commodities and even slaves were sold. The main Eastern Naga markets were, Margherita, Jaipur, Naharkatiya and Namrup; (attended by the Noctes) Wanchos went to Borhat, Namrup, Sonari. The Tangsa visited the nearby markets at Ledo, Lekhapani, and Margherita). Sadiya was the central one for the people of the hills inhabiting the extreme northeast. Barter played a large part in all transactions, subsequently, cowries served the purpose. For example, the Ao and Lotha exchanged honey, cotton and bay leaf for dried fish, rice, and salt from the Ahom.[23] The economy of the plains which produced a large quantity of rice was inseparably connected with the Nagas. Products like cotton, ginger, salt, forests products, animal skin and fur, were procured from the Nagas.[24]

The foothills were considered special zones where inhabitants from the hill and the valley transacted in the markets (*hat*), which functioned once or twice a week in the regional centres catering to the local needs and trade.[25] As noticed by the British, the Nagas were keen barterers; they traded in all the hill products.

1. The Konyak exchanged their products in these markets viz: Naganimorah, Charaideo, Meothrabor, Singmu, Sonari, Sapakati, Benenaga Bari haat, Raja pukuri haat, Namtolao, Sontok, and Geleki.
2. The Lotha villagerss ventured to the foothills market viz. Akok, Champang, Golaghat, Tsuroi, Yingsung, Bhandari, Yanmhon, Longchum, Pangti, Lakhuti, Furkating, Borholla (Porholla), Titapur, Tokenegara, and Merapani (also known as Maraju).
3. The commercial transactions of the Ao with the Ahoms took place through various duars such as;
   (a) **Dopdar *duar*/Dobuka *duar***: Frequented by the villages of Longjang, Orbong, Borolange, Sooso, Bhugalage, Longtang, Luraong, Eang, Nowgaon, Dekhahaimong, Borahaimong, Merankong, Yaongyimsen, Changtongia, Akhoia, Unger Chuchuyimlang, Mongsenyimti, Sangratsu, Mopungchuket (Molutobia), Ungma, Chuchuyimbang, Mokokchung, Longsa, and Longmisa (In this *duar* there were 7 *katakis*).

(b) **Assirangia *duar* or Charingia *duar***: Frequented by villages of Kampongiah, Lasso, Assiringia, Boragoan, Mongche, Kharee (Kari), Longjang, Changdang, Waromong, some other villages from the upper region of the country travelled to the Assiringia *Duar* through Nokpoh village (In this *duar's* there were 3 *kataki*'s)

(c) **Hatiguria (Bordobia) *duar***: Frequented by villages of Barobia (Changki), Samsa (Longjemdang), Japu, Lakhuni, Chungliyimsen, Chungtia, Chemchea, Aliba, Khemsa, Mekuli, Longkhum, Kubza, Mangmetong, Mikolai.[26] (In this *duar* there were 2 *katakis*)

There are references to Ahom Swargadeos opening *haat*. Swargadeo Pratap Singha is reported having opened a *haat* at Dibrugarh.[27] Exchange of surplus produce was the primary objective of these markets. Dihingia Raja (1497-1539) set up a mart at Dalanguri, while his son successor Suklengmung (1539-52) established another one on the river bank of Dikhou for the new settlers after clearing the jungles on the two river banks.[28] Satyunpha alias Nariya Raja (1644-48) established a market at Marangi to foster amicable relations with Cachar.[29] Gadadhar Singha (1681-96) set up two markets Chakihat and Rajahat located in erstwhile Sibsagar. Rajeswar Singha (1751-67) established a market near Disoi in Upper Assam. At almost all the upper Assam districts, transactions were mainly done in the *haat*, which was held bi-weekly or weekly. The tradition continued even after the British occupation in the Brahmaputra valley; only the number of *haats* had increased considerably. From colonial records, we get references to the haat markets and marketing system during the Ahom period. The internal trade of Nowgoan district was mostly conducted through the barter system.[30]

W.W. Hunter, in 1879 stated that in Darrang district, trade was chiefly carried on at weekly markets, which were held in several villages all over the district. Most significant were those held on Sundays at Kaligaon mouza in the Mangoldoi Sub-division, known as the Singhmari *haat*. The attendance in this market was immensely in number, usually numbering from a few to five thousand people would come to sell and buy the products. Some Nagas were reported to come from a distance of twenty- five miles with their surplus stock of grain, vegetables, fruits, betel nuts, firewood etc., to barter with the valley people.[31] The most important markets were, Naduar, Kacharihat, Dopbar, Lahing, Haatnu (Sonari), Dopdoi and Geleki in Sibsagar district and Makumduar, Namsang, Barduar, and Taratali in Dibrugarh district.[32] For instance, Shri. Asen Konyak, a 98-year- old man, a village elders from Jaboka (Konyak village), recalled that he had to walked by foot three to four days' trip to the plains of Assam for exchange. They will moved from their village in a groups at dawn and slept at night in the rest house, which they built especially for this purpose, as a resting place before continuing their journey towards the plains to sell their products at the *hat* or markets.

They bartered animal skin, medicinal plants, cane baskets, elephant tusks, bamboo mats, etc. There was no specific amount in exchange for food and the essential commodities they needed. The bartering was done mainly by women. However, they were accompanied by some men, and this tradition survives in the markets to this day.[33]

Items bartered between the Valley kingdom and Nagas

The Nagas in the pre-colonial period were engaged in barter trade with the people of Brahmaputra valley. Hill-ox (*Bosfrastails* or Mithun) were the most valuable cattle and were highly treasured by the Nagas (Ao, Lotha, Konyak). It was used for consumption and traded at high amount.[34] *Mithun* was linked with the allocation of politico-ritual positioning of different clans, and sacrificing of *Mithun* was linked to the fertility cult.[35] For the Nagas, barter was the core form of exchange within and outside the tribes, and with the people of plains. There was long-distance trade which took in some cases several days to go and come back with the outside tribes.[36] Mills Report of 1854 also describes the Nagas as keen barterers; the Ao, Lothas, and Rengma Nagas visited annually in the cold season to the plains to barter, betel nuts, cotton, chillies, ginger, broom, gourds, palm-leaf mats, and the gum of a tree called *hyang* (Ao dialect) being the main articles. The products brought by the Lothas to barter were bamboo mats, cane and bamboo, products, wooden images, spears, *daos*, ornaments, walking sticks, ginger, arum, chillis, pan (betel leaves), sweet potatoes, oranges and lemon etc., in different places like Rajapar, Furkating, Borholla, Titapur, Tokenegara. Cotton was exchanged for the best quality dried chilli, ginger, and dried fish.

Maraju (Merapani) was not only a market but a transit point used as a resting place for the Lothas while travelling to the Ahom kingdom. Lotha men, sometimes accompanied by a group of women, travelled about two to three days to trade with the plains.[37] Cotton and black sesames were the main products which the Lotha carried and sold in the plain of Assam.[38] Raw cotton was brought down by the westerly *duar*'s, particularly by the Paneeput (Lotha). This cotton, or the bulk of it, was exchanged at first for instance, by the Abor (independent Nagas) to the *Bori* (dependent Nagas), for their products of the plains, and it was then brought down by the *Boree* (dependent Nagas) and exchanged with the Assamese traders. A small quantity of the cotton was brought down at Dopduar and larger quantities at the *duar's* west of it.[39]

A report made by Captain Brodie in 1840s mention about Lotha cotton trader, exporting a bulk of about 4500 maunds of cotton to Golaghat.[40] Mr. Davis also stated, "cotton export through the boat in the cold weather was duly watered at a Doyang river half a day's journey towards Golaghat in order to increase its weight." The Lotha traders would deceitfully apply this trick so that the wet cotton could put more weight and sell it for higher prices.[41] A considerable quality of cotton was cultivated in the hills, which they exchanged for salt, beads, dry fish, eggs, vegetables, hoes, clothes, etc., for the items that are not available in the hill regions.[42]

The Lothas also traded varieties of commodities like ginger, dried chilies, yam, wet and dried bamboo shoots, and ivory. The betel vine grows wild along the Dikhu and Saffrai, and the villages that own it made a good deal by its sale. The Lotha did not use any kind of medium therefore; they usually bartered their commodities with salt, iron utensils used for curry pots and iron implement tools for agricultural usages, dried fish, rice, duck, hen, cow, jute etc., from the Ahoms. Salt was one of the most essential commodities for Lothas Nagas. They purchased salt and sold it to the other neighbouring Nagas village at a higher price. The Lotha bartered cattle which they acquired from the plains to the neighbours Ao and Sema Nagas. Goods were mainly bartered.[43] Colonial sources give an idea 1 kg of cotton was exchanged with 15 kg of salt, 10 kg of black sesame was exchanged for 30 kg of salt, 1 kg of chili was exchanged for 3 kg of dry fish.[44]

The Konyak villages which carried on trade with the Ahoms were Phongkong (named Buragoan by Ahom) Wanching, Wakching, Kongngam, Naganimora (Ahom called this village Lekan). More Konyak villages like Jaboka, Nokzang, Niausa-(Kanubari), Nokyan, Kanubari (Banfera), Runu, Rusa, Niausa, Pongchau and Wakka had maintained a regular trade.

Hunting of Elephants in Naga Hills

Besides salt, the elephant trade also played an important role in trade relations with the Ahoms. In Naga hills, wild elephants were plentiful, moved in large herds (even to these days, and were highly destructive to the crops and human life, entering villages in daylight and plundering granaries and stores of salt, of which latter they are fond). Numerous numbers of elephants were caught every season from the Naga hills and transported to the Ahom Kingdom.[45]

Furthermore, because of dependence on the hill elephants, a post called *Hatidhar* (elephant capturer) was created by the Ahom Raja.[46] The people who tamed wild elephants were known as *Mahut* or *Fandi* during the Ahom days.[47] Products like elephant tusks, ivory, woods of aloes and agar fetched profitable revenue to the Ahom revenue. According, to Ao folklore, the Ahom Raja's elephant hunter who came to the Ao country to hunt elephant, met the two Imchen brothers, befriended them, and later took notice of a great beauty called Sentishila and reported back to their Raja of the Naga girl. The Ahom Raja Godapani had a matrimonial alliance with the Ao Naga; he married Sentisila. Later he established the *Assiringia duar*, a market which was opened in the name of his father-in-law to trade with the Ao Naga.[48] Through this *duar*, the Ahoms were able to go to the hills to capture elephants from Naga hills with the help of Naga chiefs, all this enhanced the economic prosperity of the Ahom kingdom.

In fact, the name *Hatigorias* (literally meaning in the Ahom language, 'wild elephant's area') was given by the Ahoms to the Aos. The Ahom army predominantly depended on the elephants caught from the Naga hills. In the hill tracts, plenty of wild elephants were available. The Ahoms regularly used the elephants as their carrier on the road; they were also used to transport arms and ammunition and carry water for the soldiers on the battlefield. The Ahom monarchs maintained a state department of elephants under '*Hatibarua*'s' supervision. The *kheddah* system and *mela shikar* were the principal methods for catching elephants. *Hatibarua* supervised the *kheddah* in operating the elephant hunting's. The female elephants called *koonkis*, were used for trapping the wild male elephants; in the course of the courtship, the mahouts contrived to shackle the unsuspecting animals in a suitable tree that they were fixed to the spot immovably, and they were allowed to remain till confinement and want of food rendered them easily tamable.[49]

After catching the elephants, they were kept in east Jorhat, known as *Hatigar* (in Assamese means elephants house).[50] Shihabuddin, who accompanied Mirjumla in his Assam expedition (1662 AD) reported, 'large high-spirited and well-proportioned elephants abound in the hills and wilderness of Assam.'[51] Often, chiefs of the neighbouring hill tribes like the Lothas, and Aos gifted elephants, elephant ivory to the Ahom kingdom.[52] *Deodhai Asam* and *Tungkhungia Buranjis* also mentioned various accounts of Ahom monarch's pastime, such as elephant-fights, tiger-bear contests, buffalo-fight, cock-fights, hawk-fights, etc.[53]

The Konyaks would undertake arduous expeditions into the forests during the quiet winter and hunt elephants for ivory and meat. A slain elephant must be kept lying for three days. Only then is it possible to cut into its thick skin. After removing the skin, the hunters cut the body of the dead elephant into pieces and divided all the meat among the villagers. However, one of the hind legs and the head of the animals including the precious tusks are traditionally reserved for the *wangham* (chief). The rows of the massive white tusks displayed on the walls of the front hall of the *morung* testified to their power and prosperity.[54] In the olden days, elephant hunting was common; the Nagas often presented or would sell an elephant, elephant material, weapons of elephant ivory, ivory pearls to the Ahom Raja.[55] The abundance of hill elephants, and the use of ivory as an article of trade point to the conclusion that the Nagas raids on the plains of Assam were retaliation for trespassing in the hills and the other is that the elephants were caught for various purposes and sometimes killed for ivory.[56] The Ahom kings would again present gifts made of ivory to the rulers of Delhi. For instance, Rudra Singha (1696-1714 AD), presented mats, fans and chessmen made of ivory to a ruler of Delhi.[57] The *Tungkhungia Buranji* also gives a brief reference of the Naga chief's often gifting elephants to the Ahom Raja.[58]

Besides, the name of the village Jaboka (Konyak) was given by the Ahom (*Ja-bo-ka* meaning lazy people in Ahom language). The Ahom Raja succeeded in negotiating to obtain gifts from certain Naga villages. Then they gave names to the Nagas based on the areas where they came down to different *duar*'s.[59] Wanching village (Ahoms called it Jaktoong, under it there were eight villages)[60] was known for producing iron implements which they brought down to the markets. Iron tools were used to make *daos*, spear heads, spade, and chisels. Wakching played an important role in terms of internal trade and also giving protection to the plains people from the interior hill tribes who would often be a threat to the people residing in the plains, and that would create tension in the trade with the Ahoms.[61]

Betel nut and *Ganja* (marijuan) was important commodity for the Konyak, some Konyak villages that did not have salt wells exchanged betel nut for salt from the Ahoms. For instance, betel nut per bunch was equivalent to 1 kg of salt, also known as *Choba*.[62] Earlier, the Konyaks did not have the knowledge of salt in powder form. Traditionally salt was prepared locally from the *humlo* (saline water). It was only after contact with the Ahoms that they were introduced to salt powder or dried salt. Charaideo (Haatnu in Konyak dialect) was the market where they sold the salt.[63]

A small quantity of Eastern Naga salt reached the Ao villages by a roundabout route. The Konyaks sold it at Nazira (Sibsagar) markets, and then Aos bought it from there, later resold it to Phom and Chang across the Dikhu for pigs, fowls, etc. The Aos made about 300 percent of profits from the frontier tribes.[64] Trade was not controlled by any particular group in Naga-Ahom relations. Everyone was a consumer and a seller, the foothill Naga villages served as a middleman for the interior Naga villages. It was a part time occupation of all the able men and women; whenever the need arose, they traded.

Betel nut

The story of the betel nut holds a significant implication in the Naga- Ahom relations. According to the Jaboka village tradition, the betel nut sapling was a gift from Ahom Raja to Namsang and Konyak chiefs when they visited the Ahom kingdom to collect *sei sai* (in Konyak dialect, meaning to collect grains, livestock etc., from Ahom foothill villages). The Konyaks are highly fond of chewing betel leaves filled with a little lime and a few bits of slightly bitter bark of a tree (*pankhon* in Konyak dialect) with the betel nut. They grow betel bushes not only for consumption, also for sale.

The betel vine grows wild along the Dikhu and the Saffrai in Naga hills, the villagers that own it made a good bargain by selling down to the plains. Most of the vines were planted and owned by individuals, though the Nagas do not give the elaborate care bestowed on them in the plains.[65]

Betel nut became popular amongst the Naga tribes when Ahoms came to Naga hills to take refuge during the Burmese incursion. Among the Nagas (Mon, Mokokchung, Wokha, and Longleng), became the center for the production of areca nut; betel nut trees and *paan* (leaves) came to be planted in their garden or the fields. Shri. Gohain an old trader from Sonari narrated that hill betel nut and pan leaves are much sweeter and tastier than the plain products, so most people from plains prefer hill products, even though the prices are highly expensive.[66] The influence of chewing betel nut/*paan* on the Nagas, especially on the Konyak and the Ao are prominent even today. Almost all the households in contact with the Ahoms are fond of chewing betel nut.[67] Besides, cane mats, betel leaves are the chief commodity that the Naga tribes carried out to markets in the foothills markets of Brahmaputra valley.

The Ao oral narratives mention that machetes and other metal work were largely imported from Maibong (16th-century Kachari capital in the North Cachar hills) and Assam. In the olden days, the Ao traded with the Ahom, Kacharis, Manipuris, and Burmese. Later contacts with the plains also brought items like *daos*. Later, they were made in certain villages of the Ao region. The Ao village of Merankong talks about Ahom coming and staying in their region, from which they learned how to make *daos* (machete). Nokpu village oral traditions also narrate about learning how to make *daos* from the Ahoms during the early days. According to Mills,[68] around 1706, when Rudra Singha, the Ahom king, attacked the Kacharis at Maibong, when Mir Jumla's expedition against the Ahom king must have significantly disturbed the Ahom people, a body of immigrants came up from the plains and built a village on the hills. Later as the situation became safer in the plains, they went back leaving behind four men who settled in Kulingmen (Ao village). These men migrated to different Ao villages and even performed the *mithun* sacrifice. These people integrated into the Ao clan, and their descendants were the smiths of the Ao country, where later villages like Ungma learned the art and started making tools.[69] There were groups of blacksmiths settled along the roadside of Dodhar Ali at *Assiring khat*. They produced all kinds of agricultural tools for domestic use and weapons. The Ao called these groups *Alimenyinsem* (*Alimen* means roadside and *Yinsem* means blacksmith). Depending on the location, it took two to three days for the Aos to reach the *khat* market. They would return after the trading and sleep in their rest house. The Ao usually went down to the market in groups; at least five to six people would go down to the *khat* markets for security reasons. Sometimes the women folks accompanied the men group. The group did not require permission to visit the *khat* market. The Nokpu village of *Assiring khat* enjoyed the rights and privileges of agricultural products and of any trading items, they were given particular concessions before other customers from other regions and were allowed to purchase of their liking.[70] The Nagas also supplied pig hairs as the Ahoms were good in making brushes.

Table 4: List of Articles which the Nagas/Nyishis[71] used to take from Ahom and the approximate price of each products

Items	Rupee	Anna	Paise
Eria cloth	5	8	0
Saloo	1	0	0
Eria gamcha	0	2	0
Mats(bamboo)	0	2	0
Ducks	0	2	0
Drakes	0	8	0
Fowls	0	4	0
Hoes	0	6	0
Salt	0	2	3
Gur (base)	0	2	0

Brass for pan	0	1	0
Knife	0	1	0
Kani (opium)	0	8	0
Riha	0	0	0
Chakoli (necklace)	0	2	0
Oil	0	8	0
Rice	0	12	0
Sandhal	0	6	0
Cotton gamcha	0	2	0

Sources: Assam secretariat, File No. 177J, Nos. 1-6, serial No.6, 1882.[72]

In 1855, the British official had reported that trade had come to occupy an important place among the Eastern Nagas, which appears to have contributed to "a good mutual understanding between these communities (with the Naga hills), in consequence having always been accessible to the people of the plains."[73] Hence, the trade between the Naga hills and the surrounding plains is only an index to what Johnstone termed as "the self- sufficient condition of the Naga tribes."[74]

Market Taxes

Beepari/Bepari (male broker) and *Poharis* (female broker) bartered directly from the Nagas for a discount, and they resold the hills product to the plains with a higher sum. The product items bartered by the *Beepari* for salt from the Nagas were: rice, dried fish, opium, gur (jiggery), cotton, edi cloths, rice etc. The Ahom Raja Suhungmung (1497-1539) was reported to have taken one-seventh or one-fifth of that to himself and another one-fifth again at the salt wells. Of the salt purchased, out of four lumps, he had to give the Raja one piece and a half to the manager (*hatkhowa*).[75] The Raja families would take their share for their monthly use and the rest of the salt was sold in markets.[76]

During the reign of Pratap Singha, a new high official called 'Borbaruah' was created, Momai Tamuli was the first person to hold the post of 'Borbaruah.' He initiated an administrative reform of systematic exploiting of salt wells from Mohong wells. The Nagas were taxed in all kinds produced in hills, including salt. The taxation terms indicate that up to this point; the salt producers were mainly the Nagas. Though the Ahoms Raja took the possession of the salt wells, the production was still under the control of the Nagas. The Nagas enjoyed their right on the salt wells after paying a nominal tax. It was during the reign of Gadadhar Singha, the Ahom tried to control its salt-extracting units in Borhat area, causing tension and hostility between the Nagas and the Ahoms. To avoid such a situation, the Ahom Raja appointed an official in the Borhat-Namsang area and supervised the salt extracting activity. During the reign of King Rudra Singha (1696-1714), one officer known as 'Mohongia Baruah,' was appointed to look after the extracting work. From that time, the officers and workers of the Ahom king were directly involved in salt production. Both Nocte and Ahom had the right to salt production and would help each other in extracting salt. In Sadiya region, another officer known as 'Mohanghat Baruah' was appointed.[77]

To collect duties and to control the illegal transportation of goods *chauki's* or *chokie's* (toll gates) were established at strategic locations. The Ahom monarchs not only granted certain right to foothill tribes in the adjoining plains but also set up *hat* and fairs for the exchange of commodities at convenient places.[78] *Dan*[79] (sale-tax), *hat*[80] (tax on buying and selling in the market), *ghat* (tax for using rivers for trade), *phat* (duty on marketing places), *katal*[81] (payment made in lieu of personal service), *pad* (fee to be paid by *paik* on getting assignment), *panchak* (contributions), *beth* (to catch wild elephants from the forest for the state), *beggar* (force labour obtained from paiks), *chor* (fined taken from the thief'), *chinla* (fined on *paiks* for adultery), *dhumuchi* (king's claim on the properties of those who died without heir), *marecha* (tax for acquiring land through a marriage according to Vedicrites), *ghamecha* (tax to be paid to the king for marriage), *danda* (fine for crimes), *bandha* (keeping in confinement and compelled to do work), *khut* (tax on movable articles), *jalkar* (tax for fishing), *yabakshar* (tax for production of gunpowder)[82] etc., were the numerous taxes imposed on the subjects under the Ahom state.

Taxes and all sorts of revenue were mainly in the form of personal labour and in kind. Less produce and lack of trade and commerce meant an undeveloped feudal economy.[83] It was only after the Ahoms had come into contact with the Mughals that there was an elaboration and some sophistication of their economic system. As a result, towards the close of the Ahom rule, monetisation of the economy slowly came in.[84]

Salt production in the Naga Hills

The Ahom *Buranjis* repeatedly used the term 'Naga' with their village name for salt-producing hill people. The British used the term Eastern Nagas. They are now called by different tribal names and live in different districts of Arunachal Pradesh and Nagaland.

The Eastern Naga salt spring wells are locally called '*hum/sum*' (literally meaning salt in Konyak, Wancho, Nocte, Tutsa language). The Nocte (Eastern Nagas) was one of the important sources of salt suppliers for the Brahmaputra Valley.[85] The Mughal account also tells us that salt was mainly procured from the eastern region in the Naga-Patkai ranges.[86] The Eastern Naga salt springs had a reputation among the Ahom. During the medieval period, salt became a politico-economic item in hill and valley relations. Wars broke out between villages and, later, between the Nagas and the Ahom for control of salt mines, especially in the Wancho-Nocte regions.

Salt obtained from these springs was believed to be purer than the one imported from Bengal.[87] It was one of the principal sources of income. According to Buchanan Hamilton, in 1809, the revenue derived from Sadiya springs was about Rs 40,000 rupees per annum.[88] At one time, the quantity amounted to be no less than 1,00,000 maunds.[89] C.P. Strong Sub-Assistant Commissioner of Sibsagar identified 85 salt wells (Namsangia area-54, Borduaria area-19, Paniduaria area 12) in 1838.[90]

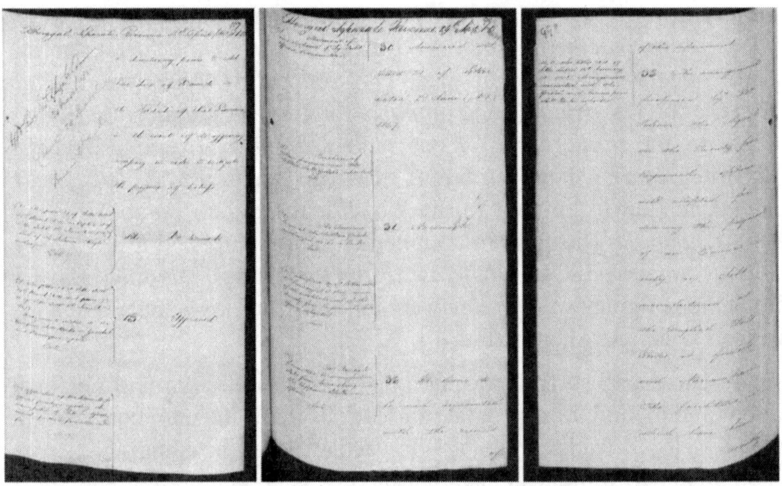

Figure 2. Bonsal's report on Eastern Nagas salt brine springs preserved in British Library

The quantity of salt springs was numerous and was found scattered all over Borhath, Joypur, and Sadiya. A considerable quantity of salt was obtained from Borduaria, Khonsa, Namchangias, Niaunu, Kalagaon, Paniduaria, Kalagaon, Yangkang, Tutnu,Tutsas, Tangshah and several Wancho villages of Longding, Pongchau, Wakka and Laju circles (at Changlang, Tirap, and Longding districts of Arunachal Pradesh).[91] The following are the groups who were involved in the process of salt production, Dimasa,[92] Semsas,[93] Lopungias (Lonpuriyas),[94] Noctes,[95] Borduarias,[96] Tutsas,[97] Tangsa,[98] and Mattaks.[99] The existence of salt-wells in the Naga Hills was revealed to the British after the explorations of Wilcox, and M'Cosh stated "at Borhath, on the river Disung, there are about twenty of these brine-springs from most of which Nagas are in the habit of making salt."[100] Pemberton also stated that "salt-springs of Burhath and Sadiya" were well known and the quality of salt obtained was "much purer and higher priced than that imported from Bengal." [101] However, the indigenous salt being expensive and inadequate, a large quantity of Bengal salt had to be imported to Assam every year.[102] Only after a commercial treaty between Captain Welsh and Gaurinath Singha, then Ahom Raja of Assam on 28th February 1793, salt from Bengal entered Assam. Slowly the demand for hill salt declined and now it exists as ritual practice and medicinal purpose. The chemical composition of these brines resembles with rock salt.[103]

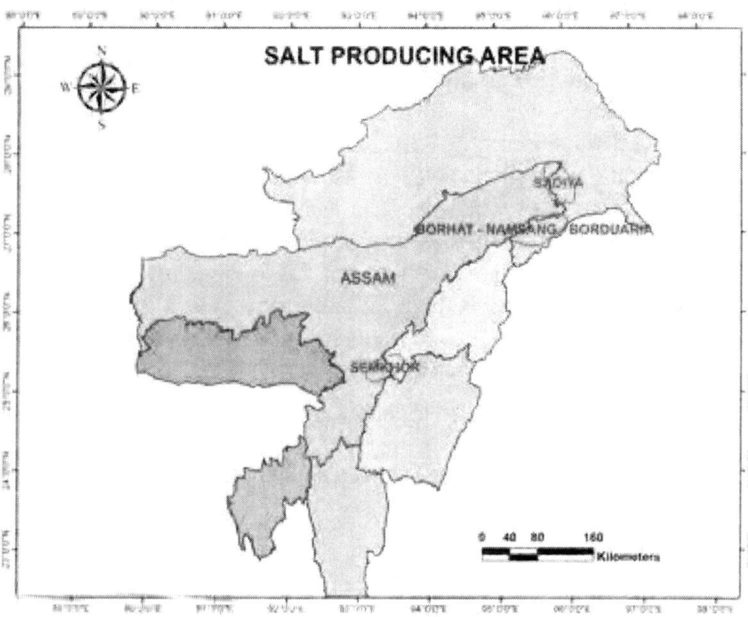

Source: Internet, accessed 2020.

Figure 3. The Map showing 3 ancient salt production villages in Medieval Assam chronicles.

Miles Bronson, the first Christian missionary who visited the area near Namsang, described the extraction of salt by the Noctes and Tutsa. He described the evaporation was carried on in green bamboos; the salt presented was generally grey, rugged, and compact, having the form of the bamboo in which it had been boiled for 12 to 13 hours, possessing the radiated structure in perfection.[104] Salt extracting usually began in November and continued till March or April as the wells being situated in a valley were subject to inundation during the rainy seasons. The wells found in the beds of rapids were only available for salt extraction in the cold season. They prepare clay-coated bamboo tubes filled with brine, and the tubes are placed in the furnace. When brine water boils are evaporated, they again add more brine water to the clay-coated bamboo tubes. The clay layers protect the bamboo tubes from burning. This repeated evaporation process yields a cylindrical-shaped salt piece.[105]

Miles Bronson, as early as 1839, stated that Purandar had the Nagas "much more under control than the Government now has…He made them look to him in all important matters, and when they did wrong, he chastised."[106] About Purandar's ability to compel the Nagas to serve his interest, Bronson remarked:

> There were about fourteen or sixteen houses among the Borduarias who were obliged to work every men ten days out of thirty in working the salt-wells for Purandar. These twenty days, they cultivated their rice and worked their salt but the remaining ten days' work was all received by the Rajas. There was one village called Khila gong, which the Raja had made arrangements with the Namsangias and Borduarias to remove to another place when the Raja designed to form a village of his own. The Khila gongias were to labour for the Raja in the same way. It was considered as a tribute paid by the Nagas to the Raja and would have brought in a vast amount of salt to the Raja.[107]

Soon, both parties worked together day and night to extract the salt; the quantity manufactured during the night belonged to the Ahom Raja and that obtained during the day went to the frontier chief. The share of the salt was made into *topolas* (bundles). The men who made these bundles were called *topolakatia*. The *topolas* were then carried to the royal store, from which they were distributed among the different officers for consumption for a year according to the sanctioned scale.[108] Jenkins, Borhat, stated on 8 February 1838:

> The Rajah raises a revenue of about 3000 rupees a year from this source. But the manner in which he manages the concern does not seem well adopted to make the most of ages the concern does not seem well adopted to make the most of it. Of the articles brought to barter for salt, the Rajah takes here one-seventh or one-fifth according to the kind of articles and the manager of the *hat* taxes (¹/) that quantity to himself, another fifth was again taken at the wells

and of the salt purchased. Out of 4 lumps of salt he had to give Rajah one piece and a half to the manage (*Hathkhow*). Articles that cannot be divided were valued and the same or a lesser proportion of their value taken. Thus, about 50 percent was take on the trade upwards and near 40 percent on the trade downwards which was not likely to contribute much to the encouragement of traffic or the development of the resources of the country, but it would be difficult to imagine and persuade the Rajah that a remission of tax it might be practicable to retain the same amount of revenue or even to increase it. The Rajah has however lately sent two Assamese of rank to superintend the wells and taken into his own hands and as the men he has employed are apparently intelligent men there is some prospect of an improvement.[109]

Intending to ensure a regular supply of salt and to regulate proper networks with the Ahom capital, the Ahom monarchs constructed several roadways. The earliest Kachari rulers mostly made these roads from about 1040 A.D., such as Dhodur Ali running from Nagura near Golghat on the Dansuri river through Titabar, Charaideo and Borhat, ending at Tipam on the Bori Dihing river; Garh Ali, and its continuation in the Seoni and Bogota Ali, starting from the junction of the Kolliani and Dunsiri Rivers, running parallel with the north of the Dhodur Ali through Jorhat, Rangpore near Sibsagor, Garhgaon, to the Bori Dihing River at Rangarora.[110]

The Ahom Raja Suklenmung (1539-52 AD) built the roadway called the Naga Ali, running from Bar-Ali to the Naga hills. This tangible measure adopted by the Ahom kings had succeeded in maintaining good relations with their neighbours Nagas, by repairing the old roadways and adding new roads it facilitated easy communication with the hills and the plains, haats were set up for exchange of goods at the foothills in the plains. Accordingly, by the time Gadadhar Singha and his successor Rudra Singha, the Ahom rulers had succeeded in maintaining tranquility with the Naga tribes: the Nocte, Wancho, Tutsa, Tangsa, Konyak, Ao, and Lotha.[111]

Purunder Singha (1833-1838) was known to have successfully asserted his rights to share with the Nagas the produce of salt manufacture of the lower hills. He maintained a duty of 20 percent levied on all the salt brought down by the Nagas to the *haat* of Borhat and Joypur for sale. The revenue collectors were stationed at the springs on the hills as well as in the markets below and tolls were levied both at the salt produced and on the articles the Nagas obtained in barter for the salt they sold.[112]

Though the measures of reciprocal of salt wells was prepared, the Nagas often continued to give trouble to the Ahoms and would come at night to ransack and attack the Ahom villages. Salt created mutual respect and destroyed the relations simultaneously; the Ahoms could not restrain the Nagas completely. The Ahom Rajas had to maintain goodwill with the Konyak through various means. In some cases, they were given important positions in the king's court, while sometimes they were motivated or controlled by sending Vaishnavite spiritual leaders or saints.[113] Even today some Naga villages in Sibsagar sub-division, Charaideo district and Tirap district follow Hindu practices. These conditions prevailed till the advent of the British rule to this region.

As discussed, salt was very dear and difficult to obtain, only found in Eastern Nagas villages. Salt thereby played a significant factor or role in inter Naga socio-economic relations, who often used it as a medium of payment for labour work or considered it as a valued medium of exchange. There are no salt springs in the Western Naga hills, so the- Lotha, Aos, Rengmas, Semas had to obtain their supplies from the plains and from the Konyak and Khianmungan tribes. The Lhotas in the foothills used to go down and buy it and also used it for exchange with the Phom and Chang tribes for pigs, fowls etc.[114] However, the standard of weighing and measuring varies from village to village. An old Naga barter table is given below:

30 medium *Lah* (gong)	1 slave
1 big *Lah*	1 mithun
1 small *Lah*	1 cow
1 *jabili*	1 day's wage
1 *mithun*	5 cows or a pair of ivory armlets
3 cows	1 conch shells
1 bamboo tube of salt (small)	1 *dao* or spearhead
1 packet of salt (1.5 kilograms)	3 baskets of paddy or one *dao*

The salt, being an essential ingredient for household consumption, was used as a form of currency for trading purposes.[115]

The Lotha resold salt to the Rengmas for-profits, who passed it on to Sema and Angami villages for distribution. The Rengmas paid one cow for two, three, or four parcels of salt, according to the state of the market. Later, certain Rengma local traders resold within their villages a large lump of salt; they got a cow for one parcel of salt, which was the standard wage for a day's work. In order to trade directly with the plains, the Rengmas used to be involved in a war with the Lhotas.

Nevertheless, they used to endeavor with the idea of cutting out the mediator's profit.[116] Their camping places were well hidden, and they had the curious custom of planting onions that would be ready for eating by the time they returned some two months later.[117] A depiction of the great interacting of trade during the early days was given by Jacob where he mentions on the trading of salt circularly. The Konyak traded in salt with the valley, and the other Naga tribes like, Ao and Lotha purchased this salt from the valley and later traded it to other Naga inhabitants.[118]

There was another system of loan, debt, mortgage and sale among the Nagas. Rice was the main article for lending and borrowing with interest. The interest was cent per annum and collected at the end of the year. The minimum amount of rice loaned was six baskets, and interest was calculated for three years as under:

Interest in first year	10 baskets
Interest in second year	20 baskets
Interest in third year	40 baskets

Interest on a loan of paddy-seeds had to be paid before any other loan could be secured. The traditional method of recovery of non-payment of loan was the outright appropriation of land. Another system that prevailed at Mon district that involved the bondage of the debtors's children or even their grandchildren along with an attachment of land.[119]

Trade was not controlled by any particular group within the Naga tribes. Those who sold were often the producers or gatherers of the goods sold. The Naga chiefs' were given his share of products and the superfluous would be taken to the markets for exchange. Any unfortunate confrontation occurs during the trading activities then the chief's role was to negotiate the issues with the other parties. As the villagers paid their dues to their chief, so it was chief duty to solve any matters with the support from the council of village elders.[120]

Oral narrative of Ao-Ahom relations

An Ao oral tradition of the Nokpu *Puto Menden* (generation of the council), [121] gives a glimpse into the economic nature of the Naga-Ahom relations. This oral tradition describes how the *Assiringia duar* or *Saring Rongpang* was originated among the Ao tribe. The *duar* of Merinokpu (Nokpu), was named in honour of the marriage of *tongdi* (headman) Assiring's daughter with *raja* Godapani (Gadadhar Singha 1681-1696). The Nokpu tradition claims that after shifting from the ancient settlement at *Atsu* hills, their permanent home Nokpu was established. During the latter part of its history, it was during the third *neso/aso*[122] that *Saring duar* (now

Assiringia duar) was opened. This *duar* facilitated the interaction between the plainsmen and the Nokpu villages,[123] also, like many other *duar*s at the Ao region. Through the efforts of Imchen clan elders, namely Asomsangba (Asom=Ahom, Sangba=flattered by) and his brother Yimyudangba this *duar* was originated.

According to this tradition available among Ao Nagas, there once lived in Nokpu village two brothers named Asomsangba and Yimyudangba Imchen. One day the two Imchen brothers were steaming a bamboo vessel full of fish at the bank of a river when they met a group of the Ahom Raja's elephant hunters who were unsuccessful to apprehend elephants that day and was in great despair. The Ahoms or plainsmen befriended the two brothers and took them to the Ahom Raja court. Their intention was to accused the two Imchen brothers. They reported to the Raja that their guests had driven away the elephants, and hence they returned empty-handed. Fortunately, their story did not convince the Raja. So the Ahom Raja demanded to see the brothers. It was almost the middle of the day that Asomsangba and Yimyudangba Imchen were led to meet the Ahom Raja. The two brothers walked about fifty yards before they reached the well of the throne. Both of them were deeply impressed by the grandeur, having paid their respect to the Raja; after which, they resumed their seats. The king waved his hand and both the brothers were taken close to their seats. The king again made a gesture and the grand older man on whose face authority of a powerful lord was manifested rose and addressed the two brothers. The integrity of the brothers had satisfied the investigators and the king. The Imchen brothers later learned that the investigating Gohain, in power was next to the king in the kingdom. Now the investigations had ended, the king addressed the meeting, particularly pointing at the two brothers and said, "I am pleased to have you in my kingdom, I want to maintain a peaceful relationship with you Nagas. Our friendship will go a long way." The peers then rose in their seats, and drank for good health and a long happy new friendship. Subsequently, the two brothers agreed to have mutual reciprocity with the Ahoms.[124]

The Ahom Raja constructed a road leading up to the hills. The road connects on the bank of *Ponu* stream, and both parties feasted together, the hills and the plains people exchange their products. Opening of the road between Merinokpu and Rongpur (Sibsagar) led to a greater socio-cultural exchange between Ahom and the Ao. The villagers were often on occasion honoured as 'guest' in Rongpur. This cemented the mutual admiration and friendship between the two communities. Through the efforts of Imchen clan elders, and *Asomsangba,* the *Saringduar*

(*Assiringia duar*) was opened. Thus, the opening of this *duar* allowed free interaction between the Ahoms and Nokpu.

Another oral tradition relates the marriage of Sentishila to an Ahom king. One day, a group of the Ahom Raja*'s* men took notice of a beautiful girl, named Sentishila and the Ahom groups reported back to their Raja about the beautiful girl. She was the daughter of Saring alias *Assiring* of the Walling clan. The Raja pursued a propose to Sentishila's father, seeking his wishes to marry his daughter. However, being a widower, his intense attachment to his daughter dissuaded him from parting with her. Raja Godapani was hurt by the refusal. One day he sent his noble men, along with a trained bird (*mynah*) to lure Sentishila. The bird *osen* (mynah) with the sounding bells approached Sentishila house. Who was then basking rice at back of her house. Suddenly, she saw the cute bird, so, she set out her tools at once to catch the bird, instead the trained *mynah* jumped lured her outside the house. Sentishila raced towards the bird with a step or two with her soft feet lest the *mynah* flew far away. Then the bird lured her beyond the fortified gate of Nokpu village. In no time, the Ahom nobles apprehended and rushed Sentishila down to the plains and reached the Raja*'s* palace, they did successed in abducted Sentishila with the help of the trained bird and she was presented to their Raja.[125] Much later in the day, a tired *Assiring* came home with a load of firewood. His neighbours told him that Sentishila was seen running off chasing a talking *osen* bird beyond the gate and yonder. *Assiring* knew it was the conspiracy of the Ahom Raja. Infuriated, he went chasing, and to search for his lost daughter and on his way, he killed and cut the heads, legs, and hands of some Ahom soldiers whom he met on the way. He did not know that the Raja had ordered his soldiers that no harm should come to him. A *Borahi* or *Borahi* (medicine woman) was dispatched by the Raja, a kind of envoy to persuade *Assiring's* inorder to clear up the misunderstanding between the Raja nelwy would be father-in-law. She informed *Assiring* that Sentishila has already become the wife of the Ahom Raja. She beseeched him to accept the fact and return to Nokpu village and were told to come back to the plains meet her in four days.

On the appointed day, *Assiring* arrived at plains and was escort by the medicine woman to the Ahom raja and reconciled with his lost daughter. Thus, *Assiring* and Raja Godapani established a reciprocal agreement. On the notion of contracting marriage and alliances, the Ahom Raja declared that the name of Nokpu was to be known as *Assiringia*, calling Merinokpu (Nokpu) after the name of his father-in-law. Secondly, the Ahom Raja declared that the Asomsangba-Yimyudangba was to be renamed as *Assiringia duar*, the path where *Assiring* travelled.[126] Thirdly, the Raja declared that a Naga *khat* (literally *khat* meaning a portion of land or revenue assigned by the Ahom ruler to the Ao Nagas perpetually) will be granted to *Assiringia*. The name of the *khat* was called *Assiring khat.*

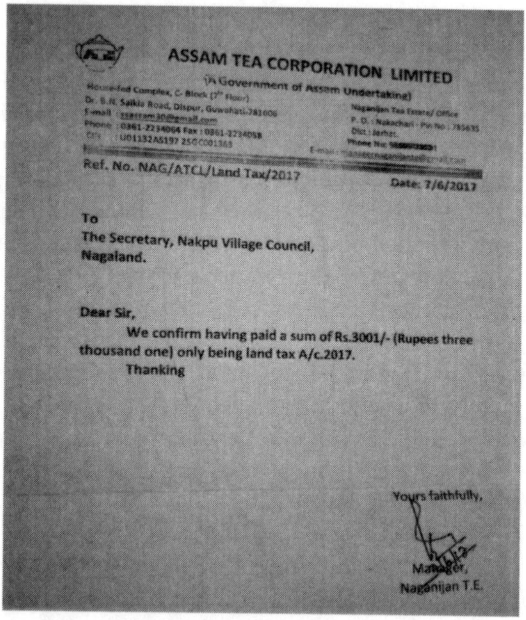

ASSAM TEA CORPORATION LIMITED

(A Government of Assam Undertaking)

Ref. No. NAG/ATCL/Land Tax/2017

Date: 7/6/2017

To
The Secretary, Nakpu Village Council,
Nagaland.

Dear Sir,

We confirm having paid a sum of Rs.3001/- (Rupees three thousand one) only being land tax A/c.2017.

Thanking

Yours faithfully,

Manager,
Naganijan T.E.

Figure 4. Payment receipt from Assam Tea Corporation Ltd to Nokpu village, 2017.

In 1842, captain T. Brodie and Nokpu elders came to an agreement to use some part of the *khat* land near Naganijan for a tea plantation. Subsequently, the British established *Naginijan* tea estate in 1844 and agreed that the tax would be paid to Nokpu in honour of Sentishila.[127] *Naginijan* was named after Sentishila as '*Naginijan*' meaning that a Naga girl had gone away. After the nuptials, the Ahom Raja called Sentishila as Dalimi and later, Ahom people started a weekly bazaar called *Naginijan* bazaar at Jorhat in memory of Sentishila. This was the beginning of commercial interaction, the market *Assiringia khat* gradually developed and shifted from its original place near *Naganijan* tea factory into the Saturday market, which are used more for the interest and needs of the tea garden labour. The Nokpu villagers get a certain amount of payment from the *Naganijan* tea Factory as *khats*, remunerated to the land owners and as part of what they cultivate from the land called *posa*. By April 1861, the *duar*s were closed to the Naga traders by order of the Commissioner of Assam.[128]

In 1924, the British Government converted the *posa* into an annual payment of Rs 70, which was paid till 1974.

According to Ao oral narratives, there were six different types of *duars* between the river Dikhu and Doyang. These were *Assiring duar*, *Namsangia duar, Dopdoria duar, Doyangia duar, Hatiguari duar* and *Panee path duar*. Three *duar's* belonged to Aos, *Assiring duar* (Charringia), *Dopdoria duar* (Doboka) and *Hatiguari duar* (Bordobia).[129] The Ao villages who passed through the Assiring *duar* to barter with Ahom at Naganijan were *Longjang, Debuia, Khar, Mongchen, Nokpu, Leremin* and *Waromung*.[130] The name Sentishila (Dalimi) continues among the Walling clan till-date.[131]It is a culturally defined relationship that exists even to these days.

During the reign of Godapani, *Dodhar Ali* and *Akar Ali* roads were constructed. Several tanks were made, wells dug, a rest stop made for the convenience of the travellers. Several Naga *katakis* were posted at *Assiring khat*. Furthermore, the functional aspects of the *khat* and *duar* was announced by Bargohain, who stated that the Ahoms shall finance the repairing and maintenance work of *Assiring duar*, the '*Chokies*' were assigned at *Assiring's duar*. At *Assiring duar* the *pokhori* (well) was built which are now located in the following historical places:

1. Garhgaon namely: *Assiring Pokhori,* 2. *Namti Ali,* 3. *Namsoso Ali* and *Pokhori* (wells) were also known as *Assiring Pokhori*.[132]

Among the Ao villages the *Assiringias duar*, served as one of the most vital pass for the Ao Naga villages. The *Assiring duar* was established along the roadside of the Dodhar Ali, as one of the boundary lines. In the *Assiring duar* the Ahoms settled three distinct occupational groups, viz., the peasants, traders, and blacksmiths, to help the Nagas at *Assiring duar*. They catered to the needs of the Nagas in transit either on trading expeditions or on militia movement in aid of the Ahoms during external threats. The cultivator groups who occupied the *khat* supplied the produce of paddy to Nokpu twice a year (once in the month of May-June and once in November) as *posa*.

In order to maintain good relations with the Nagas payment of *posa* continued even after the British occupation of Assam, with some changes (abolished *paik* labour offered to Nagas), *Posa* was given to Nokpu, Changki, and Longmdang by the Assam Government till 1974, through the Deputy Commissioner of Mokokchung.[133] To cite another example, in an Ao village called Changki (two and a half hours' journey from Mariani, Assam), there is a tradition, according to which members of the village council make annual trips to Ahom villages in the foothill areas to collect 'tributes or land ownership allowance' in the form of livestock like a duck, chickens, rice, betel nuts and leaves. Later on, it developed into a friendlier and neighbourly relationship so that when the Changki villagers went on this errand, they carried small gifts, such as ginger, yam etc. Whatever was collected from the Assamese villages was shared by all during any community feast.[134] Even to this day, the Ao and the Konyak still exchange gifts with the Ahoms and invite each other during their festivals.[135] The foothill Konyak villagers at present visit Ahom villages annually during the festival month of April.

Bamboo baskets and Handicrafts among Nagas

Baskets made of bamboo and cane were one of the extensive items used at home and in the fields for storing goods and transporting most commodities by the Nagas to the plain. Bamboos of several species are plentiful, and there is a great deal of cane in some parts. The Nagas were naturally experts in basket-making, every man could make his household baskets, but the manufacture of difficult things such as cane helmets *(kiven)* is generally left to an expert.[136] Each family make baskets of various kinds, and large mats from bamboo splits.[137] Mats that retain the cool of the earth are used for sleeping and for drying grains. In fact, to these days, the demands for Konyak mats and winnowing fans at Naganimora and Sonari (Charaideo district) markets in upper Assam continues.[138] Moreover, bamboo wattles were used as house walls and as flooring on the open platforms of houses and *morung* (dormitory for men's).[139] Mat-making is even today a major cottage industry among the Nagas. Ptolemy opines, that to the east of Serica, bamboo cultivation and its use for various purposes are well-known. They have mentioned Assam, and there were hills and marshes where canes were full-grown and used as bridges.[140] Evidence of the production of other cane articles were also indicated by the Harsacarita, which mentioned stone stools of cane.[141] Bãna again affirms to this highly developed craft. He states that Bhãskaravarman the ruler of Kamarupa, sent to Harsavardhana "baskets of variously coloured reeds," "thick bamboo tubes" and various birds in 'bamboo cages.' All these prove that varied manufacturing arts were developed in Assam at an early period and were continued to be practiced till recent times, can be seen as a part of their daily cultural and material life. It is important to note that most tribes have been experts in these amalgamated arts.[142]

The most convenient and usual way of carrying the goods to the plains by the hill tribes was by bamboo or cane basket on their heads. The trader loaded their produce in the basket and carried them to visit Brahmaputra valley, Burmese or Naga villages too exchange goods. The small traders also included female counterparts. Heavy large quantities of goods which could not be carried on the heads, back or shoulders as a single load were divided into two and tied at two ends of a bamboo bar called *dang,* or flat bamboo piece called *biriya* or *baoka* (by the Konyak). The *dang* alone with the loads was called *bhar*, when the goods were too heavy to be carried on by a single man in *bhar*, two men did it by binding the loads in the middle of a strong bamboo-pole, and depending on the weight of the load, even by four men by putting the goods on a square or rectangular size flat bamboo appliance bound to two strong bamboo poles called *sangi* or *changi*.[143]

Figure 5. The Konyak women carrying bamboo mat on their heads to sell at the foothill haat, photographer Haimendorf, 1937.

Colonial records and the traditions of Konyak say that different bamboo appliances were used as a commercial good. These included baskets of different sizes like *duli, pachi, tom, japa,* etc.[144] Earthen pots like *kalah* and *tekeli* were also use.[145] Goods like cotton were bound in the form of bales, and sugarcane, betel leaf, pig hair etc., were in the form of bundles.

Transportation of goods to distant land was not only conditioned by lack of good overland routes, but also by the geographical and topographical condition of Assam. Subsequently, distant trade was the business of wealthy people who could collect labour and take the risk of riverine trade. Small traders, therefore, confined their business to their locality.[146] Also, low production of the commodities was one of the significant factors that limited extensive trade.

Medium of Exchange-Weight and Measures

For exchanges, different mediums were used in the form of livestock goods in the early period. In fact, barter had been the major form of trade. Over time, the Nagas evolved from the barter system to a new trading system using currencies as a transaction medium. The Ao Nagas learnt the use of the currency system from the Ahoms. Evidence of the iron-made arrow-shaped *Jábilee*, which wasused as currency in circulation for at least three centuries by Ao Nagas was discovered. It is the oldest currency so far noticed and recorded by the British among the Nagas. *Jabilee* was not introduced by any sovereign authority; it may have resulted from the necessity to do trade transaction with the Ahoms. The existence of *Jabilee* as a medium of exchange among the Naga tribes came to light when the British occupied the Ao country in A.D. 1889.[147] The *Jabilee* has a narrow strip of iron, six to eight inches long with a triangular projection at the end. It represents a demi form of the conventional *dao* (a sort of bill or chopper) of an obsolete type.[148] It is made of iron; the selection of this metal was probably due because iron was scarce in the hills. According to John Owen, there was an extraordinary value attached to iron by the Nagas.[149] This was a significant accomplishment that an ethnic tribe living in the most isolated and difficult landscape with a simple organisation could introduce a currency more or less of standard weight.[150] The iron *Jabilee* (mode of currency) was used as a means of payment and regarded as a symbol of wealth; it was introduced long before the arrival of British among the Aos, Sema, and Lothas.[151]

The foothill Nagas learnt to operate the market economy by bringing the items preferred by the Ahoms and also make sure to take back commodities required for the neighbouring hill tribes who were far away from Ahom.[152] The Ao Nagas profoundly treasured the *Jabilee* and it became a hereditary family heirloom. The eldest member had the largest share of it, and the punishment for stealing a *Jabilee*, could be confiscation of the property and excommunicate in from the village.[153] The approximate value of a *Jabilee* can be guessed from the following table: 50 *Jabilees* = one slave, 100 *Jabilees* = one mithun (wild cow), 1 *Jabilee*= equivalent of a day's labour.[154] The Sema, neighbours of Ao Nagas, also used the blades of worn-out knife weapons as primitive money, which was worth eight annas a piece.[155]

British colonial officials like Hutton described the *Jabilee* as calculated it was equivalent to a day's labour.[156] Mills also stated that a *terolung* or *changklung* was the weight of salt due to a man for a day's wage.[157] A *terolung* was equivalent to almost one *seer*, among the Nagas.[158] *Nyam* (a brass disc in Konyak dialect) made of bronze was used as a medium of exchange by the Konyak, Chang and Phom. Originally procured from Myanmar, the value of a *Nyam* was is about 2-3 *mithuns*.[159]

Table 5: The measurement of *Jabilees* which are given below

No. of Length	Weight	Thickness
1. 23.4 cm	6.2 gms.	1 mm
2. 25.2 cm	7.4 gms.	1 mm
3. 25.1 cm	10.4 gms.	1 mm
4. 21.8 cm	5.9 gms.	1 mm
5. 26.3 cm	7.6 gms.	1 mm
6. 24.5 cm	7.6 gms.	1 mm
7. 265.8 cm	13.5 gms.	1 mm
8. 26.6 cm	10.4 gms.	1 mm

The Lotha Nagas used conch-shell as a medium of exchange. In fact, all the Nagas are fond of marine shells; for instance, they use cowries and conch shells as decoration in their ornaments, without which their traditional attire is incomplete, and it also shows the wealth and status of the families. Butler also reported in 1874 on the importance of conch-shells among the Naga societies.[160] *Mithun* was one of the most important mechanisms of exchange among the Nagas. It is used for both consumption and farming, for instance, one *mithun* was worth fifty baskets of rice. Besides, spear heads, and *daos* were also used as currency. Stones were used for weighing precious ornaments.[161]

Figure 6. Jabili is another form of currency used by the Aos. It is made from the edge (rongnok) of obsolete daos at Mopungchuket Senso Mungdang Library and Museum. (Photo by N Nyejat K, 2017).

Figure 7. Discs (laya) or Nyam an old form of currency, used by the Konyak, Phom, and Chang villages, State Museum Kohima, Nagaland. (Photo by N Nyejat K, 2017).

Bigge, who set out on a reconciliation mission in the Naga country in December A.D. 1840, observed that the Naga had never seen coins till its distributed a few pieces of coins.[162] Similarly, Hunter also commented in 1879, the Nagas were beginning to appreciate the value of money. However, Naga villagers were not overwhelmed by seeing the coins issued by the British officers.[163] These indicate that the Nagas already had their medium of exchange and payment even before the British advent, consisting of articles such as *Jabilee,* laya, conch shell, salt, spear head, iron tips, etc.,[164] Since, beads were not locally manufactured (oral and literary sources), it highlights that they were acquired through trade and exchanges with Myanmar and Ahoms and other nearby regions.

Within the villages, exchanges were in the form of a kind such as vegetables, grains, meat, pot, clothes and other essential commodities. Changki (Ao) village was the main center for manufacturing handmade pots, which garnered the needs of the whole region of the Ao's besides some small scale manufacturing in villages like Khar and Nokpu.[165] There was no common currency circulated in the Naga Hills.

Lending and Borrowing within the Nagas

Many families had enough stock of food to wait for the harvest, and only a few families could lend surplus food to others. Those who could not produce enough to last the entire year usually borrowed from the rich people or sometimes rendered service as labour in the fields in exchange for a paddy borrowed. A person borrowing one basket of paddy is to pay back two baskets the following year. This practice is common among the Ao, Lotha, Konyak etc., tribes of Nagaland. If the principal is repaid at time, the interest may remain unpaid and will remain the same as it was when paying the principal. However, if the principal is not paid the next year, the outstanding sum re-doubles for two years at 100% compound interest, and then the interest ceases to occur. Every creditor, therefore, wisely pays off the principal. In times of scarcity, crop failure, and dispute with the plains, the Nagas from one village go to the other to buy paddy from the rich men, who will generally have obliged to sell them. In this way, the villagers used to help each other in times of scarcity.[166]

Slavery

The practice of slavery in hills and valleys has also influenced the mechanism of trade in northeast India. Verrier Elwin has rightly expressed that "The institution of slavery is essentially a business matter, with its investments in human lives, its dividends in human toil. The result of this is that some of the tribes are keen traders.[167] Often the Nagas sold off habitual thieves or criminals to adjoining tribal segments or the Ahoms, for they had no customs or moral sanction of executing their erstwhile kinsmen.[168] As recorded by Butler on the Naga slaves, a male slave was worth one cow and three conch shells, a female slave three cows and four or five conch shells.[169] Hornell also recorded that a male slave at that time was worth one cow and three conch shells, and a female slave much more valuable. A cow was valued at ten conch shells, a pig and a goat at two each; a fowl was worth only one packet of salt.[170] Based on British colonial, sources the Ahoms procured some slaves from the Aos, Lotha, and Konyak Nagas.[171] The commonality as well as the difference in the nature and severity of slavery, which varied with each respective tribes and regions. For instance, the Ao, slaves were never allowed to rest but were made to carry stones when there was no work left to be done. While among the Konyak, the slave's hair was shaved to prevent it from falling on the food they cooked for the masters and to identify their identity. It was belived that taking of heads would earn a man glory in this world and a slave in the next. The Nagas also view that headhunting brought prosperity to the village in the form of bumper crops, many children, and good hunting.[172]

During the Ahom period, when the Naga chiefs came down to the valley kingdom annually, they bought gifts in kind such as, slaves, elephant teeth, spear shafts, clothes, cotton etc. and the Nagas, in their turn, received presents of various kinds in return. The Assamese considered the offering of the Naga chief as dues; but the hill tribes no doubt looked on the presents they received in the same light and viewed the matter as a mere interchange of presents.[173]

Raiding, warfare and enslaving of the captives on the valley kingdom and Upper Burma by the Konyak, Wancho, Noctes, Phom, and Khuanmiungan were main mechanism of acquiring slaves, with poverty, debt-bondage, destitution, and orphans being the other sources. The captives were generally offered for human sacrifices, especially by Konyak, Wancho, Nocte, with whom they had more interactions. The socio-cultural requirement for skulls and tattoos also led to the procuring of slaves. Headhunting raids and slaves were considered necessary to procure human heads for the last rites of the chief among the Konyak, Wancho, Nocte. Caputuring the slave labour and the sale and exchange of slaves and produce, were part of an elaborate tribute system of political control and economic transactions between powerful patron and less powerful client villages.[174]

Slavery was abolished in British Indian Penal Code of 1843. However, it continued to be practiced in "Unadministered" areas of northern Burma, in the northeast of Assam, and among the Lushai tribes. With regards to the Naga hills, on 8th March 1889, A Porteous, Esq., Offg. Deputy Commissioner hills, in his letter to Secretary to the Chief Commissioner of Assam, wrote that slavery in the 'domestic form' was 'widely prevalent' among the Aos and that children born of female slaves were 'usually put to death.' Porteous also added that "such a state of things cannot be allowed in British territory," and asked if the Government was declare all slaves in the Naga hills as emancipated with or without compensation or to leave the institution to disappear slowly but refuse to acknowledge the supposed rights of the slave owners.[175]

Analysis of the colonial records and reports of the punitive expeditions undertaken in the different areas of the Naga hills as well as the missionaries account suggest that the slavery ended by the 1940s.[176]

The tradition of 'women mediators' in pre-colonial Naga society was another important custom. As per Naga customary laws pertaining to warfare, slave capturing, inter-village marriage alliance was a tradition. The existence of such traditions was prevails even during the Ahom period; the oral narratives of Nagas mentioned repeatedly, the Ahom Raja matrimonial alliance with the Naga chiefs' daughter, that we will discuss further in details in the next chapter.

The economic condition of medieval Assam, according to contemporary observers like Shihabuddin Talish[177] has been described as under developed because the Ahom state did not fully exploit the economic potential of the region. Overall the economy was agricultural and rural in character. The *paiks* and respective *khels* supplied all the basic needs of the Ahom state. The state gave in kind and received mainly in kind and labour services. In a way, the mode of appropriation by the Ahom state in the form of labour services and in kind also limited the range of trading activities at various levels.[178] After the Mughal invasion during the seventeenth century, the Ahom state not only regulated trade and controlled it but also exercised overall supervision over all trading activities both within and outside the region. Severe restrictions were imposed on traders coming from outside. They thought exporters with political power might undermine their authority as a sovereign state and reduce their profits.[179] The Ahoms considered local trade with the hill people as an essential element of the economy preferring it to long-distance trade.[180] The economy of the Nagas was a traditional self-subsistence economy based on land, its produce and forest resources.

The Ahom Raja's recognised the importance of peaceful relations with neighbouring tribes by using trade as state policy. As the Ahom state expanded and grew it sought to control the natural resources of the kingdom and also those of the surrounding hills. The Ahom kings during the later period took his share of the resources by splitting the salt wells mutually with the Nagas and opening several market networks in all the main trade sites. *Duarias'* were appointed to man the *chowkeys'* and collect tax from the traders. As mentioned previously, the policy followed by the Ahom rulers in dealing with the hill tribes was wise, based on the principle of political expediency. It was advantageous for both the parties concerned. The Ahoms, in their dealings with the hill tribes, were conciliatory; nevertheless, they did not hesitate to employ coercive measures when necessary.

Summary

The trade between the hills and valley were based on exchange of goods and services. For the tribes, the element or question of profit making did not exist. The producers or gatheres were often the sellers of the goods sold or bartered. Trade, in general was managed by the local inhabitants. The hill and plain territory have been described as a country where no extra-ordinary prosperity or distressing undernourishment occurs. The Assamese proverb *Akalo nai, Bharalo nai* (there is no scarcity or overflow), indicates the economic condition under the Ahoms. Though self-sufficiency in the absolute sense did not exist, yet most of the limited demands of the people were satisfied within the household and village itself. Through commercial transactions with the Nagas, salt, cotton, spears, ginger, honey, red chillies, ivory, etc., were obtained and exchanged for cattle, goat, rice, tobacco, cloths, dried fish, silk, iron etc. Such commercial transactions encouraged the trading pursuits of the people, and to facilitate these Ahom rulers opened *haat*/markets which were attached to each *duar*s[181] Often the Ahom state manipulated the economic needs of the hill people to their benefit by compelling the Nagas to pay taxes in kinds (elephant teeth, ivory, spear- shafts, cotton etc.) for bringing the products to the plain markets. The trade relations between the Nagas-Ahoms were conducted by duly appointed frontier warden of *chawkies'* at the *duar*s' to deal with the hill tribes. To encourage and foster trade and peaceful interaction the Ahom state even gave grants of *khats, bheels, posa* to the Nagas; this policy was so practical that the British followed the same in their dealing with the hill tribes.[182]

Notes

1. For details, see Robin Skeates, "Trade and Interaction," in Chris Gosden, Berry Cunliffe, and Rosemary A. Joyce (eds.), *The Oxford Handbook of Archaeology*, Oxford University Press, 2009, p. 409; J. Allen, "Fishing for Wallabies: Trade as a Mechanism of Social Interaction, and Elaboration on the Papuan South Coast," in M. Rowlands, J. Friedman (ed.), *The Evolution of Social Systems,* Duckworth, London, 1976, pp. 419-455; J. Allen & O. Rye, "The importance of being earnest in archaeological investigations of pre-historic trade in Papua," in Dutton (ed.), *The Hiri in History, Pacific Research Monograph,* No. 8, Australia National University, Canberra, 1982, pp. 99-116. In the case of northeast India, see Amrendra Kr Thakur*'s* "Pattern of Pre-Colonial Trade and Polity Formations in Arunachal Pradesh: A Study of their Relationship" in *Proceedings of North East India History Association*, Imphal Session, 2002, pp. 299-318; *Idem*, "Polity of pre-colonial Arunachal Pradesh: Interactions in Trade, Culture, State and Buddhism," in S. Dutta and B. Tripathy (eds.), *Buddhism in North-East India*, Indus Publishing Company, New Delhi, 2006, pp. 241-263.
2. Namsangia are Nocte from the Namchang village and its adjacent area. There are 45 subordinate villages under Namchang. Nocte now live at Tirap and Changlang districts, Arunachal Pradesh.
3. There are 51 Wancho villages, upper Wancho has 31 villages, and lower Wancho has 20 villages. These villages are scattered over the circles of Kanubari, Longding, Pumao, Pongahu, and Wakka. The name of the villages are: 1. Kanubari, 2. Dasathong, 3. Olington, 4. Luaksim, 5. Mopakhat, 6. Banfera, 7. Wanu, 8. Longhua, 9. Rusa, 10. Pong, 11. Ronglua, 12. Nokfan, 13. Naitong, 14. Otongkua, 15. Chopsa, 16. Chopnu, 17. Chatong, 18. Ozakho, 19. Chanu, 20. Longsom, 21. Maihua, 22. Longkhaw, 23. Pumao, 24. Longphong, 25. Mintong, 26. Niausa, 27. Niaunu, 28. Longding, 29. Zedua, 30. Senua, 31. Tissa, 32. Senua, 33. Bonia, 34. Pongchau, 35. Konsa, 36. Jagan, 37. Khasa, 38. Konnu, 39. Votnu, 40. Kamhua, 41. Kamhua, 42. Kampong, 43. Chop, 44. Khanu, 45. Wakka, 46. Chongkhaw, 47. Nginu, 48. Nissa, 49. Kaimoi, 50. Khogla.
4. The growth of the *Nagamese* (a pato is Assamese mixed with certain local words) as a language is evidence of this relationship.
5. Lalit Kumar Baruah, *Oral Tradition And Folk Heritage of North-East India*, Guwahati, 1999, p. 43.
6. S.K. Bhuyan, *Anglo-Assamese Relations, op.cit.*, p. 33.

7. William Robinson, *A Descriptive Account of Assam*, *op.cit.*, pp. 386-398.
8. Tajenyuba Ao, *British Occupation of Naga Country*, *op.cit.*, p. 183.
9. Report of visit by Captain Welsh to the Singpho and Naga Frontier of Luckhimpore, No. 225, January 4, 1842.
10. John Owen, *Notes On the Naga Tribes in Communication with Assam,* W.H. Carey and Co., Cossitollaii, Calcutta, 1844, p. 13.
11. The native Nagas (Konyak-Wancho) inhabits at present-day Mon and Longleng districts in Nagaland; the eastern strips of Sibsagar and Tinsukia districts of Assam; and the north western part of Saigaing province of Myanmar. The, eastern Nagas have been divided up under various sub-group official names like Konyak, Phom, Tangsa, Tutsa, Wancho, Ollo, Nocte, etc. Ollo tribe (also known as Lazu), is one of the Naga tribes that mainly resides in Arunachal Pradesh and the Naga Self-Administered Zone in Myanmar. However, due to lack of official recognition from the Government of Arunachal Pradesh they are considered a sub-tribe of the Nocte.
12. When the Ahoms entered Assam in the 13th century, the Kacharis had already attained a stable polity covering an area extending from the river Dikhu in the east to the river Kopili in the west. An Ao Naga tradition talks about the existence of Kachari settlements in the lower ranges of their hill. The *Buranjis* speak of Sukapha encountering many Kacharis at the Naga hills (Present Tirap District of Arunachal Pradesh). It was either Sukapha (1228-1268) or Supimpha (Subinphaa, 1281-1293), who pushed out the Kachari Raja Dersongpha to the hills. The Kacharis were then removed to the south bank of river Dikhu by Dihingia Raja; S. Dutta Choudhury, *Gazetteer of India Arunachal Pradesh, Tirap District,* 1980, Published by Shri R. N. Bagchi, Director of Information and Public Relations Government of Arunachal Pradesh, Shillong, 1980, pp. 1 and 228.
13. William Robinson, *A Descriptive Account of Assam, op.cit.*, p. 243.
14. The Nocte have divided themselves into two groups: The Upper Nocte and the Lower Nocte. They believed that Nocte Bordumsa come from Dadom and Chingkoi villages which is the Upper Nocte. The Upper Noctes are believed to have originated from the Wanchos (the Wanchos mostly inhabit in Tirap, Longding, districts). The Lower Konyak are believed to have originated from Wancho groups, which now inhabit in Mon district. The Bordumsa town is a border area between Arunachal Pradesh and Assam. Originally Bordumsa was a Singpho settlement, the word '*bor*' is an Assamese word meaning big and '*dumsa*' is the name of a Singpho clan (a traditional Singpho priest). The Bordumsa areas falls under the jurisdiction of the states (Assam and Arunachal Pradesh) and Assamese is the dominant language there; S. L Baruah, *A Comprehensive History of Assam, op.cit.*, pp. 203-219. The term Konyak in the study is used to refer to the Upper Noctes, Wancho, Tangsa, and Lower Konyak, who were then singled-out as Eastern Nagas by the British.
15. Foreign Department proceedings, Extension of the eastern boundary of the Naga Hills District. Restriction regarding trans-frontier tours, External-A, Government of India, No. 130-131, March 1904.
16. J. D. Soul, *The Nagas of Burma. Their Festival, Customs and Way of Life*, Orchid Press, Bangkok, Thailand, 2005, pp. 133-134.
17. C.L. Imchen, "History of the Relations between the Nagas and the Valley Kingdoms," in F.A. Qadri (ed.), *Society and Economy in North-East India,* Vol. 2. Regency Publications, New Delhi, p. 118.
18. *Ibid.*, p. 118.
19. V. Elwin, *India's North-Eastern Frontier in the Nineteenth* Century, *op.cit.*
20. E.A. Gait, *A History of Assam*, *op.cit.*, p. 301.

21. W. Robinson, *A Descriptive Account of Assam, op.cit.*, pp. 386-398.
22. H.K. Barpujari, (ed.), *The Comprehensive History of Assam* (1st edition), Vol. III, Publication Board of Assam, Guwahati, 1994, pp. 124-126.
23. S.K. Bhuyan, *Early British Relations with Assam A Study of the Original Sources and Records Elucidating the History of Assam for the Period from Its First Contact With the Honourable East India Company to the Transfer of the Company's Territories to the Crown in 1858*, Department of Historical and Antiquarian Studies in Assam, 1949 p. 15.
24. Jahnabi Gogoi, *Agrarian System of Medieval Assam, op.cit.*, p. 60.
25. *Haat* (weekly market) were held on certain days of the week in almost all the foothill Naga hill villages; also see, Dolly Kikon, "Borders, Bagaans, and Bazaars, Locating the foothills along the Naga hills in Northeast India," in *Essay Biblio,* May-June 2008, p. 21.
26. R. H. Rattan, *Moina of Ancient Ahom-Nokpu Naga Relation, op.cit.*, p. 54; B.B. Ghosh, *Nagaland District Gazetteer*, Mokokchung District, Published 1979, p. 40.
27. Liza Talukdar, Mundunsungkham, "The Casket of Gold; Aspects of the Economy, Society and Culture Under the Ahom rule circa 13th -18th," M.Phil. thesis, Centre for Historical Studies School of Social Sciences, Jawaharlal Nehru University, New Delhi, 2004, p. 32.
28. *Ibid.*, p. 33.
29. S.K. Bhuyan (ed.), *Kachari Buranji,* Department of Historical and Antiquarian Studies, Guwahati, 2010, p. 36.
30. D.P. Barooah, *Assam District Gazetteer: Nowgoan District*, publisher Government of Assam, Gauhati, 1978.
31. W.W. Hunter, *A Statistical Account of Assam,* Vol. I, Spectrum Publications: New Delhi, 1897 (Reprint 1998).
32. *Ibid.*, pp. 243-244; External Affairs Department, Tour of the Konyak Foothills of the Political officer, Tirap Frontier Tract, 1946.
33. Information recorded by the author from Shri Asen 98-year-old village elder in January 2017 from Jaboka village, Nagaland and Shri Khamo Wangham (chief) 50-year-old in March 2018 from Shangnyu village, Nagaland.
34. Foreign Political Proceedings (FPP), Pol A, 1841, pp. 71-74.
35. C.L. Imchen, "Naga Myths of Origin and Historical Reconstruction," (eds.), in Mignonette Momin and Cecile A. Mawlong, *Society and Economy in North-East India*, Vol.1, Regency Publication, New Delhi, 2004, p. 126.
36. J.H. Hutton, *The Angami Nagas, op.cit.*, p. 71.
37. Luchymo Enie, "Trade Relationship between Naga and Ahom," Ph.D. thesis, Department of History and Archaeology, Nagaland, 2016, pp. 43-44.
38. S. Dutta Choudhury, *Gazetteer of India Arunachal Pradesh, Tirap District,* 1980, Published by Shri R. N. Bagchi, Director of Information and Public Relations, Government of Arunachal Pradesh, Shillong, 1980, Appendix I.
39. Foreign Political Proceeding by T. Brodie, Principal Assistant, Governor General's Agent, No. 5, Dated the 15th September, Seebsaugar, 1841.
40. Foreign Political Proceeding by T. Brodie, Reports on, No. 6, 26th February 1844, pp. 294-295.
41. Gertrude M. Godden, "Naga and Other Frontier Tribes of North-East India," in *The Journal of the Anthropological Institute of Great Britain and Ireland,* Vol. 26, 1897, p. 10.
42. *Ibid.*, p. 10.
43. Information recorded by the author from Shri. Khongthungia (Michael) 65-year-old, at Bhandari, Wokha on 11th May 2018.

44. S.E. Peal, "Notes on a visit to the tribes inhabiting the hills south of Sibsagar Assam," in *JASB*, No. I, 1872, p. 124; J.P. Mills, *The Ao Nagas, op.cit.*, p. 98.
45. John M'Cosh, *Topography of Assam, op.cit.*, p. 44.
46. P. D. Stracey, *Nagaland Nightmare*, applied publishers, New Delhi, 1968, p. 12. The Ahom military organisation consists of well-equipped elephant cavalry known as the *khel* system composed of *paik*. According to the Naga oral traditions, i.e., of the Aos and Konyaks, they exported wild elephants to the valley kingdom. Mills and Stracey frequently recorded the frequent elephant hunting expeditions at Lotha and Ao villages.
47. G.C. Barua (ed.), *Ahom Buranji, op.cit.*, p. 185.
48. R. H. Rattan, *op.cit*; The author recorded this oral narrative from the Nokpu village council member Shri Senti Walling, Shri. T. Tia Aier (77 yrs) at Nokpu village, Mokokchung on 26th March 2018.
49. John M'Cosh, *Topography of Assam, op.cit.*, p. 44.
50. Surya Kumar Bhuyan, (ed.), *An Account of Assam,* first compiled in 1807-1814 by Francis Hamilton, DHAS, Guwahati,1963, pp. 180-183; Gait, *op.cit.*, p. 78; P. D. Stracey, *Nagaland Nightmare, op.cit.*, p. 12. The name Hatigoria was given by the Ahom, which means where elephants are found. Certain *paiks* were assigned to lure and train elephants from the Naga hills.
51. B.K. Barua, *A Cultural History of Assam (Early Period)* Vol. I, Satya Rajan Dev, Guwahati, 1951 (Reprint 1986), p. 69.
52. *Ibid*., p. 70.
53. S.K. Bhuyan, *A History of Kamrupa with Reference to its Relations with Neighbouring Kingdom* (tr.), 22, Vol. V, Pt. II, Intro. XV, DHAS, Guwahati.
54. S.E. Peal, "Notes on a visit to the tribes inhabiting the hills south of Sibsagar Assam," *op.cit.*, p. 124.
55. Surya Kumar Bhuyan (ed.), *An Account of Assam*, *op.cit.*, pp. 60-62; Kamal Hussain Ahmed and Projit Kumar Palit, "The Role of Elephant in Assam in the Medieval and Late Medieval Period," in *EAS Journal of Humanities and Cultural Studies*, Vol. 2, July-August 2020, p. 217; see Report on the Trans-Dikhu Tour, File No.469, Government of Nagaland, 1913, p. 10.
56. Pratap Chandra Choudhury, *The History of Civilisation of the People of Assam to the twelfth century A.D.*, Spectrum publications, Guwahati, first published 1959, (Reprint 2017), p. 338.
57. Kamal Hussain Ahmen & Kumar Palit, "The Role of Elephant in Assam in the Medieval and Late Medieval Period," *op.cit.*, p. 216.
58. S.K. Bhuyan, *Tungkhungia Buranji, op.cit.*, pp. 60-62.
59. J.P. Mills, *The Ao Nagas, op.cit.*, pp. 4 and 20.
60. Alexander Mackenzie, *The North-East Frontier of Bengal*, *op.cit.*, p. 93.
61. Information recorded by the author from Shri Nyakwang Konyak (Gaobura or village head) at Shangnyu village, Mon Nagaland, March, 2016.
62. Information recorded by the author from Shri Nyakwang Konyak (Gaobura or village head man) at Shangnyu village, Mon Nagaland, March, 2016.
63. Information recorded by the author at Niausa-Kanubari (Longding) and Kanubari (Banfera) Longding (Arunachal Pradesh) on October 29, 2016.
64. J.P. Mills, *The Ao Nagas, op.cit.*, p. 103.
65. Report on the Trans-Dikhu Tour, File No. 469, Government of Nagaland, 1913, p. 10.
66. Information recorded by the author from Shri. Shomwang Jabuka chief, Mon, Nagaland, on 2017 and Sri. Hazarika 79-year-old trader from Sonari town, on 7 May 2019.

67. K.S. Singh and C.L. Imchen, *People of India Nagaland,* Vol. XXXIV, Anthropological Survey of India, Seagull Books, Calcutta, 1994; Field observation by the author at Jaboka, Nokzang (Mon) Namsang (Tirap) and Nokpu, Leremin (Mokokchung), from 2016-2019.
68. J.P. Mills, *The Ao Nagas*, *op.cit.*, p. 96.
69. *Ibid.*, p. 98.
70. T. Rattan, *op.cit.*, p. 56.
71. The Daflas (Nishis) who called themselves as '*Nishis*' lived in the hills stretching from the Bharali River on the west and the upper courses of the Somdiri (Suvansiri River), on the east in Kameng and Suvansiri districts of present day Arunachal Pradesh. The Assamese people called the Daflas living near the Darrang *duar's* Pachima Daflas, and those on the border of Lakhimpur, Tagin Daflas. The Daflas are not a single tribe but a collection of petty clans, independent of each other. The chiefs or heads of the clans are known as *Gams*.
72. Assam Secretariat, File No.177J, Nos.1-6, serial No. 06, 1882.
73. Foreign Political Proceedings (FPP), 1845, p. 49.
74. J. Johnstone, (1896), "My Experience in Munnipore and the Naga Hills," V. Elwin (ed.), *Nagas*, 1969, p. 598. Especially the Nocte, Wancho, and Konyak polities supplemented their swidden agriculture with various forms of economic transactions, i.e., salt production, trans-polity barter trade, and control over trade routes.
75. H.K. Barpujari, *The Comprehensive History of Assam,* Vol.V, Publication Board Assam Guwahati, 2007, p. 76.
76. *Ibid.*, p. 76; Jenkins, Foreign Proceeding Periodical (FPP), No.46, 28th March 1838, paras 86-90; The *beepari* were small traders, who bought things from both hills and plains and sold them outside the state at higher prices. Thus, the possibility of having a sufficient scope of profitable trade in Assam attracted the attention of the British's in the 18th century, who first concluded a commercial treaty with the king of Assam in 1793 A.D.
77. Foreign Political Proceeding, No. 82, November 9, 1840.
78. H.K. Barpujari (ed.), *The Comprehensive History of Assam* (1st edition), Vol. III, *op.cit.*, pp. 124-126.
79. Darrang people had to pay a tax on every animal sold; see, Jahnabi Gogoi, *Agrarian system of Medieval Assam, op.cit.*, p. 108.
80. Several *hat* or market places were established by the Ahom rulers. King Pratap Singha is said to have established *haat* in Namsang, Barhat, etc. on the Assam Kachari borders; see, S.K. Bhuyan, *Atan Burangohain and His Times: A History of Assam, from the invasion of Nawab Mir Jumla in 1662-63 to the termination of Assam-Mogul conflicts in 1682*, Lawyer's Book Stall, Guwahati, 1957, p. 40.
81. Jahnabi Gogoi, *Agrarian System of Medieval Assam*, *op.cit.*, p. 108.
82. *Ibid*; Towards the end of their supremacy the Ahom rulers introduced new taxes, e.g., *Khatiyadhan* or a kind of poll tax and *Dewaldhan* (land tax).
83. R.S. Sharma (ed.), *Land Revenue in India: Historical Studies*, Motilal Banarsidass, Delhi, 1971, p. 1.
84. The contact with the Mughals brought many changes in the court of Ahom, for instance, food habits, dresses, pursuits in fine arts including music, musical instruments etc.
85. S. Dutta Choudhury, *Gazetteer of India Arunachal Pradesh, Tirap District,* 1980, Published by Shri R.N. Bagchi, Director of Information and Public Relations, Government of Arunachal Pradesh, Shillong, 1980, p. 133.
86. R. Wilcox, "Memory of the Survey of Assam and the Neighbouring Countries, Executed in 1825," in *Hill tracts between Assam and Burma Selection of Papers*, Delhi, 1873 (Reprint 1978), p. 5.

87. Shrutidev Goswami, "The Eastern Nagas and the Salt Trade of Upper Assam," in *Proceedings of North Eastern India History Association,* Fifth Session, Aizawl, 1984, pp. 93-100. Bamboo barrel salt had always played a vital role in Naga culture; bamboo baked salt has been used for traditional Naga medicine for centuries. Proponents for bamboo salt states that it helps in digestion, oral health, skincare, etc.
88. F. Buchanan Hamilton, *An Account of Assam, op.cit.,* p. 47.
89. R.B. Pemberton, *Report on the Eastern Frontier of British India*, DHAS, (Reprint 2015), p. 82.
90. Foreign Political Proceedings, No. 83, April, 1838.
91. R. Wilcox, "Memoir of a Survey of Assam and the Neighbouring Countries, executed in 1825-6-7-8," in *Selection of Papers Regarding the Hill Tracts between Assam and Burmah and on the Upper Brahmaputra,* Vivek Publishing Company, Delhi, 1978, p. 5; The Sadiya is a frontier area to the eastern part of Assam, which was a part of historic "Mohong" area. Several British reports have mentioned the availability of salt wells in Sandiya. The Sadiya salt mine was for many centuries under the superintendence of an officer called Mohonghat Barua, who paid not less than forty thousand rupees a year to the Ahom royal exchequer; Narayan Singh Rao, *The Tutsa tribes of North East India Origin, Migration and History (Two parts*), Krishan Mittal Publications, New Delhi, (First Published 2010), p. 16.
92. Dimasa are also known as the Kachari and are the first tribes to produced salt from Mohong areas. This production was practiced before the advent of the Ahom in 1228. When the Ahom occupied the Dimasa territory, they engaged some Dimasa people to extract the salt. The six Kachari groups residing in the salt producing area of Sodiya and Mohong are (1) Sonowal (2) Khamyang (3) Mohong (4) Duania (5) Hazong 6). Kheremial.
93. Semsas are known as Semkhor (Dima Hasao, District Assam). From 16th century, the Semsas protected the salt wells from any outsiders; they share cultural and language traits with the Dimasa tribes.
94. Lonpuriyas/ Lonpurias (salt-makers) were the contingent of Ahom kings sent to the salt springs to prepare salt. The Lonpurias were recruited from different tribes, such as Chutias, Ahoms, Kacharis and Moran. The groups that supply firewood for salt making were known as Borkheremiya and Sarukheremiya.
95. The Noctes called *sum* (salt), and the clan which produce salt are Barduria, Paniduria, Namchangia, Takam and Khampa Nagas.
96. Borduarias (Borduar meaning big door), are Noctes living around the village Borduar. They guard the eastern land route to Ahom kingdom. Under Borduarias, they have 20 villages; the village Paniduar (Paniduarias) is situated on the right bank of the river Disang, which flows from Patkai Mountain Range. Disang River was the eastern water route to the Ahom kingdom which was guarded by the Paniduaria Noctes. Namchangias are Noctes, and under Namchang there are 45 subordinate villages.
97. Tutsas live in Changlang and Tirap districts of Arunachal Pradesh. They share cultural traits with Nocte, Wancho and Lower Konyak. There were reports of several salt wells in Tutsa village.
98. Tangsa inhabitant at Tirap and Changlang districts migrated from Myanmar during the 12th century.
99. Francis Hamilton Buchanan, *An Account of Assam: With Some Notices Concerning the Neighbouring Territories in 1807-1814,* Department of History and Antiquarian Society, Gauhati, 1884 (Reprint 1963), p. 46; Mattaks reside in the eastern part of the Ahom kingdom. The word Moran is synonymously used for Mattaks; in 1805, they established a short-lived tiny kingdom on the easternmost border of Assam. The Tutsa oral history says Mattaks sought to exploit the salt wells of Tutsa areas.

100. S.K. Barpujari, "Raja Purandar Singha's Management of Salt-wells in the Naga hills," *op.cit.*, pp. 73-83.
101. R.B. Pemberton, *Report on the Eastern Frontier of British India*, DHAS, Gauhati, 1966, pp. 84-85.
102. S.K. Bhuyan, *Anglo-Assamese Relations, op.cit.,* p. 68.
103. Rakim Ranjan Saikia and Nurul Amin, "A Study on the Salt production on Ancient Assam," in *IJHS* Vol. 54.4, December 2019, p. 495.
104. R. Wilcox, "Memoir of a Survey of Assam and the Neighbouring Countries, executed in 1825-1828," *op.cit.*, p. 5.
105. J.P. Mills, *The Rengma Nagas*, *op.cit*; see, Foreign Political Proceeding, No. 82, 9 November 1840.
106. Foreign Political Proceedings, No. 82, 9th November, 1840.
107. Foreign Political Proceedings, No. 82, 9th November, 1840.
108. Lila Gogoi, *The Buranjis: Historical Literature of Assam, (A Critical Survey),* New Delhi, 1986, p. 179; Raktim Rajan Saikia and Nurul Amin, "A Study on the Salt production of Ancient Assam," *op.cit.*, pp. 485-495.
109. Journal of Jenkins on the South Bank from 30 January to 20 February, 1838.
110. L.W. Shakespear, *History of Assam Rifles*, MacMillan and Co., Limited St. Martin Street, London, 1929, p. 273.
111. J.P. Mills, *The Ao Nagas, op.cit.*, pp. 102-107; Lakshmi Devi, *op.cit.,* p. 36.
112. *Ibid.*, pp. 385-386.
113. As a case in point, the Nocte and Konyak Nagas came under the influence of the Vaishnavite Goswami of *Baragarh xatra* near Nazira and Sibsagar, it appears that the *xatra* exercised a considerable amount of influence in seculars matters like the involvement of the Goswami in settling a dispute between Namsang and Borduria on the share of tribute from six villages. Subsequently, there was a manipulation of their origin myths to legitimize a developing polity. For instance, the Noctes, though considered themselves the offsprings of the union between the sky god's daughter and the spirit of the earth, would rather give precedence to their Lowang in reckoning their origin. The Lowang (chief) of Namsang recounts a tradition about the migration of the Noctes from Burma led by Wanghang. They are said to have ridden horses and brought over water buffaloes on their trek. The present Lowang of Namsang, Borduria and Laptang claim descent from Khungbao, the first Nocte chief. According to the tradition, he sired two sons, namely, Khunlung and Khunlai. This story linked them with the Ahoms. However, the Ahoms had their genealogies attached to the Hindu pantheon, i.e., Khenkham (son of Indra), who was the progenitor of Khunlung and Khunlai; E.A. Gait, *A History of Assam*, p. 336; S.N. Barua, *Tribes of Indo-Burma Border*, (New Delhi, 1991) indicates the strategic nature of the territory and the relations that ensued thereon: "There was a time when Namsangias and the Borduarias were capable of waging war even against the most powerful Ahoms, who ruled Assam for six hundred years. The former was, however, brought to defeat and made an alliance with the Ahoms. They too have an alliance of matrimonial relations. The Borduarias had to maintain sharp look out at the principal point of entry to the plains so that no undesirable elements made an inroad to the Ahom territory. There was a Paniduar also at the Tisa or Dilih or Disang River which flows from the Patkai border. It was to be looked after by a Nocte chief whose country was the right bank of the river."
114. J. Jacob, *The Nagas-Hills people of Northeast India: Society, Culture and the Colonial Encounter*, Themaes and Hudson Ltd. London, 1990.
115. J.P. Mills, *The Ao Nagas, op.cit.*, pp. 102-107; C. L Imchen, "Naga Myths of Origin and Historical Reconstruction," in (eds.) Mignonette Momin and Cecile A. Mawlong,

Society and Economy in North-East India, Vol.1, Regency Publication, New Delhi, 2004, pp. 162-163.

116. J.P. Mills, *The Rengma Nagas*, *op.cit*., pp. 72-73.
117. J.P. Mills, *The Rengma Nagas*, *op.cit*., p. 73.
118. J. Jacob, *The Nagas-Hills people of Northeast India, op.cit.*
119. C.L. Imchen, "Naga Myths of Origin and Historical Reconstruction," *op.cit*., p. 163; The Abors (Nishi), hill Miri, Nagas were given the privilege of the *posa* system.
120. Information recorded by the author from Borduria chief Shri. Paiwang Lowang, on 21.11.2021.
121. Every Ao village is governed by a ruling body called *putu Menden,* (*puto*-council, *Menden* - seat). The word *putu* is from *Chungli* language and *Menden* from *Mongsen* language. This governing body consists of a group of people selected from the villagers representing all the founder clans (those that established the village) of the village. Each founder clan select senior and qualified men of the clan, those capable of running the village administration and who have a good knowledge of Ao customary law and practices, as their representatives. The members of the *puto Menden/Samen Menchen* exercise legislative, executive and judicial powers of the village. The Ao *putu menden* have a standardized cycle of five generations (*putu*). On the other hand, every individual inducted into an *Ariju/Zuki* (Morung for boys and girls respectively, *Ariju/Zuki* serves as a learning institution for the youngster about the customary law of the village) got slotted into one of the five political generations, namely Mechensanger (Chongli moiety)/Mechenjanger (Mongsen moiety); Mepungsanger (C)/Mevungjanger (M); Kosanger (C)/ Kojahjanger (M); Riongsanger (C)/Riongjanger (M) and Medemsanger (C)/ Medemjanger (M). This system is directly linked with *Ariju/Zuki* (Morung). This system is also linked with the Medemsanger in the distant past; it was coordinated with the simultaneous induction of a *zünga* or age group in the *Ariju/Züki*. The concurrent recruitment of young people attaining the age of ten every spring continued till one of the male inductees got a male child. Then a process known as *Mendang* (blockade) occurred, and the Medemsanger generation was considered complete. A new *puto* would then be ready to start, i.e. the Mechensanger *puto*. This way, successive *zünga* groups filled up the remaining *puto* in an endless cycle. Here the demographic attribute played a crucial role, as one generation may have four *züngas* or even six *züngas* depending on how early the members got married and procreated. Nevertheless, no account is fixed cyclic generation, the government was hindered, i.e. even if a generation had six age groups when their turn came for powers, the first and second age groups might have died out, and the rest would take up the *tatar* or councillor position of a particular ruling generation. When an old generation demitted office after every thirty years, a ceremony known as *atsüngtepba* (pushing out) marked this occasion. In these rituals, every member of the incoming *puto* contributed a pig or else he would forfeit his rights to have any say in the decisive matters taken up by his *puto*. This ruling generation would then throw up elders to fill official posts in the *Tatar Menden/ Samen* These positions were assigned based on the seniority of clans (This system is still in vogue among the Ao Nagas).
122. The *aso/ neso* or biological generation in the sense that it is reckoned from the transfer of parental authority to the eldest son. It is generally affected by the demise of the head of a family; Based on oral narratives recorded from Shri. Senti Walling and Shri. T. Tia Aier of Nokpu village, on 26th March to 19 July 2018.
123. The Naga*'s* addresses valley peoples of Assam as plainsmen.
124. Information recorded by author from Nokpu village council Shri Senti Walling, Shri. T. Tia Aier (77yrs) at Nokpu village Mokokchung, on 26 March 2018; Also

See, R.H. Rattan, *Moina of Ancient Ahom-Nokpu Naga Relation,* Shree Venkateswara Printing Press, New Delhi, 1985.

125. C.L. Imchen, "History of the relations between the Nagas and the Valley Kingdom," in F.A. Qadri (ed.), *Society and Economy in North-East India,* Vol. 2, Regency Publications, New Delhi, 2004, p. 115.
126. Bendangangshi, *Glimpses of Naga History,* Published by Naga Patriots of Soyim, Mokukchung, Nagaland, 1993, p. 11.
127. Letter No. LR-8/71-72/1996 dated 14th July 1972 by Shri S.C Dey Commissioner of Nagaland, Kohima, address to the Chief Secretary of Nagaland Kohima; see Letter No. 4400-R dated Shillong, the 5th December 1921 from the Chief Secretary of the Government of Assam to Commissioner of Suma Valley and Hill divisions in response to Letter No. 899-T dates the 24th October 1921 regarding the resumption of certain Naga *khat* and payment of revenue to *khat* owners including *Assiring khat* owners with the copy to Deputy Commissioner of Naga Hills.
128. Alexander Mackenzie, *op. cit., p.* 97.
129. *Ibid*., p. 97.
130. R.H. Rattan, *op.cit.,* p. 44.
131. Based on an oral information recorded by the author from Smt. Sentishila or Dalime (70 yrs.) of walling clan of Nokpu village, on 12th May 2018. My informant told me naming of Sentishila or Dalime continues every generation to date among the walling clan.
132. Garhgaon was the capital of Ahom kingdom, built by Suklenmung in 1540, presently located near Sivasagar town. In Garhgaon, the Ahom king constructed these three resting houses with potable water (wells) facilities for the travellers from (Assaringias) and later, the Garhgaon well was named Assiring well. The Mughal general, Mir Jumlah, when he seized the Ahom capital in March 1662, he mentioned the daily bazaar at Garhgaon, where he said the availability of betel leaves (and nuts) were on sale. He also mentions that no eatables were available in the daily bazaar.
133. C.L. Imchen, "History of the Relations between the Nagas and the Valley Kingdoms," *op.cit*., p. 126.
134. Temsula Ao, *The Ao-Naga Oral Tradition*, *op.cit*., pp. 10-11; Elwin Verrier, *The Nagas in the 19th Century, op.cit.*, p. 18.
135. Based on information recorded by the author from Shri. Chao Memanta Changmai, President of Tai Ahom Parisad, Sibsagar Assam, on 15 December 2016.
136. '*Kiven*' means cane helmets in Lhota dialects. A cane is far more valuable and reserved for articles which are meant to last a long time, it is used to make hamlet, shields (*otsung*), rain-shields (*phuchyo*), cane seat chair and grain baskets. For rough work, a checkered pattern is generally used.
137. William Carlson Smith, *The Ao Naga Tribe of Assam: A Study in Ethnology and Sociology*, Macmillan and Co. Limited, London, 1925, p. 44.
138. Information recorded by the author from Smt. Shongna, a 90 years old woman from Wanching village. She narrated how when she was young, they (groups of women's) walked 3 days carrying mats or cotton to sell at Naganimora or Geleki *haat,* 26.2.2018.
139. Christoph von Furer-Haimendorf, *The Konyak Nagas, op.cit.,* p. 17.
140. P. C. Choudhury, *The History of Civilisation of the People of Assam to the Twelfth Century,* Spectrum publication, Guwahati,1959, (Reprint 2017), p. 352.
141. 141. *Ibid*., p. 352.
142. 142. *Ibid*., p. 352.
143. Jahnabi Gogoi, *Agrarian System of Medieval Assam*, *op.cit.*
144. S.K. *Jayantiya Buranji,* Department of Historical and Antiquarian Studies, Gauhati, 1937, p. 99ff; see, *Changrung Phukanar Buranji,* p. 6ff.
145. *Ibid.*

146. Jahnabi Gogoi, *Agrarian System of Medieval Assam, op.cit.*, p. 155.
147. J.P. Mills, *The Ao Nagas, op.cit.*, p. 102.
148. S.K. Bose, "The Ao Nagas and their Medium of Exchange," in Fozail Ahmad Qadri (ed.), *Society and Economy in North-East India,* Regency Publication, New Delhi, 2006 p. 145.
149. J. Owen, *Notes on the Nagas Tribes in Communication with Assam*, British library, Historical print editions, first editions 1884, (Reprint 2011), p. 13.
150. *Ibid.*, p. 13; S.K. Bose, "The Ao Nagas and their Medium of Exchange," *op.cit.*, p. 146.
151. S.C. Goswami, "Jabilee or the Nagas Coin," in *Journal of Assam Research Society*, Gauhati, Vol. II, 1939.
152. S.K. Bose, "The Ao Nagas and their Medium of Exchange," *op.cit.*, p. 145; see, Hutton, *The Angami Nagas*, *op.cit.*, p. 71.
153. S.C. Goswami, "Jabilee of the Naga Coin," *op.cit.*, p. 97.
154. J.H. Hutton, T*he Angami Nagas*, *op.cit.*, p. 72.
155. J.P. Singh (ed.), *The Coinage and Economy of North Eastern States*, N.S.I, Varanasi, 1977, p. 140.
156. J.H. Hutton, *The Angami Nagas*, *op.cit.*, p. 72.
157. J.P. Mills, *The Ao Nagas*, *op.cit.*, p. 398.
158. J.P. Singh (ed.), *The Coinage and Economy of North-Eastern States*, *op.cit.*, p. 140.
159. Information recorded by the author from Shri Chuiwang Wangham, the *Nyam* (brass disk) was found at the Wangham house at Nokzang village Tizit Nagaland, 11.12.2017.
160. B.B. Ghosh, *Nagaland District Gazetteers,* Mokokchung district, Published by Government of Nagaland, 1979, p. 29.
161. J. Jacobs, *The Nagas, Hill People of North East India Society, Culture And the Colonial Encounter*, Edition Hanhsorg Mayer, West Germany, 1990, p. 34.
162. H.K. Barpujari, *Problems of the Hills tribes- Northeast Frontie*r, Lawyer*'s* Book Stall, Guwahati, 1970, p. 182.
163. W.W. Hunter, *A Statistical Account of Assam*, Vol. II, Trubner and Co., London, 1897, p. 193.
164. S.C. Goswami, "Jabilee or the Nagas Coin," *op.cit.*
165. Information recorded by the author from Shri. S. Nokan Lonchar 81-year-old retired lawyer of Liremin (Kampangia) village, Mokokchung, on 29th March 2018.
166. Joseph S. Thong, *Glimpse of Naga Legacy and Culture*, published by Society for Naga Students Welfare, Kottayam Kerala, 2011, pp. 209-211; Information recorded by the scholar from Shri Micheal, members of village elders Bhandari town, Wokha district, on 26th to 29th November 2019.
167. V. Elwin, *A Philosophy for NEFA*, Directorate of Research Government of Arunachal Pradesh, Itanagar, first published 1957 (Reprint 1998), p. 9.
168. William Robinson, *A Descriptive Account of Assam*, *op.cit.*, pp. 380-398.
169. J. Butler, *Travels and Adventures in the Province of Assam: During a Residence of Fourteen Years*, Smith Elder & Co, London, 1855, p. 157.
170. J. Hornell, The Chank shell cult of India, *Antiquity* 16:113 33, 1942, p. 121; see, Alok Kumar Kanungo, "Naga Ornaments and the Indian Ocean," in *Indo-Pacific Pre-History Association Bulletin 26*, 2006, p. 161.
171. Report of a visit by Captain Vetch to the Singphos and Naga Frontier of Luckhimpore, No. 05, 15th September 1841.
172. J.P. Mills, *The Ao Nagas*, Macmillan & Co Ltd., London, 1926, p. 200.
173. Report of a visit by Captain Vetch to the Singphos and Naga Frontier of Luckhimpore, No. 05, 15th September 1841.

174. Gordon, P. Mean, "Human Sacrifice and Slavery in 'administered' Upper Burma During the Colonial Era" in *Sojourn: Journal of Social Issues in Southeast Asia,* Vol. 15, no. 2, October, 2000, pp. 184-221, ISEAS, Yusof Ishak Institute, *Source:* http://www.jstor.org./stable/41057039 p. 2.
175. Foreign Political Proceeding External Affairs, February 1890, No. 156, Assam State Archives. Porteous also mentioned that slavery in the 'domestic form' was 'widely prevalent' among the Aos and that children born of female slaves were usually put to death.
176. Political Department, "Report on the Operation Undertaken against Chinglong and Certain Other Independent Villages lying outside the Boundary of the Naga Hills District", 1913.
177. Mazhar Asif, *Tarikhe-e-Aasham*, Department of Historical and Antiquarian Studies, Guwahati, 2009; see Edward Gait, *A History of Assam, op.cit,* pp. 273-277.
178. See Tejimala Gurung, "Social Formation in Eighteenth Century Assam", Ph.D. thesis, Dept. of History, NEHU, Shillong, 1990.
179. B.K. Barua, *A Cultural History of Assam*, Bina Library, Guwahati, 2003.
180. Johh M'Cosh, *Topography of Assam*, *op.cit.*, p. 75.
181. L. Devi, Ahom-Tribal Relations, *op.cit.,* p. 271.
182. Mackenzie, *The North-East Frontier of India*, *op.cit.,* p. 36.

4

Socio-Cultural Relations

The long centuries of interaction and contact of the Nagas with the Ahoms during the medieval period, contributed to the process of socio-cultural development. From ancient to medieval times, powerful states have used various means to expand and strengthen their kingdom. Besides conquest and aggression, marriage alliance and adoptions were part of their diplomatic policies, which helped them strengthen and defend their territories.[1] The process of Naga-Ahom socio-cultural relations were also furthered due to matrimonial alliances and adoption. The Ahoms were liberal in their social outlooks[2] guided by the principle of *'Sama-dama-bheda-danda'* (conciliation, concession, disagreement and forces). Frequent conflicts with the Nagas offered wide scope for flexibility within the framework of what they considered to be their diplomatic norms.[3] Social and cultural assimilation between the Ahoms and hill tribes was a matter of political expediency for the Ahom rulers.[4] The tribes from hills and plains families were generally admitted to the Ahom fold for their heroic and meritorious deeds on the part of their founders or due to their particularly attractive manners and features or indications of their unique and potential capacity. Thoroughly integrated, these new families had no disabilities regarding holding rank, offices and enjoyment of other usual privileges which the older Ahoms were entitled.[5]

The orthodox and the 'blue' section of the Ahoms were, however, annoyed if too much prominence was given to the new entrants in the first stage of their affiliation, but their opposition reduced as the new members proved their ability and identified themselves with the ideals and aspirations. Throughout the whole of their history, the Ahom has always had a remarkable capacity for assimilation, and whenever they settled, they have always been seen to acquire the cultural traits necessary for the process of raising themselves to the level of a most enlightened section of the society of their adoption.[6]

Even in the last part of the 18th and the beginning of the 19th centuries, when the decline of the Ahom power set in and some of the hill tribes could have availed themselves of the opportunity to plunder territory and enrich themselves, the hill tribes did not make any disturbances or ally themselves with the enemies of the Ahom sovereigns.

Ahom matrimonial alliance with the tribes

The Ahomisation process was also carried out through the policy of matrimonial relations established among the Ahom and the local communities. There are many examples of inter- marriages that took place between the Ahom royal families and of different tribes during the period of their rule. The Ahom Rajas encouraged these efforts to integrate the community, entering into a matrimonial alliance with the local community's hills and plains inhabitants. Sukapha himself married two non-commoner Moran, and Borahi women each.[7] As the number of womenfolk (from original place) was less in numbers accompanying Sukapha's group, it was relatively natural for its male members to take wives from the newly occupied areas. Moreover, the Ahoms had to depend upon the guidance of the old settlers in obtaining knowledge themselves as "guest" and the old settlers as "ancient lords of the country."[8] The message ran as follows,

> They should come to us for a personal meeting. We have come from the east, and they are *Sthana-giris* (ancient lords of the country). We are guests, and they should, therefore, acquaint us with the villages and the lands.[9]

Bhuyan opined

> There was an admixture of blood; the Ahom community had a mixed origin as they adopted an intermarriage policy when they first came from Nara, and they accepted wives only when they came here.[10]

According to Amalendu Guha, the reason behind the Ahomisation process was the liberal matrimony policy adopted by the Ahom and the similar level of the animistic belief system between the autochthonous groups.[11] He concludes that this Ahomisation process was followed by the Hinduisation process that brought in enormous changes in the matter of language, living styles, food habits and even in agricultural techniques of the autochthonous people. All these constituted an essential dimension in the early formation of the Ahom states.[12]

Initially, the Ahoms married only from the officially recognised chiefly families; towards the later part of their rule, the Ahom monarchs married even from Hindu families.[13] Raja Suhummung (Dihingia Raja, 1497-1539) had married the daughter of a goldsmith and made her chief queen to the utter displeasure of his eldest son Suklenmung (Gargayan Raja or Deka) 1539-1552.[14] Sukhampha (Khora Raja) 1552-1603 married two Sonari Hindu girls, who became the monarch favourites to the humiliation and resentment of the rivals and at the displeasure of his nobles.[15] To honour the pride of his wives, he promoted several commoner families into the noble status. The king bestowed the status of the noble families to many handsome youths, equipping them with gold-mounted muskets and declaring them as families of royals. These 'princes' were given the title Konwar-Hiloidaris (musketeer Princes). Sutanpha (Siva Singha) 1714-1744 married Phulmati, a Nat girl, and after her death, the Ahom Raja re-married her younger sister, Damayati. Both of them were granted a prominent status in the court, and were given the title of Pramatheswari Devi and Ambika Devi.[16] Both became patronesses of art and literature; their brother Harinath was made Barpatra Gohain after being formally admitted to the Ahom noble families. Other relatives, including their mother Sita were honoured and was given a high position in the society. Siva Singha successor Pramatta Singha also married several Hindu girls. Rajeswar Singha married the Manipuri princess, Kuranganayani, who had played an important role in reinstalling king Gaurinath Singha to the Ahom throne. There are records of King Gaurinath Singha marrying the daughter of one Kalita Deka of the Dihingia family following Brahmanical rites.[17] In 1812, king Sudingpha (Chandrakanta Singha 1811-1818), married Padmavati, the daughter of a devotee attached to Bengena-Ati Satra, against the opposition from his Prime Minister Purnananda.[18]

Pratap Singha was offered two Jayantia princesses by Jayantia king Jasamanik who wanted to strengthen his relations with the Ahoms.[19] With similar intention, the Koch king Raghudev offered his daughter Mangaldai to Pratab Singha.[20] At the request of the Kachari king Bhimbal, Pratab Singha offered daughter of a Handikoi family to enhance the friendly relationship with Kachari kingdom.[21] Ahoms also acculturated with Chutias, Nagas, Morans, Barahis, Kacharis, etc., and many plain tribes in the process of state formation.[22] Since that time, there was an admixture of blood, and children were of mixed origin.

Amongst the Nagas there exists a rich oral tradition of matrimonial alliances and socio-cultural relations with the Ahoms. Some of these narratives are given below to highlight the relationship.

Konyak-Ahom relations

A popular legend among the Konyak tribes of Nagaland is the story of the intermarriage of an Ahom king with the Konyak chief's daughter.[23] The Konyak tradition narrates the story of a beautiful young woman, Watlong, daughter of Longmoi the *Angh* (chief) of Tanhai village (located in Mon district, Nagaland).[24] Watlong lost her father at an early age; so her mother sought a home in her uncle's village of Wanching (located in Mon district, Nagaland). Her uncle, the *Angh* (chief) of Wanching took them into his household and raised her as his daughter. During 1679-1681 AD in the Ahom capital, the tyrannical Sulikpha (Lora *raja*), on the advice of Laluki Borpukhan, ordered the mutilation of all the royal families in order to disqualify them from becoming heir to the throne.[25] Traditionally an Ahom king was selected from among the noble royal families. Another custom was that a prince selected for the throne should not have any scars on his body. Taking advantage of this, the Lora Raja attempted to inflict injuries or scars on the bodies of the able princes so that none of them could claim for the throne.[26] Consequently, Godapani (1681-1696 AD) the heir-apparent, fled to the hills and through his sympathizers escaped via Ponkong and Tanhai villages and took up shelter in Wakching village and made it his home. Godapani's wife, Joymoti, who swore by biting her finger that she would not tell anyone about his whereabouts, was tortured to death by Lora Raja (Sulikpha 1679-1681) after the failed interrogation. While hiding in the jungle near a village close to the Assam plains for a long time, Godapani stayed in several places in the Naga hills, and eventually, Godapani reached Aokeang Morung[27] (located in Wakching village Mon District). Wakching village then was divided under five clans – these were Palang, Pala, Aokeang, Tupong, Angpang and each clan had separate Morungs with an *Angh* (chief) attached to it. The *Angpa* (great chief) were from the Palang clan. The villagers noticed Godapani; he was caught and brought to the house of the Aokeang *Angh* (small chief, Morung).[28] When he reached Aokeang Morung, lightning and thunder rolled nine times from the sky. The Aokeang Morung could not provide shelter, due to their belief in the phenomenon as a bad omen. So, they decided to help the Ahom prince, and he was sent to the house of the *Angh* (chief) of Palang Morung.[29] Ultimately, the thunder and lightning stopped immediately to prove that the stranger Godapani was of royal birth. Godapani lived like the son of the Palang *Angh* (the great chiefs). The Ahom Raja learned the value of life and accepted the law of Wakching village as they were doing their best to save his life from his enemy. The villagers from Palang Morung cut his hair, dressed him in traditional Naga attires and assigned him the local name Bongyong Tikshshai to help perfect his camouflage.

It was stated that many omens were witnessed in the Ahom kingdom during the period of exile of Gadadhar Singha. The cultivation of paddy and vegetables were down and there was no harvest. The Ahom people started to enquire about the omens through the astrologer and priests. They found in their calculation that the ruler (realm) of the country was in Konyak land. If he could be brought back and enthroned, the misfortunes of the country would end. So the Ahom people went in search of their king in the Konyak country, no one could recognise their king and they returned back to their kingdom. A second attempt was made by the Ahom people, an old wise man immediately recognised the king's eyes and face of the changed raja and identified him. However, the Ahom raja did not trust the people who had come to call him, and hence put on a disguise by putting on the same attire as the people of Wakching and pretended not to recognise his people. Subsequently a singer from Assam was bought inside the Morung, who sang a song in Assamese language about how everything was falling apart in the plains. The Ahom prince heard the song and as the only person in the Morung to understand the meaning of the song- started to shed tears on hearing the words. Nobody else had understood the Assamese language, and this is how the Ahom soldiers identified him and brought prince Gadadhar back to their land and reclaimed his kingdom. However, the Ahom king could not regain the happiness that he felt in the hills; Joymoti, his former wife, had been killed by her tormentors and he was missing his beloved Watlong whom he had met and fallen in love with her when he was in Wakching. In the olden days the men folk and the Ahom prince usually visited Wanching Morung to exchange songs and dialogues where they learnt a lot not only about the person whose praises are sung, but also about the collective history of the village and the people. A kind of courtship begins when young males from their dormitories (among Konyak villages they have a dormitory for both male *Baan/Morung* and female *Ywo*) visit young females in theirs and acquaintance is struck. The beauty of Watlong captivated Gadadhar. He told his Ahom people that there was a beautiful girl named Watlong *Angya* (chief's daughter) at the village and he wished to marry her.

Coming back to the story, the royal attendants went to the Konyak village in search of Watlong. However, she was afraid to go to Assam, and in order to protect her, the villagers told the attendants that she had died in the meantime. But Godapani had seen Watlong in his dream and so the king ordered all women from the villages to be brought to his palace.

As told, all the women went down to Sibsagar but were dressed in identical clothes to confuse the king. One after the other they were brought before Gadadhar Singha. When it was Watlong's turn he recognised her immediately and said '*hoi*' (yes). Godapani ascended the throne in 1681 (after the coronation he took the Ahom name Supaatpha and the 'Hindu' name Gadadhar Singha).

The Ahoms approved the wishes of Gadadhar Singha (Gadapani) and allowed him to marry Watlong Angya. As a gesture of binding relationship between them, the Ahom raja granted Mezenga Borthar, Lingiri and Pukhiri Chunpura lands to the *Anghs* (chiefs) of Wanching and Wakching. Until very recent times, the *Angh* of Wanching used to collect annual revenue of Rs 140 from his share of land grants.[30] Subsequently the wedding ceremony was performed and the Ahom king invited the Palang *Angh* (chief) and Wanching *Angh* (great chief) to the Ahom court for his wedding. They bade farewell to their beloved daughter Watlong by arranging a feast. The whole city was in a festive mood, drums were beaten and groups of people were singing and dancing in a place called Bihuber (Sivasagar). Some attendants, who came up to the Ahom capital and did not return, settled in Baligain near Sontok and Sripur near Charaideo. Gadadhar Singha presented a buffalo to each and every villager involved and special presents were given to some of them. Wakching and Shangnu (located in Mon District, Nagaland) were granted to make annual trips to villages in the border areas to collect 'taxes' in the form of livestock. When the Konyak villagers went for errand they too carried small gifts of ginger,

Fig. 1. Shovel-shaped metal object given by the Ahom Raja, kept at Wanching village. Photo by the author, 2017.

betel nut leaves, yam, chilly etc.[31] In addition, Wanching were gifted text documents and a shovel-shaped heart metal object which are kept in the village even to this day (Figure 1). Furthermore, a bowl was gifted to Wanching, whichwas later presented to Chui village as well as a cock-shaped piece of iron.[32] Before Watlong left for the plains, she had asked her mother Shianglih and the villagers to remember her at the time of the annual *Aoleang* festival. During every *Aoleang* festival, they were to throw the blooming flower of '*Jitwangpeang*' (Erythrina Indica tree-a special kind of flower that bloom in March and April) into Dikhu River, so she could remember her village by seeing the floating flowers down in Assam. Her request to throw flowers into the Dikho River is reminisced in a song.[33]

Watlong wangya sumlan-a	*Wanglong, Queen of us.*
Lun he jon pu mai	*Secret Love.*
O shung wangha	*O King of the plains.*
Mai mong mam pü üi	*Hurry up to get married.*
Shongwang naomaa watlong sub	*Watlong got married to an Assam King and cried*
Hum longnyu tho ayu kah yeü-e-o *O shung wangha*	*without telling your mother a farewell words.* *O King of the plains*
Ayu shanglih ei yoüngjong wai	*Mother Shanglih is crying for her beloved daughter.*
Jitpong müwalaa.	*The Jitpong flower reminds you.*
Yeiangma pongbo jitpong mawan.	*you remember when you see the jitpong flower on the Dikhu river.*
Pangwang üoling pua	*Blessing of üoling (Aoleang) should be conveyed*
Yeng ma phong. Püjel-wang pong *Ngin lah eiya*	*When seeing the Jetwang flowers flowing in the rivers, Watlong cried.*
Shongwang naomaa watlong sab	*she is crying inside the large house.*
Yongtiam pong.	*Missing her people.*
Pang wang Aoleng pejü üle shuphi *Yong*	*because she understood that the Aoleang festival is coming.*
Tuowei kunmah lakshum pü yang	*She died of loneliness and sorrow in the plains of Assam.*

The Konyak tradition also aphorism that Sheanglih obeyed her daughter and threw flowers called '*Jitwangpeang*' (Erythrina indica) in the Dikhu River every year during the Aoleang festival.[34]

According to the Konyak legend, the utmost significant and best known object relating to the Watlong story, is the slab of rock 'Longtem' (called Longtem Longnyu at Tanhai) that is today located on the way up to the village, right next to a National Highway leading to Assam. On it there are different marks, which were explained by the inhabitants of Konyak as imprints of the visit of the Ahom king had left on it. Roughly in the middle of the stone, right next to the imprint of the royal walking stick and the marks of the royal buttocks, circles can be seen where he had placed his beer mug and foot plate. Another shape is understood as a hoof mark of the royal horse. It was on this stone the Ahom Raja sat on when he visited his wife village of origin.[35] The Konyak tradition says that the grandparents used to predict prophesy through this stone. So the villagers were afraid of the stone and even to go near the stone or touch it. They believe that if anyone touched that stone then it will bode ill to the villagers.

Fig. 2. This slab of rock, on which the Ahom king Gadadhar Singha is said to have sat on. Photo by scholar, 2017.

The Konyak legend also says, the Raja took the name Gadadhar Singha after the coronation. Watlong agreed to marry him, however, she made a request to her husband that she wished to see her parents once. Accordingly, the Raja made a road from her village to Assam for the parents of his wife Watlong, so that they could visit their daughter anytime at the valley kingdom. The name of the road constructed by Godapani laid through Naginimora (Lehkaan) and Borhan is known as *Longmoi Ali* (*Longmoi*- named after Watlong's father and *Ali*- meaning road in Assamese). The Raja also made a promise to Watlong that he would take her to her native village once a year. One day Watlong and Gadadhar were returning from his wife's native village to the valley kingdom, an unfortunate circumstance occurred; she suddenly fell sick and died. The place where she breathed her last is called Naginimora (located at present sub-division of Mon district in Nagaland).[36]

The last request of Watlong to her husband was after her death her body should be taken back to her native place to be buried there. As per as her wishes, her body was buried at Naginimora which is near to Wanching village. Naginimora means the place where the Naga-Ahom noblewoman was buried. It exists till today as a mark of matrimonial relation between the Konyak Naga and the Ahom.[37]

Another oral narrative about the Konyak-Ahom relations, relates to a *Maan* (Burmese) battle that took place in the Ahom kingdom, in which the Ahoms were defeated. During that period many Ahoms sought refuge at *Soatingsheang* (meaning place for the Ahom refugees), near Shangnyu village. The Ahoms with the help of Konyak warriors could manage to win the battle against the *Maan*. The Konyak and Ahom soldiers marched through Ladoigarh and fought the battle at a place called *Zoaka* (at present a tea garden in Assam). In that battle the enemies were completely destroyed, many Burmese soldiers were killed. To honour the victory of the *Maan* battle Shangnyu village named the place as *Saphakati* (completely destroyed). The two famous warriors from Shangnyu who fought in the battle were, Manlei and Manting. The descendants of these two warriors still live in Shangnyu village. In the battle many men were killed and it was difficult to identify the bodies of Nagas and the Burmese. Therefore, the chief suggested that '*chos*' (Wanchos) which means Konyak- Wanchos shall be bearing *nakha* (meaning 'pierce in the ear' in Konyak-Wancho dialects).

There is also another oral narrative among the Hongphoi a Konyak village. It is said that during the *Maan* (Burmese and Singpho attack on the Ahoms) many Ahoms fled to the Konyak villages of Hongphoi, Wangla and Yansa. During that time (early nineteenth century) the Konyak people had adopted certain new technology and customs from Ahom refugees, like superior gun making, knives and cultivating wet rice. When the battle was over, some Ahoms stayed back at the respective villages and they intermarried with the Konyak. The descendants of the chief of Wangla said they learned to cultivate wet rice from Ahoms in a fertile valley below their village by ploughing with oxen.

It becomes apparent that a great deal of admixture among the Konyak and Ahom segments had taken place.

Lotha-Ahom relations

According to one of the Lotha myths of migration the Lotha migrated to the present place from China via Burma, Manipur, Chakhesang, and Angami areas. They first arrived at Honoho hillock near Tseminyu, the present Rengma land. They stayed briefly in Honoho hillock. They saw a picturesque land (now Lotha area) and decided to settle there. Since they were many in number, they agreed that whosoever wanted to stay in the hills and valley would be as per their choice. Subsequently, they split into three groups. One group went down and established Phiro village; another group established Tiyi Longchum (near Wokha), and the third group moved down with a view to create a new village at (Pyangsa), however misguidedly crossed the area and went towards the plains and established a village at a place called Koro. It is believed that Koro village is approximately 1000 years old.

Slowly the Koro village expanded their territory to the vast forest area and in course of time came in contact with people at the other side of the forest. They found these people friendly and kind and so befriended them. They later started to exchange goods on barter system with them. The Koro village were the first to come into contact with the Ahoms, and also the first to introduce salt to the Lotha villages. During the period, the Ahom Raja saw the cane baskets. He admired it and wanted it for himself; he requested the Lotha chief to supply canes to the kingdom. Accordingly, the forefather of Koro village collected canes from the forests and supplied cane since then to Ahom kingdom. In this context one of the Lotha folklore narrates the friendship of one Thungbemo with an Ahom ruler which goes like this

> In one of their visits to the Ahom kingdom to supply canes, a boy named Thungbemo accompanied the groups to help in fetching water, cooking food and watching over their things on their journey to the valley kingdom. He was a timid boy and rarely spoke. When the group went to deliver their goods to the Ahom Raja, Thungbemo was left at the camp. He could not join the group as he had wounded his leg, and when the flies disturbed him, Thungbemo stamped the ground while jumping with an intention to get rid of the flies. That jumping shook the ground with such force that even the Ahom Raja could felt the rumble. Thungbemo, though a shy boy, was a supernatural gifted boy. The Ahom Raja asked for the visiting Lotha Nagas and examined them one after another to find out the person who possessed such powers but was not successful. He then enquired whether they had another man with them. The Raja, came to know that only Thungbemo was left in the camp taking care of their stuffs. The Ahom Raja summoned to bring the boy, accordingly, he was brought before the Ahom Raja and since he came to know the cause of earthquake by Thungbemo.

The Ahom Raja became immediately fascinated with Thungbemo, took out some betel nut from his mouth and put it into the mouth of Thungbemo. Astonishingly, the boy started speaking in Assamese language after chewing the betel nut. Soon the two became good friends. Then the Ahom Raja ordered his servants to clothed Thungbemo with Assamese attire, gave him gifts. In this way, a long enduring friendship sprang up between the Ahom Raja and Thungbemo whom the Ahoms called Naga Raja. The Ahom Raja often sent his men to call his friend Thungbemo and asked him to stay with him. Thungbemo loyally extended his help to the Ahom Raja whenever needed and in return the Ahom Raja showered him with gifts.

Once, the Ahom Raja requested Thungbemo to bring a horse for him. At that time there were no horses in the Ahom kingdom, hence the Ahom Raja desired to own a horse. Thungbemo knew that horses were available in the valley of Manipur. He therefore, undertook a long journey through the hills, rivers and valley and finally reached Imphal. Thungbemo's aunt was married to a Manipuri man and was living in Imphal. Thungbemo stayed with his aunty to find out where the horses were available. Fortunately, he could find two horses, one male and one female. He then brought them to his aunty's place and stayed for the night. The next morning, his aunt cooked food for him including 60 nos of swallow birds. His aunt came to know that some Manipuri men were searching for Thungbemo to have him killed. In order to shield her nephew from being caught, she told Thungbemo to leave her home early. Thungbemo did not listen to his aunt's warning and went on eating up all the dishes her aunty had cooked for him. Meanwhile, the Manipuri soldiers came and surrounded his aunt's house, suspecting the danger, his aunt shouted roughly at Thungbemo to leave the place. Then she took off all her clothes and struck the earth with her *mekhela*. While the Manipuris were diverted, looking on what was going on, Thungbemo took the opportunity to escape taking two horses with him. Thungbemo reached his native village with the horses after three days. (There is a footpath road that still exists in Pyangsa village which is called "Thungbemo Kuresulan" literally meaning the road where Thungbemo pulled the horses). After reaching his native village Koro, Thungbemo fell sick with dysentery.

Meanwhile in the Ahom kingdom, the Raja sent his faithful men to enquire about the arrival of his friend Thungbemo. They learned that Thungbemo was seriously ill, so the informer straight away reported to their Raja about his friend's illness. The Ahom Raja delivered medicines as soon as he heard the news through his informers to Thungbemo.

After taking the medicine, he soon recovered from his illness. Later, he took both the horses to the valley kingdom and presented to his friend Ahom Raja. The Ahom Raja accepted the gifts with immense pleasure and showered with gifts to Thungbemo. Following this, the Ahom Raja arranged a big feast, invited his friend Thungbemo and also the entire Koro village for a feast. Furthermore, strengthened their ties of friendship in that feast, they exchanged gifts with each other, vowed to continue the friendship in the future generations too. Another astonishing promise was made between the Ahom Raja and Thungbemo, they vowed in front of their kinsmen and friends that they would die on the same day Some years later, the Ahom Raja fell sick and died. The Ahom Rani thought that the Naga Raja Thungbemo, would also die on the same day. So, she sent a contingent of soldiers including 50 men to Koro village to bury Thungbemo's death body. But they were surprised to discover Thungbemo alive. The Ahom soldiers went back and reported the matter to the Ahom Rani. The Ahom Rani therefore sent one fly tied with poison in its body to kill Thungbemo. The fly manoeuvred around Thungbemo to get a chance to poison him. Thungbemo came to know the plan of Ahom Rani and so he didn't open his mouth for some days. Unfortunately, he opened his mouth to yawn, taking advantage of that moment the fly immediately entered his mouth and so Thungbemo was killed with the poison.

Since the fly did not return, the Ahom Rani believed that the Naga Raja had died too. So, she again dispatched a contingent of 50 men with all the musical instruments to bury Thungbemo at his native village Koro. In this way, the dead body of Thungbemo was buried at the outskirt of Koro village with all the honours. They also put some costly ornaments along with the dead body and placed nine numbers of big cauldron (*karahi*) one after another and planted a banyan tree on top of the grave. This banyan tree is believed to still exist at Koro village and the folklore of Lotha-Ahom friendship are still narrated to this day. There is a proverb in the village that sounds of drums, trumpets and other musical instruments are heard from time to time. When these sounds are heard, people die in Koro village.[38]

This folklore was narrated to the scholar by the village elders of Pyangsa and its neigbouring villages too.[39] According to the village elders, occurrence of the story is believed to have happened when the Ahom capital was in and around the present Golaghat area. It was narrated that the Ahom Raja lived in a palace near the adjoining of two rivers, the present Doyang and Dhansiri rivers, the Kora village elders called as '*Tchunyiko*' (black water) and 'Tchunyomo' (red water). In those days, only Ahom and some native people of plains lived in Golaghat. They became great friends with the Nagas and lived in peaceful co-existence. In this way the alliance between the ancestor (Nagas) and the Ahoms developed enhancing smooth trade and commerce up to these days.

Another traditional narrative of Lotha-Ahom friendship goes like this as given below.

> Long time ago in a village called Pyangsa there lived a man named Tsokashan. He was charming, smart and energetic. He often accompanied his fellow villagers to the *haat/*market to sell the products from the hills. He became well known for his talent of work ethic among the Ahom. By seeing his talent, the Ahom *Mahajon* (shopkeeper) employed him in his shop. Thereafter he became an expert in his profession. One day while he was busy weighing the goods, the daughter of the *Mahajon* saw him and started to admire him. Soon, she came near Tsokashan and put a love charm pill into his mouth. Then, Tsokashan too started to like the girl and got married to her. Tsokashan was not allowed to go back to his native village by the *Mahajon*'s daughter after getting married to her. They lived a happy marriage life at Ahom *Mahajon*'s place. In course of time, they were blessed with seven sons. However, inspite of living many years with his Ahom wife and their seven children, Tsokashan constantly remembered his first wife and his two sons at his native village. Often he was unhappy and kept reminiscing of them, seeing her husband miserable; she felt pity for her husband and asked him to visit his native village. Before leaving the place, his Ahom wife gave him a bamboo tube and instructed him not to open it until he reached his native village. Tsokashan started his journey to his village. However, out of curiosity he wanted to know what is there inside the bamboo tube. He stopped and broke open the bamboo tube; there he saw a ribbon-like piece of cloth nicely folded inside the tube. He started pulling out the cloth slowly but the more he pulled the more the cloth that remained inside the tube came out, and so the end of the cloth could not be found. He tried to insert the cloth back inside the bamboo tube but could not do so. So, he took the whole lot in his hand and went back to his Ahom wife to seek for an answer, but then he never got a chance to go back to his native village after that incident. It is believed that the descendants

of Tsokashan are still living somewhere around Golaghat.[40] This story highlights the social relation which had evolved between communities of the hills and the plains.

Ao-Ahom Relations

The Ao inhabited area of erstwhile Mokokchung district in Nagaland lies adjacent to Assam on its north-western frontier. Contact between the two was inevitable from the early days. There was a saying among the Aos since they lived atop hills, water ran down, flooding the plains. Therefore, the Aos called the plains as '*tsumar*' (meaning people of the plains near the water or people living near the water).

The Ao-Ahom relations are mentioned in many oral narratives of the Ao Nagas. There are references of raiding, conflicts, friendship, intermarriages and even Ahoms migrating to Ao lands. Initially the interactions of Ao- Ahom were primarily on the economic exchanges while social and marital relations followed subsequently. Most often the foothill Nagas raided the plains and this led the Ahom Raja to retaliate and intervene in the affairs. The oral narratives of Ao also talk about taking the help of Ahom *Chuba* (Raja) for settling internal disputes between the villages. Besides, strategically the Ahoms needed Nagas and often took refuge in times of turmoil in the Ahom kingdom.

Such events are mentioned both in the Ahom *Buranjis* and the oral narratives where Ahoms came and settled in different areas of the hill hitherto occupied by the tribes. Social and economic contacts in the form of friendship and exchanges existed. This was maintained through the channel of *duar*'s. However, the plainsmen whosoever willing to stay in the hills were received into the fold of the Ao and Konyak tribes, which shows acceptance of outsiders into the community.

The challenge to trace Naga-Ahom relations are the diverse Naga group names given in the *Buranjis* which do not coincide with the contemporary names of the Nagas. Thus, it becomes essential to look at the oral narratives to understand the Ao-Ahom relations.

An Ao oral narrative of *Chuchuyimlang* village[41] tells about the wife of a wealthy man of *Pongen* clan who was due to deliver a baby, and she was in great labour pain but could not deliver the child. By seeing her pain, her relatives were worried for her, so they went to meet the *arasentsur* (soothsayer) to seek help from him. The soothsayer told them to spread a mat outside the *kilang-i* (uplift platform behind the house) and let her deliver the child, for she was carrying the child of *ita anu* (mystical child of sun and moon), the child was blessed with supernatural power.

When they took her outside, she immediately delivered a baby boy, and they named him Imkonglemba.

Imkonglemba grew up to be handsome, wealthy, fearless, wise young man. He was well-known not only in his village but also in other Ao villages.

Imkonglemba had four sons, one of his sons named Imadangmeren was like his father who was well built, good-looking, rich and famous all over the Ao region as well as outside. During that time the Aos frequently visited the plains to barter their products for salt and other necessities needs. Shortly, the Ahom Raja (based on the Ahoms king genealogies, Rudra Singha 1696-1714), who resided at Rongpur the capital (Sibsagar), heard about the achievement of Imdangmeren Pongen, and so the Raja wanted to meet and know him more.

One day Imdangmeren Pongen was invited by the Ahom Raja to his palace at Rongpur. When he met the Raja at Rongpur, Imadangmeren immediately impressed the Ahom Raja with his charismatic personality. On meeting him, the Ahom Raja directly addressed him as Naga Raja and as a sign of the long lasting friendship the Ahom Raja gifted him a brass anklet.[42]

Fig. 3. Brass Anklet gifted by Ahom Raja to Pongen clan of *Chuchuyimlang* village, as a token of friendship. Photo by the author in 2018.

To this day, the brass anklet is preserved as a family heirloom of Pongen clan (Chuchuyimlang village), which they still wore during the Maotsu Ao festival (held on 1st week of May by the Ao tribe) as a way of honouring the memory of their long lasting friendship and goodwill with the Ahom.

Another oral narrative is from Merangkong (*Merang* = trying or try hard, *kong*= land, literally meaning getting through and settling by working hard on an elevated land), which is situated on the foothills of the Assam and had a close contact with the Ahom during the pre-colonial period.[43] The Ahoms called Merankong village as *Naorokong* or *Naogong* (literally means a village which could not be defeated by the Ahoms). Their interaction began when the Ahoms started to make wooden boats on the river bank of *Melak* (Jhanzi river), which was on the territory of the Merangkong village. Seeing the movement of Ahoms trespassing their territory, the Ao villagers went to defend their ancestral land, leading to war with the Ahom soldiers. However, considering their need for protection, shelter and procure resources like wood, cotton, elephants, herbs, fertile river banks etc., the Ahoms decided to made an alliance with the village of Pangkalong (olden name, currently, *Amguri* train station, Assam).[44]

Later, Ahoms extended their interactions with other Ao villages. For the Ahoms the river bank was necessary to support their economy and they put huge logs to demarcate the land and in exchange the villagers were given gifts such as *jaapi* (Ahom hat), clothes, salt, and iron for making *dao*. Besides, the Ahom Raja even granted a plot of land at Rongpur (capital of the Ahom) to the villagers. The Merangkong oral narrative also says during that time, the area of the Merangkong village extended up to Amguri (Assam), where the Ahoms dwelt now. The village collected *bond* (Ao term for tax) on those lands in the form of rice and other essential commodities.[45] These are some place names within Merangkong village where Ahoms settled, such as Lemtala Kimong, *Hapart* (meaning Ahom sepoys shelter area) etc. After the conflict with the *Maan* or Burmese ended, some of the Ahoms left Merangkong to go back to their homeland. However, many Ahoms decided to stay back, integrated with the Aos, intermarried within the villager and so on etc. It is believed that the Ahoms bought the technique of *dao* making traditions along with them. Though the Ahoms made curved *dao*, which could not be used by the villagers for all their works. The Ao made their own version.

Ahom Settlements in Ao village areas

In 1546 and 1563 when the Koches invaded the Ahom kingdom, many of them fled for shelter in Ao and Konyak villages. Again during the Burmese attack against the Ahom, the Merankong village extended their help towards the Ahoms by allowing them to take shelter and even two of its villagers, Azukolak, and Yangpidangnok were taken as prisoners by the Burmese for helping the Ahoms. The following[46] were some of the areas inhabited by the Ahoms.

Tuli Lenden

One day the Ao villagers on their way to their field they saw a group of Ahoms taking bath at their area. When the villagers asked what they were doing in their land, to which the Ahoms responded, '*kaotuli*' (meaning taking bath in Ahom language). The villager thought they were saying their name, and thus named this area as *Tuli*. The area Tuli Lenden near Jorhat was the place where the Ahom refugees took refuge in Ao country.[47]

Borbarua Lenden

Certain groups of Ahoms under the name *Borbarua* took refuge in Ao area. Since then it was named as *Borbarua Lenden* (plains of *Borbarua*).

Chuba Toba Ayong (also known as Ahomlar Yimkong)

Under a great Ahom Raja, *Chouba* a group of Ahoms crossed a river, thus the villagers named the river as – *choubatobaayong*- River where the king went up (tributary of Melak) and occupied an elevated plain, taking refuge during the Burmese aggression. The Ao villagers named the area as *Ahom lar yimkong*- residence area of Ahoms.

Longli Lenden.

During the period of *Kashinath Tamuli Phukan* (17th century), a group of Ahoms came to the area called *Longli lenden* (in Ao, meaning a stony plain area). Within *Longli lenden* there is an area called as, *Horu Morile* (a young boy died while taking bath at the river *Melak/Jhanzi*). Because of that incident the area is known as *Horu Morile* till date.

Places within Merangkong village where Ahoms settled are as follows:

Lemtala Kimong

Lemtalu (meaning a group of Ahoms came and settled here).

Hapart

This was the name on an area given by the Aos to the Ahom sepoys to settle during the *Maan* War. After the war ended many Ahom soldiers stayed back making *dao* and the villagers learned how to make *dao* from the sepoys. They intermarried with the Merankong village and were assimilated into the fold of the Ao clans.

Mopungchuket (Ahoms called it as Molotopias)

According to the oral narrative of the Ao villages of Mopungchuket, Pongendong and Sabangnenba on its relations with the Ahoms, it is stated that once when they were on the way to Brahmaputra valley they were suddenly attacked by the small Ao village of Yajang. The villagers of Mopungchuket (during that period the territory of Mopungchuket village extended upto *Togat Ali*, towards Amguri, Assam), were infuriated that a small village had the imperity to attack a big village. So, they decided to retaliate against the village. Hearing about the impending attack by Mopungchuket, Yajang villagers escaped and took refuge at nearby Leremin village. Mopungchuket attacked Yajang and turned it into rubble. Fearing the Mopungchuket village would again attack them any moment, Leremin sought help from Raja Chandrakanta Singha (1810-1818) for armies with guns to guard the village.

> When Mopungchuket villagers went to attack Leremin, they saw the Ahom army guarding Leremin village with lamps, guns and *daos*. Since they could not win in open fields, they decided to attack Leremin at dark hours, slowly went inside the village to see the Ahom soldiers on duty fast asleep. Taking the opportunity, they killed many Ahom soldiers. Leremin villagers went to the Ahom king and reported the incident. The Ahom king got furious and sent many good fighter soldiers to fight against Mopunchuket village. On the way to the village, the Ahom soldiers rested at Sungkotenem Lake. One of the Mopungchuket villagers prayed to the lake spirit saying 'there are many gathered to defeat our village. Rise up, why are you not making a move'.
>
> After offering prayer to the Lake spirit, he left the lake. It is narrated that the Spirit stood up tall and mighty in front of the Ahom troops. Seeing the mighty figure, the Ahom soldiers got scared and fled the area. In this way, Mopungchuket village could succeed in chasing the Ahom troops.[48] Since then, the forefathers regarded this lake as place of God, where God resided, the God who protects the village and since then the villagers come to worship the Lake god twice a year, by making sacrifices of pigs. It is said that some *daos* (machete) were collected while clearing the lake recently, which the elders of the villager narrated that it belongs to the Ahom soldiers, who left it behind while fleeing during the Ahom-Molutopia battle at Sungkotenem Lake.

Fig. 4. Sungkotenem Lake. Photo taken in 2018.

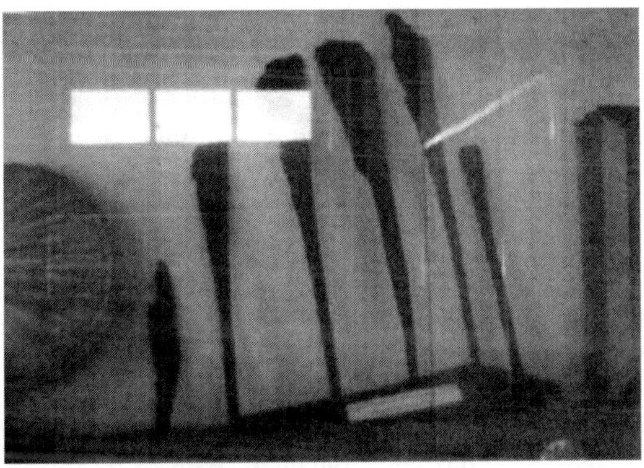

Fig. 5. Daos (machete) recovered from the lake, Mopungchuket Museum Mokukchung. Photo taken in 2019.

According to the oral narrative of Nokpu village[49] there was a time when the Ao*'s* were settled at Koridang, a group went towards the east leaving the rest. It was said that this group were seen leaving Koridang, carrying *daos* on their shoulder, singing and dancing. Thus, they were called by the rest as Nokpu (Nok-dao, pu-carrying) meaning going carrying *dao*.

Nokpu followed the Tzula tzu (Dikhu River) and from the bank of the river, they saw a mount towards the Phom area (Naga) resembling a hat. Henceforth, named the mount as *Korangkong* (mount of hat), and settled there for a while. Their neighbour was the *Owengyenching* village of Phom tribe, the Nokpu maintained cordial relations with the

Phom. Nokpu resided at Korangkong for more than three generations. Unfortunate enmity with their close neighbours, i.e., Yaonger, Tsungkhor, Nangdanger compelled them to migrate again, they could no longer stay at Korangkong, and decided to proceed further and settled at an elevated area called *Sungmerongkong Ali* (land) or *Akholongshi*. Even there they could not stay for long period because of the dispute with *Tzusa* village and had to relocate further to the west and settled at *Natushi tenem* where they succeeded in establishing an influential village. It is said that many of the villagers became wealthy. One of the rich man in the village by the name *Natushi,* decided to have a feast of accomplishment in the village. He invited all the villagers to celebrate the feast by killing a massive pig. It is described that several villagers had tried to catch the pig but could not as the pig was too large. At that time a person called *Ongpangsangba* tried to catch the pig by jumping near the pig but got hit and fell dead beside the pig. Because of this incident, the villager declared that place as '*menenkimong*' meaning unclean place. So, they left the site and migrated to a new site called as *Atu tenem* (mount).

They lived there for 70 years; one day they, saw a new group coming from *Yaong Yanchem* (Phom), who occupied an area near *Atu tenem*. Nokpu gave a name to that place where the group had settled at '*Tongar Teland*' (meaning others have come with more than 100 families). These people brought with them anvils and used them to make *daos*. Thus, they named this group '*Anokranger*' or '*Nokranger*' (meaning *dao* maker), and for around *putu* (around 30 years), Nokpur at *Atu tenem* and *Nokranger* at Tongar Telang stayed as neighbours. During that time, Nokranger started a war against Longkhum village, and since then the Nokrang and Longkhum have been enemies.[50]

Nokpu had to abandon *Atutenem* (mount) and move again to a new place since they could not stay near their nemesis. Around 1210 A.D (according to the Ao tradition of calculation called *Nokpu putu menden*), they shifted to a new higher mount village from *Atutenem*. However, due to the steep landscape and shortage of water, the village had to be shifted down towards a less elevated area just below the village, and by the year 1985, a new Nokpu model village was founded.

There are still around 7 to 8 families occupying the old Nokpu village, and the villagers call these two areas under the Nokpu village jurisdiction (Nokpu old village and Nokpu new village). According to this oral narrative the relationship between the Nokpu and the Ahoms started around 1335 AD during the time of Ahom king Sukrangpha with the opening of a *duar* (pass). This was called *Asheimba-Yimyudangba duar*, which was established to celebrate the friendship between king Sukrangpha and Nokpu.[51] The relationship between Nokpu and Ahom grew when King Godapani married a Nokpu girl.

The Nokpu villager also helped the Ahoms during the Burmese invasion (the *Maan Singpho* war). They were given refuge at Naganijan (Naga *khat*) by the Nokpu villager on their land. Oral narratives of Nokpu villagers say that three groups of Ahoms took refuge in different Nokpu areas, such as:

1. A group of traders under the leadership of *Dellai*, who was placed at *Lisemyong Ayongkum* Lenden (the plains of the river bank of Lisemyong), the *Dellai* lenden-plain of *Dellai* valley, where the Nokpu villagers carried on wet rice cultivation.
2. A group of blacksmith was given a plot of land near the village gate; they made all the tools, such as daos, utensil, weapons, etc. The area is called *Anokjangjen Yenden* (dao making area by the plain).
3. Under the leadership of Ahom *Kahulong* a group of farmers were given refuge at *Tzurong* Lenden or *Tzurong* plain. The area is known as *Kahulonglushi* or *Kahulong* cultivation land.

After the Burmese war ended, some of the group stayed back and became Ao.[52]

Naga cultural elements: Linkages of material culture

One of the reasons for the success of the Ahoms in dealing with the Nagas and other tribes (both in the hills and plains) was their liberal attitude and affinity that is related in one of the rare references to the tribes in the *Buranjis*. It relates the great satisfaction of the tribes when Ahom soldiers ate with them, saying, 'These people eat the things we eat; they are therefore men of our fraternity.'[53] The Ahoms typical common method of cooking was

1. cooked with boiling water in an open clay pot
2. cooked meat or vegetables in a covered pot
3. cooked by baking under hot charcoal or ashes
4. cooked in a bamboo tube
5. cooked by steam
6. prepared by using sour or fermented stuff
7. roasted on the fire

The main food of the Ahom was rice, and they liked sticky rice, and different kinds of steam rice cake. Their other favourite foods were *Tao Nao* (soya bean), *Khaw nu* (special rice), *Nomo* (pig), *Tap Fu Phet*, *Phal Soum* (pickled leaf), *Lo/No-mai* (bamboo shoot), *No Sum* (fermented bamboo shoot), *Phak Keng* (boiled leaves), *Pa Heng* (dry fish), *Nou Heng* (dry beef), *Pa Soum* (sour fish/fermented fish), *Kong Soum* (sour pawn/fermented prawn), bamboo worm, red ants etc.[54] These have a lot of similarity with the food eaten by the Nagas too.

The Ahoms adopted the policy of conciliation.[55] For instance, the Ahoms adopted the manners and customs of the land and also the language and later contributed to the growth of the Assamese nationality. Such assimilation between the conqueror and conquered is rare in the history.

For instance, rearing live stocks another socio-economic activity of the Nagas had a significant contribution to the socio-economic life of the Ahoms. The Nagas normally ate pork, and they rarely ate beef. Milk was also not a part of the Naga diet, and there is no dairy farming by Nagas. Pigs on the other hand were raised both for household consumptions and for barter in the market. Pigs sty can be found in every household compound and pig breeding is a major source of revenue for the villagers, taking care of a pig is mostly women's work. There is an average of four to five pigs per family in the Naga villages. Fowl and pig rearing was significantly common among the tribes. Later on, Ahom learned this domesticated method. However, the influence of Vaishnavism among the Ahom communities led to the abandoning of pig rearing and consumption of beef.[56]

To take another example, the Naga festivals are generally related to agriculture and nature. In every season of sowing and harvesting of the crops, the Nagas and Ahoms observe different rituals and festivals. In the first week of April, the Konyak observe their most significant festival called *Aoleang/Oriah* (sowing festival/Konyak new year and spring festival), the Ao festival *Maotsu* (blessing for a good harvest/ welcoming new year and spring festival) in the first week of May, the Lotha observed festival *Tokhuemong* (harvest festival/autumn festival), in the first week of November. Similarly, the Ahoms observe the spring festival and the harvesting festivals. *Bihu* (under *Bihu* three, set of festivals: *Rongali* celebrated in April, *kongali* celebrated in October, and *Bhogali* celebrated in January). While observing the festival of the new harvest, food, and rice beer are shared and offered among the households, also the popular music and *bihu* dance, and festivals, which are celebrated during the harvest and new years' arrival or sowing festival, had been primarily reinforced by borrowing from the tribes.

During the festival *bohag* bihu in Assam rituals are performed in a similar way to the Nagas. During the season of harvesting the crops, the Ahoms observe the ritual of welcoming the new crop to their granaries, known as *lakhimi-ana* in Assam. They have a community feast prepared with newly gathered crops called the *magh-bihu*, similar to *chahchia-ven* (harvest festival celebrated in October) by the Konyak. There is also the custom of having a family feast or *na-khowa* (Ahom) with newly grown rice. While observing all these rituals, great attention is given to ancestor worship. The first seasonal crops, vegetables and fruits of household are offered to them first. They are worshipped on the eve of any occasion related to cultivation, before planting rice, after harvesting, during the annual feast of first crops, social festivals like *Bihu* etc.

Ahom Social outlook on the Nagas

The Ahom kings were aware of their numerical minority given the hostile and freedom-loving unfriendly hill tribes. Therefore, they adopted a wise policy of cultural assimilation with the plainsmen of Assam, being dominated in their action mainly by considerations of practical necessity and political expediency, unaccompanied by any desire to propagate their way of life. The number of Ahoms who had come with the first conqueror Sukapha was smaller in number, and those who came in later were restricted in number as Shans were reluctant to leave their homes where there was plenty of food and happiness in their self-sufficient village situated amidst pastoral surroundings. With such small numbers, the Ahoms found it impossible to maintain their extensive dominion in the Brahmaputra valley, surrounded by people of heterogeneous tribes, with the Muslim and Koch rulers on the west as a source of perpetual danger with whom the Ahoms had frequent conflicts. The Ahoms, therefore, were compelled to increase their community by conferring upon the locals the status and privilege of the members of the ruling race. [57]

Emergence of Nagamese as Lingua Franca

One of the most significant outcome of Naga-Ahom relations was the development of the pidgin language called *Nagamese* which helped them to communicate efficiently and conveniently. Nagamese evolved as a common lingua-franca due to several types of contact socio-political, trade, adoption, and marriages between the Naga-Ahom.[58] The Ahom's integrated with the tribesmen of the hills and the plains in the process of state formation, which has been seen in social and linguistic spheres. Assamese proverbs are full of brimful references concerning the customs of the tribal neighbour. The popular music and dance of Assam have been reinforced mainly by borrowing from the tribes.[59]

By the 17th century, the Assamese language was used in historical writing and in the markets. Friendship with the tribes, both hills, and plains, was assiduously nurtured with great care. When the Ahoms adopted Vaishnavism a large number of experts conversant with the languages and customs of the tribes of hills and valley, and the experienced councillors were summoned in all diplomatic negotiations.[60] Simultaneously, a kind of bilingualism emerged amongst the hill tribes of Naga, especially those of the foothills who had frequent contact with the plains-folk and carried on their trade. So knowledge of Assamese had to be acquired by the visiting tribesmen through necessity and the same case with the people of the plains who had to carry on a trade or transact the state's business. There was also a tribal expert in the king's court, and their service was utilised.[61] Significantly, the outcome of Naga-Ahom trade exchange was the development of Nagamese among the Nagas.

Nagamese as a common trade speech developed several centuries ago, over a loosely defined geographical space covering the present state of Nagaland and Arunachal with Assam. The term communilect has been considered more appropriate as 'vehicular' or 'bridge' language transgressing the margins of the multiple tribes, and used as a second language for communiqué between the inhabitants of Nagas and Ahoms; the term lingua franca implies a usage in a much wider context. According to Simionescu and Simion, lingua franca as 'a tool for multinational integration, a language of inter-ethnic communication does not replace the native language, its purpose is to make language the common ground of comprehension and understanding instead of a barrier between nations."[62] Again lingua franca has been described as a vernacular language which allows inter-comprehension among people speaking different mother- tongues, as a neutral language of which nobody can claim ownership, but also as the mother tongue of one of the parties in the exchange.[63] Compared to Kiswahili in Kenya or Afrikaan in South Africa, historically and in the world context as well, Nagamese has a relatively low level of adoption and uses. Hence the term communilect seem more appropriate. As the term communilects suggests, the 'community' is the core component behind the dynamism of this language. The sense of language ownership is a core component of community membership.

The adoption of Nagamese as a communilect reveals as stated by Holcombe, 'the shared reactive construction of identity' in a historical context.[64]

Historically its origin can be traced to Naga-Ahom relations which dates back to the early decades of the 15th century, if not earlier. For instances, when an Ahom Raja had a child from the Naga chief's daughter; Kangchng Barpatra was earlier adopted by the Banfera Nagas; the two sons of Momai- Tamuli Barbarua took shelter at Naga villages, and two Naga women got married to the Ahom king himself. This contact necessitated a language for communication; since no single Naga language was dominant. Assamese as a language eventually exerted a hegemonic impact of a newly created contact-induced language, viz., Nagamese. Parenthetically, the Naga elders at present, still refer to this communilect as 'Okhomiya' rather than 'Nagamese'[65] which is the distorted version of 'Asomiya,' the anglicized pronunciation of which is 'Assamese.'[66]

Such communilect may be termed as what Mufwene states: 'one of the competing alternatives for successful communication.'[67] Given the variation among the Naga individuals and groups, not merely as distinct tribes but also languages and dialects that do not allow inter-clan communication, it is interesting to note how Nagamese as a construct ignored some of the individual or group variation and at the same time adapted certain variation introduced by those outside their community. Mufwene had also pointed out, a variant may be preferred to another because of frequent usage.

Socio-linguistics have described this social and historical process as reciprocal, in which users of the communilect opt for only some of the variants and abandon others. Thus, 'mutual accommodation is a social mechanism through which selection operates.' Hence a 'communal phenomena' that does not evolve uniformly or independently, but matures through the interplay of various ecological factors such as topography, population structure, pattern of social interaction which determine particularly structural variants that are preferred by particular speakers, depending on location, age, gender, social class, ethnicity, race, frequency of interaction, and other such factors. Mukwene maintains that nothing about the communilect can be explained without factoring in the ecology of the population of interacting individuals, those aiming at communicating with each other but not necessarily intending to develop a language.[68]

Thus, from a historical perspective, Nagamese as a communilect evolved from a 'contact-included language' through trade and other economic activities to a system of differentiation and knowledge/power relations, a powerful social identity marker leading on to a socio-political construct–the 'Naga identity' in the colonial period, while simultaneously transformation was taking place within the communilects itself. What began as a pidgin of Assamese enriched by Naga words, metamorphosed during the colonial period with the inclusion of Bengali, Nepali, Hindi, and English words, taking the present form 'Nagamese.' Hence in understanding the historical matrix of formulation of Nagamese, the communilect appears not as a mere cultural marker of the Nagas but also as a powerful tool which the British used to implement their political and economic strategies on one hand, and the Nagas used to expand their world-view, through the transgression of several boundaries; geographical, ideological, social, political and psychological. The missionaries and the British officials too encouraged the Nagas to learn Nagamese because it would be impossible for them to learn all the dialects in use among the Naga people. They too adopted Nagamese. British officials like J.P. Mills,

J.H. Hutton, and sociologists/anthropologists like W. C. Smith, Verrier Elwin as well as the British government occasionally suggested using Nagamese as a medium of expression in the Naga hills.[69] Nagamese became a medium of communication among the different communities of Naga hills. It is in fact a living example of the Naga-Ahom socio-economic relationship.[70]

Material Culture and Food Habits of the Naga-Ahom

Each ethnic group possesses traditional knowledge; some traditional elements are practised daily. One of them is knowledge and skill of food preparation which developed the food habit of a particular group of people. Secondly, a geo-economic condition also determines the ingredients of the food culture of a community. More importantly, food culture contributes towards moulding a community's mind-set and mental attitude, vice versa, indicating whether people of that community are secular or prejudiced. Therefore, food habits reflect a community's distinct traditions and folk culture. As a result, food habit contributes towards preserving the distinct identity of a particular group of people. In light of these ideas, the traditional food culture of the Nagas, Ahom, and their affinities with other groups of Southeast Asia could be understood. The traditional diet of the Nagas and Ahoms was similar to a great extent. However, with the conversion to Neo-Vaishnavism, consuming certain food was forbidden for the Ahoms.

Naga diet

All the Nagas are non-vegetarians, and they eat both domesticate and wild animals, for instance, pig, goat, deer, cow, monkey, elephant, porcupine, bamboo rat and various types of birds. However, pork and *mithun* meat are their favourite delicacies. Most of them chew betel nuts with paan until it discoloured their teeth with intensive use. Nagas eat dogs, the meat of which is reckoned by the Ao, Konyak, and Lotha to give strength in illness or old age or for recovery. Strips of meat would be dried for off-season; dried fish is another delicacy, the Nagas make a sauce out of dried fish eaten with rice. They eat simple boil food, rice being the staple, with meat of any kind and many other wild edible plants with no spices except dried chillies, bamboo shoot, fermented soybean etc. The natural fats in the meat give a flavour to the curry, which is more the consistency of soup. They refrain from using oil in the dishes and prefer eating boiled food. It is this simple food, eaten three times a day and accompanied by plenty of home- brewed liquor called *Yu* (Konyak dialect).[71]

Sticky rice cooked in the unmatured bamboo tube, which are the main dishes during the festival, bamboo shoots, pork, chicken, duck, frog, cocoon seed of Endi and Muga worms, eggs of red ant are some of their typical favourite dishes.[72] Earthen vessels or bamboo vessels were used for cooking rice, and for bringing water. Hunting and fishing is often a ceremonial enterprise undertaken by the whole villages. One reason for eating dried food is that the meat or fish supply commonly comes all at once in large quantities, so they stock it up for unseason periods.[73]

Ahom Diet

According to the *Padshahnamah*, the Ahoms ate 'every land and water animal.'[74] King Gadadhar Singh's favourite dish was coarse spring rice, and a calf roasted in ashes.[75]At the consecration ceremony of the tank at Misagarh, cows and buffaloes were slaughtered in honour of King Pratap Singha.[76] Meat and wine were usual in the Ahom menu. The Ahom feasted on the flesh of cattle, buffaloes, swine, and fowls. They were liberal in their dietary habits until Neo-Vaisnavism brought an inevitable change in the food habits of the Ahoms in as much as the meat of 'unclean' animals became taboos. Otherwise, Ahom food habits have not undergone significant changes among common people. Vegetables chiefly consist of leaves and tender stems called 'sag' other items that require mention are seasonings, spices, chillies, mustard oil, turnips, onions, fowls, eggs, and milk etc. Tobacco is widely used.[77] Ahom king Gaurinath Singha has been described as an opium addict.

Preparation of Rice beers (*haj*) in Ahom and (*zu*) in Naga

Rice beer was the most important beverage used frequently in religious rites and festivities among the Nagas and Ahoms in northeast India. It forms a daily caloric intake and also acts as a medicine. The Ahom called rice beer '*Nam ha*' and the Nagas called *zu* or *zuthoor yi/Mejemtsu* (homemade rice beer).[78] Bamboo cups and animals horn are commonly used while serving traditional drink, food, liquor and opium. Since early times the brewing of local beer or *zu* has been practised by most of the Naga societies. It was an essential part of their daily diet and used to express joy and merry-making on festive occasions. Rice beer was also used for ritual and religious purposes; it symbolically signifies strength and life, and its inclusion in rituals and prayers forms an essential part of religious and social practises, being held in great esteem and reverence. For instance, it will warm the spirit in meeting halls and councils.[79] Rice beer is served to everyone, irrespective of age and sex. Rice is not only consumed as food but is also used in preparing rice-beer, the drink is vital to the ethnic culture. No doubt all sections of Ahom society universally consumed in the past before some of them adopted Vaisnavism and the Nagas too before they converted to Christianity. The most important fact concerning rice beer is that it forms an integral part of the religious culture of the Ahom people. In traditional Ahom and Naga society, no traditional religious function was performed without rice beer. It is an invariable item of offerings to gods and their ancestors. The best rice beer is produced from sticky variety rice. Traditionally it is a female who prepares rice beer.

Community Fishing Traditions of Naga and Ahom

Fishing was another community food gathering activity for the Ahom and the Naga tribes; both are fish and meat-eaters; evidences of the epigraph and ethnography from plains and hill tribes mention the practice of fishing and hunting. If there is a river in their respective areas- this is usually fished by the community. This communal fishing is usually carried out annually. Method used by the Nagas to intoxicate the fish: For instance, they pound the walnut leaves juice into the water, the juice poisons all the living being under the water; letting the fish stupefying lifeless for some hours, later the fish float on the surface of the water lifelessly, and then the whole community moves on to the bed of the river to catch the fish with all the traps.[80] *Naga bih,* another poison, was used to intoxicate and kill fish, it is prepared much the same way as walnut leaf juice, that is pounded up with water and macerated. There are other kinds of poison, called Lota *bih* or Deo *bih*, Bor *bih,* which was traditionally used by the tribes of Assam.[81]

The articles used for catching fish were nets, bait, means traps, baskets, and bamboo rods fitted with iron nails; another device consisted of poisoning the river or a pond with herbs. Most of the fishing methods are borrowed from the Austric or Tibeto-Burman speakers because such modern words as *láñgi* (a kind of fishing net) and *khokà* (a kind of fish trap) are of Tibeto- Burman origin.[82] Peal stated

The seeds of this shrub or tree (Koni *bih*) are used by the Assamese (plain tribals), to kill and intoxicate fish in the rivers. After the floods have subsided, they usually select the deep pools and stake the outlet and in-let to prevent the fish from escaping. It seems that both the leaf and the bark are capable of poisoning, if used in any quality…[83]

Rice Cultivation tradition

Both dry and wet rice cultivation is practiced by the Nagas, the art of wet rice cultivation was learned from the valley kingdom when they came in contact with the latter. Wet rice came to be widely practised by Nagas living in the foothills since, according to them, wet cultivation demanded less labour and higher results than dry cultivation. Around 6- 7 varieties of rice are cultivated from wet rice cultivation. Evidently, the dry cultivation was carried out by a few villagers, mostly to preserve the grains.

Each year, in February, the significant jungle was cleared and burnt, the shifting cultivation was community-oriented, where the whole village participated in the clearing of forest and '*zunga*' (in Ao dialects meaning each age group), work in the respective field taking turns. Free labour exchange was common during those seasons. Paddy was planted with the early rain and the crop reaped in autumn. As the cultivation and sowing are crudely carried out the Nagas invariably find themselves with a poor crop of rice and are compelled to work subsidiary crops of maize, cassava, millets, and yams, sweet potatoes to avoid starvation.[84] Vegetables, like pumpkins, chillies, and garlic are usually planted with the main rice crop.[85]

The agricultural tools used by the Nagas included- (1) a short handled hoe, (2) a *dao* or bill hook, (3) a bamboo rake, (4) a wooden pestle and mortar, (5) a wooden mallet to break up the clods, (6) a sickle, (7) a bamboo flail and (8) an axe.

Textile and Weaving Traditions

Like all other Tai Ahom groups in the mainland Southeast Asian countries, Southern China, Vietnam, the Ahom, and hill tribes of northeast India have a primitive and long weaving tradition. Spinning and weaving of cotton and silk, had attained a high degree of perfection. Spinning was then, as always, a part-time occupation of women.

Fig. 6. An Ahom Woman with her loom weaving at Moranjan village, Assam 2015. Photo by author

Sericulture and rearing endi-worms was used for consumption and making clothes. The tribes settled in hills, and plains are fond of eating the chrysalis; they perforate the cocoons the third day to get them; they do the same with the muga, and sell a few cocoons imperforated. The excellence and memorable characters of textiles such as the woven dresses made from cotton, muga silk bears the imprint of Ahom*'s* textile culture from tribes, including the Nagas.[86] When a marriage proposal was made, the first question asked about the bride is whether she knows *bowãkatã*, i.e., whether she is skilled in spinning and weaving. The Ahom king established a weaving section and maintained skilled weavers to supply the royal wardrobe with clothes. These weavers received grants of rent-free lands and other favours in return for their services.[87] They manufactured three principal varieties of silk, *pat*, *endi,* and *muga*. The first variety is the finest and the costliest quality. Edi is of the coarsest quality and is generally used by the poor. The last variety, *muga* is a stouter and more durable fabric than *pat* but coarser and less glossy.[88] The Ahom silk, especially *pat* was in high demand by the Nagas for making traditional clothes and attire. The natives of Ahom also used dyes to produce colourful silk cloths. The dyes chiefly used by the natives were lac, munjit, and indigo.[89] Silk became one attractive item in the markets. The silk products by the Ahoms always found favourable markets in the Naga *hats*.

Weaving among the Nagas

Weaving are a collective meterial culture to the Nagas. Weaving was more than just a utilitarian activity because each motif had symbolic meaning that were intended to strengthen solidarity. Spinning yarn entails taking a clump of fibres, sepearating some of them, and twisting them to form a thread. The weaver keeps pulling and twisting to make it longer or thicker. A neat production of skein rolls is possible with the help of the *gaichak* (bamboo wheel). Yarn leis are wrapped around the wheel, and as the spinner slowly makes a skein, the wheel rotates. This allows the fabric to roll smoothly withous becoming tangled, resulting in less waste.[90]

Weaving is largely done by using a loin loom or back strap loom or back strap loom. Naga women use two different methods, namely, plain-weave and those with supplementary-weft patterns. The loom is set up by attaching the loom bars to a wooden post affixed firmly to the wall or to a *nye-tak khong* (konyak dialect, meaning wooden-framed loom). The leather or bamboo strap wraps around the weaver's hip, ensuring the loom is sturdy. The tools such as shed sticks, heddle rod, battern or sword, a yarn bobbin, and a lower loom bar are also used. Additionaly yarn sticks of different colours are also kept ready to create any desired pattern.

Loin loom or back strap loom is the oldest and simplest device used in the weaving of cloth which is the common loom practised by the Nagas. In the loin-loom for spinning and weaving and the embroidery of the Naga clothes the girls were adept.[91] The Naga women have varying attires depending on the occasion and the wearer's position in the society.

The cloth worn by both male and female (Konyak) were woven from cotton of their production and was bordered and marked with triangular-shaped patches of red and black.[92]

Naga attires, such as shawls, loin cloths, skirts, were woven. Traditionally these were woven using naturally dyed hand-spun cotton; some villages specialised in spinning and dyeing cotton yarn. As per requirement, this was either sold as dyed cotton yarn or a shawl. Each household raised enough cotton for use.[93] The cotton was seeded by rolling around a stick on a flat stone. Each design had a norm attached to who could wear which designs and product categories. For example, *Sutsongrong*, the end piece made of dyed goat's hair and cane, could be attached to the shawls on only the head hunter, or a person who has made *mithun* sacrifice, or the chief of the villages. For instance, the Ao shawl having blue ground and black checks is named *keyisü* meaning tiger shawl. It implies that the person who wears it has a tiger spirit. It is worn by both men and female, and traditionally it is woven using cotton yarn, dyed blue using *Osak* (Strobilanctres Flaccidifolius) plant. These leaves were used by all the Nagas for dyeing. As the Nagas are fond of colours so the clothes are vibrant, which are eye-catching and aesthetic, especially during festivals. The Nagas are found of using variety of coloured clothes and dress. They used dark, blue, red and rarely yellow dye. The process of dye was carried out by women, there is also a taboos among some tribes to handle any dyed during pregnancy less fetus be affected by the colour.[94]

Besides, *Mongkotepsü*, the shawl has a white band of pictorial motifs of cock, *mithun*, spears, elephants, tigers, stars, moon, human head, etc., woven in the center of the red and black stripped shawl is a warrior shawl.[95] In the olden days the art of weaving was a task which kept women busy during the cold season. The knowledge of weaving customs was imparted to the young girl at *Ywo* (Konyak dialect, dormitory for unmarried women) by the village older women. The process of ginning and spinning of cotton is somewhat on the decline, however only among the Nagas of Aos and Konyak that they are reported as being used at the present day.[96]

The foothill Nagas (Ao, Konyak, Lothas), who had frequent contact with the plains of Assam, was introduced to little seeding machine consisting of two wooden rollers geared to revolve in opposite directions and turned by a crank with the right hand. This machine was most probably imported from the plains, few villages, like Asangma village (Tuli circle of Mokokchung district), make them.[97]

Bamboo and Basket Making Culture

The Nagas and the Ahoms used bamboo extensively, from making house to fences, rice bowl, fishing equipment's, ploughing and utensil and other household articles. This material culture and these craft making traditions are quite similar.[98] Bamboo is used as firewood and even the raw ones easily burn. Bamboo groves surround them, and their houses are protected from storms and winds by them. Bamboo was used to carry water and store grains and other precious articles. Those who are addicted to opium make good use of bamboo to make their pipes. They are experts in making bamboo baskets which are used for various purposes. There are diverse types of baskets for carrying firewood, grains and other cereals. Finer baskets with lids are made for keeping precious things at home, away from the prying eyes of others. Man always carried a flat basket with a shoulder strap whenever they went out of home and kept their essentials inside.

In comparison to other parts of the world, utility of bamboo is much more in region like South and Southeast Asia, and China as the same is found in abundantly in these regions naturally. Being an inhabitant of these regions, the Ahoms and the Nagas heavily depend on the bamboo in their day-to-day life. Bamboo was the only material found abundantly nature and at the same time could have been used as a substitute not only for timber but also for metallic and non-metallic substances that were needed in daily life.[99] Every part of bamboo is used nothing is left wasted. Besides, the bamboo shoot is a favourable traditional authentic food for all the Nagas and Ahoms.

Basketry is one art that the Naga were proficient which they required in thier daily lives. To carry firewood and grains from their fields' up to the village, baskets were the most convenient containers. Each basket is of the correct size and shape for one person to carry a load, neither too heavy nor too small and is one of the staple articles of trade for Nagas with the plains.[100]

Social Assimilation

To mention a few of the many Naga traditions, there is the story of a group of Ahoms who sought refuge in Naga villages (Konyak and Ao), during the Mughal and Burmese invasions; they stayed back and in due course of time were assimilated with the Nagas. One of the manuscripts preserved in the Tai Research Institute Moranhat, refers to the migration and settlement of some Ahom amongst the Konyak long ago. According to the *Dankhawali* (literally meaning family genealogy in Assamese) of Dulan Bailung an Ahom priest opines, a few members of his families had migrated to the Konyak region. Like his families some other Ahoms too went to Konyak area and settled there according to the Ahom priestly clan genealogies.

The Konyak (Yansa, Yannu, Shangnyu, Nokzang villages), oral narratives also state the Ahoms who came to Konyak area, they integrated with the Wangnao clan among the Konyak. Similarly, there are also groups of Konyak who came to reside in Sibsagar district at Lutumgaon and Ligiri-Pukhuri.[101] The Nagas during the time of sporadic famines coerced more people to go down to the plains to get food and shelter. The village Molungkimong elders narrates that many of the Ao villages went to sell their commodities and buy food. Similarly, there are also groups of Konyak who came to reside in Sibsagar district at Lutumgaon and Ligiri- Pukhuri.

An oral history of the Konyak villages in Hatchara Adrasa Nagagaon in upper Assam says they came to Assam, accompanying the chief daughter Watlong also known as Dalimi who was married to Ahom Raja Gudapani, an Ahom prince, during his exile in the Naga hill. The people who accompanied Watlong to help her in the plains at time of her marriage did not return to their native village. Accordingly, the Ahom Raja gave them a plot of land to settle in the plains. They first stayed in the place called Chenp-phan (present-day Sripur).

They again shifted to the bank of the Hatigharia Bheel. Finally, the Moiramora Satra offered land at their present residence.

Fig. 7. and 8 Gate and Morung of the Hatchara Adrasa Nagagaon Village.

Originally, there were only seven households, and now their total population is about 408.[102] Later on, more people from Konyak villages of Hongphoi, Oting and Longkai started to migrate to the plains, following their ancestors and searching for better livelihood. They firstly stayed in Chen-phan, in the 19th century after their conversion into Neo-Vaisnavite religion the Gohain of Moiramora Satra, took them to this village now Ting-ya, also known as Nagagoan village which was established in 1775.[103] They speak Assamese; they have all the Konyak characters, features, and tradition. They even celebrate Assamese Bihu and also celebrate Aoleang Konyak festival.

The Naga tribes on the Sibsagar border are Wancho, Nocte, Tangsa, Tutsa, Konyak etc., whereas in the past they were known as Eastern Nagas, a term used by some groups of villages east and north of the Dikhu River.[104]

The cultural exchange between the two communities still prevails.[105] The tradition of *Mita* (friendship) are still to be found among the Konyak and Ahom communities. This linkage can be established on the basis of an oral tradition narrated by Nagas (Konyak-Ao- Lotha-Wancho-Nocte).

The traditions of people to people relations, for instance Ahom marrying Konyak girls are still prevailing; however, only some few Nagas men have married Ahom women. Later on, some Nagas tribes like Zeliang, Sumi, and Rengma etc., also started to migrate to the valley and amalgamated linguistically and socially with the plains, especially in Margherita, Dibrugarh, and Sibsagar. Their religious belief is an amalgamation of their traditional and Hindu beliefs. At present there are seven Sema Naga villages at Margherita, Dibrugarh district,

Lutumgaon, and Ligiri Phukhuri Gaon (Konyak), Sibsagar district (as found out by the author). Therefore, by the time the British came to Assam, the Nagas already had a good deal of socio-economic contact with the people of Brahmaputra Valley. Such interactions enabled the Nagas to speak in broken Assamese which served as the medium of communication between the Nagas and the plainsmen.[106]

The Custom of Ceremonial visiting, Exchange of Gifts and Barter

In the word of Marcel Mauss, many ideas and principles are to be noted in this type of system. The most important of these was the one which obliges one to make a return gift for a gift received.[107] For instance, the moral reasons while discussing the Naga-Ahom relations, the influence which requires the repayment of a gift and the fulfilment of bonds of these kinds were the establishment of a matrimonial alliance followed by the exchange of diplomatic relationship between the two communities. Among the Konyak, after a ceremonial gift is presented, the regulation is that this has to be repaid by a parallel counter-gift after a time gap of one year or less than that. The gifts given by the Ahom ruler to the Konyak while going to the valley kingdom is strictly kept with the chief and highly valued. An essential principle of counter-gift's equivalence was left to the giver; any coercion cannot enforce it. Among the Konyak (Jaboka) customs, a friend/trustee who has received a gift was expected to give back a fair and total value, that is, to give as good a sack of rice he receives or vice versa. It is the essential attitude towards wealth and value.[108] The tribute of a dao (*chang*) fulfilled a political obligation among the Konyak giving; the dao means it will help in times of emergency. Moreover, killing a pig and presenting a tube of salt was to fulfill the social obligation.

For instance, according to Malinowski, observing about the Kula native in 1953, he stated:

> A partner who received a Kula gift is expected to give back fair and full value, that is, to give as good an arm-shell as the necklace he receives, or vice versa. Again, a very fine article must be replaced by one of equivalent value, and not by several minor ones. Though intermediate gifts may be given to mark time before the real repayment takes places. If the articles given as counter-gift is not equivalent, the recipient will be disappointed and angry, but he has no direct means of redress, no means of coercing his partner, or of putting an end to the whole transaction. What then are the forces at work which keep the partners to the terms of the bargain? Here we come up against a very important feature of the native's mental attitude

> towards wealth and value. The great misconception of attributing to the savage a pure economic nature, might lead us to reason incorrectly thus: "The passion of acquiring, the loathing to lose or give away, is the fundamental and most primitive element in man's attitude to wealth. In primitive man, this primitive characteristic will appear in its simplest and purest form. Grab and never let go will be the guiding principle of his life." The fundamental error in this reasoning is that it assumes that 'primitive man' as represented by the present-day savage, lives, at least in economic matters, untrammelled by conventions and social restrictions. Quite the reverse is the case. Although, like every human being, the Kula native loves to possess and therefore desires to acquire and dreads to lose, the social code of rules, with regard to give and take by far overrides his natural acquisitive tendency.[109]

The social code, to give and take also overrides the natural acquisitive tendency as we find it among the Konyak (Yansa village) tribe. For instance, when the Ahom kings paid a visit to Konyak (Yansa) chief's during the festivals, then naturally it was the chief's responsibility to give shelter, food at least by slaughtering a pig and must offered rice beer to any noble visitors, even to the loiterers from another end of the village. He will be expected to share food and lodging and any of the betel nut, tobacco, *zu* (rice beer), he has to offer to the guests.[110] It may not be expensive, but in the modest manner, he had to welcome with warm hospitablity and gracefulness. His guests must feel the warmth and hospitability and their host had behaved as chief of a superior and powerful village.

Naga-Ahom Reciprocity (*Howri*)

The most outstanding form of economic cooperation between the Ahom-Konyak village life is the exchange of labour. In Jaboka village (Konyak), reciprocal work group help to prepare each other's seedbeds to plant and harvest the rice.

The traditional labour exchange known as *howri* (labour exchange), *aiei* (literally meaning labour exchange in Konyak dialect), continues to these days. Smt. Sanu, an Ahom cultivator whom the author met in the foothills of Chairadeo near Jaboka, explained that *howri* is a *niyom* (tradition). Through labour exchange, *howri* establishes social ties among different ethnic groups in the foothill Nagas and the valley people. Smt. Kohai Konyak owned a small wet rice farm at Jaboka village. During the harvest season, she said, her *satini aru ghor manu* (friends and family members) or a group of *howri* will be waiting in the field "They will come for *howri* because they are friends" Several women who came for *howri* were family friends or had kinship ties to Smt. Sanu.[111]

The *howri* day had a festival spirit, like the festive parties among peasants from the Cauca valley in Colombia described by Micheal Taussig.[112] According to Taussing, system of teamwork, festive labour practices, and reciprocal labour exchange" formed a social organisation that was "embedded in a non-market mode of using and sharing land." The Cauca valley peasants who performed reciprocal festive labour practices did not concentrate on producing surplus or accumulating profits. Similarly, *howri* services in the foothills were not tied to monetary payment, nor did they focus on profits. The owner offered tea and snacks to the workers, who rendered free labour service in return for a grand midday meal.[113]

Everyone referred to one another as *Mitani* (friends), and *ghor manu* (family members). There were no hierarchies on that day, and no one, even landowner or the farmer, behaved like a superior or inferior with each other. During season (harvest or sowing rice), it allowed workers to collected fire wood and keep any vegetables they found in the *jhum* field, since it was mostly practised during the rice harvesting and clearing the new jungle for shifting cultivations.[114]

The *howri* workers was permitted to take the vegetable from the field, they had fun finding ripe pumpkins, yam, ginger, chillies, herbs roots covered by the rice stalks, etc. Since the rice and vegetables she grew in her garden can sustain the household only for a few months throughout the rest of the year, she manages the rest year bartering vegetables, herbs, or firewood, etc., at the *hat* market. The *howri* labours joked, sing and the young children accompanying their parents would play in the *jhum* field or catch fish during rice panting season in paddy. If a person needs help, a *howri* group of family's friend will go and helps them out. Smt. Kohai from Jaboka village explained that special skills were required for different *howri* activities.

The skills needed to clear a forest or work in a *jhum* were different from those needed for working in a vegetable garden or a paddy field. She explained that her friend Smt. Sanu (an Ahom woman) will go to her friend Smt. Kohai Konyak (Jaboka village, Mon district) to help in her *jhum* fields, and she reciprocates by going to the plain during the paddy season. They followed friendship and solidarities suitable to the family's traditions of *howri*, which provide security to those living in the foothills. Unlike the tight kin-based labour required for *jhum* in the hills of Naga hills, those engaged in *howri* were aware of the different cultivation systems in use; settled farming, regimented plantation, and shifting cultivation. These foothill agricultural practises required a more extensive network of people than in upland Naga villages. *Howri* practices constituted a different kind of labour relations that was neither coercive nor bound by rules of wage labour. *Howri* was limited to landowning families.[115] In short everything is reciprocal and presumes co-operation between the two.

Cross-cultural reflections of Naga-Ahom

The hill-valley contact has entered into the texture of Assam's music and dancing, into Assamese vocabulary and in Nagamese lingua franca. The Ahom strengthened their numerical fold by adoptions, intermarriages and integrated the non-Ahoms within their fold, this process of assimilation contributed to Ahom solidarity, which enabled them to uphold Ahom rule for 600 years. Friendship with the tribes was assiduously cultivated. The Ahom possessed a number of experts conversant with the languages and customs of the hill Nagas, and their expertise were requisitioned in all diplomatic negotiations.

Words used by the tribes have contributed to the vocabulary of the Assamese language. A few list of English-Ahom-Konyak words taken from G.A. Grierson, is given to indicate[116] I: *kau* (Ahom), *ku* (Konyak-Wancho); Come: *ma* (Ahom), *mai* (Konyak- Wancho); Go-*Ka* (Ahom), *Kha* (Konyak-Wancho); Cow: *hu* (Ahom), *mahu* (Konyak- Wancho); Cat: *men* (Ahom), *miah* (Konyak-Wancho); Three-*Sam (*Ahom), *Zam* (Konyak- Wancho) Six: *ruk/rok* (Ahom), *rok* (Konyak-Wancho); House: *ren* (Ahom), *hum* (Konyak- Wancho)., etc.[117]

Assamese proverbs are full of references to the customs of the tribes. The popular music and *bihu* dance of the Ahom have been significantly reinforced by borrowing from the tribes. Weaving which is universal among women in Assam, are also found among a large tribal population. This attitude of friendship was reflected in the universal use of the word '*mita*' (Sanskrit means a friend) '*mita*', a male friend, and '*miteni*' a female friend, in accosting a man from hills.[118] As remarked by Bhuyan

> The latter knew what the word means, and on hearing it, he/she feels an atmosphere of familiarity and love. He/she becomes disarmed of his/her scepticisms fears and reciprocates the cordial advances of his/her friends from the plains. The use of the word *mita or miteni* (Assamese means friends) summarises in a sense the whole attitude of cordiality existing between the people of the plains and the hills.[119]

The numerous Naga lores' integrate inter-village relationships of friendliness, disputes concerning land and water rights, etc. For villages bordering the plains of Assam, the lore of friendship between the Ahom kingdom and Naga villages became part of their tradition, which can be termed as the secondary tradition. For instance, houses in the foothills adopted families from the Ahoms. Such adoptions were gestures of friendship and trust. Usually, traders from the hills would rest with their adopted families after they completed their business transactions in the foothills. On reaching the Ahom territory, the Nagas would deposit their unsold vegetables and reclaim them on their next visit to plains markets in their Ahom friends' houses. The Nagas would also leave their *daos* and spear with the *katakis*. These practices prevailed as a symbol of peace in those days, periodical meetings between the Ahom and Naga were held, and they pledged to uphold and continue cordial relations.[120] Especially during harvest festivals, the foothill people and the people of the hills visited each other, exchanging gifts, which developed into a friendlier and neighbourly connection between the Naga-Ahom.[121]

The Naga (Ao, Lothas, Konyak) oral narratives also talk about Nagas, seeking help from Ahom Raja for settling their internal disputes. During times of trouble the valley inhabitants found refuge in the hills and settled in different areas of Naga hills. Such instances are mentioned in both the *Buranjis* and the oral narratives. The Ahoms respected the Naga love for independence and desisted from interfering in their internal affairs.[122] However, any Naga or Ahom willing to remain in the hills or go down to the plains were received into its fold by both. Unlike the Ahoms who assimilated with the society and culture of earlier inhabitants, the Nagas despite the contact for centuries, were neither influenced by the Hindu culture of the plains of Assam nor by the Buddhism of Burma. We see that the internal polity of the Nagas remained unaffected by the Ahoms. It was only with the advent of the British and the Christian Missionaries that tremendous changes were noticed.

Summary

The process of Naga-Ahom socio-cultural relations started in the 15th and 16th centuries, when the Ahom Raja initiated adoption and matrimonial alliance with the Nagas. Unrestricted by many taboos, the early Nagas showed a lot of flexibility in these relationships. The Nagas were even employed as soldiers in the Ahom military, and soon became indispensable because of their knowledge of local customs and their adaptability in learning the language and manners of the Ahoms

The Ahoms also cleverly raised the Nagas upto the rank of nobility, which gave them prestige within their community and also employed them as ministers.

On the part of the majority of the Ahoms, their Tai language and religion came to be forgotten, and they adopted the majority Hindu religion and adopted Assamese language. The Ahoms had gradually assimilated with the local populace in religious, social and cultural aspects for the following reasons:

(i) It was a social necessity to do so at that time in the interest of consolidation, and to hold on to their political hegemony.

(ii) Socially, it was the process of adjustment with the different ethno-cultural groups, who were already Hindus by religion.[123]

(iii) Politically it was a matter of building and maintaining a kingdom under the rule of the Ahoms.[124]

Therefore, the foundation of Assamese society was laid by all these elements, including the Austro-Asiatic, with their linguistic legacy, and the Alpine-Aryan-Tibeto-Burman elements which influenced every aspect of the life of the Ahom community. The survivals of the Austric and the Tibeto-Burman culture may be noticed particularly in the names of places, rivers and other physical features throughout Brahmaputra Valley to these days.[125] Besides, the physical features of Brahmaputra valley, dividing the hills and plains into parts, drawn by nature herself, have also preserved the distinctive identity of the region and of its cultures.

The unity of hills and valley amid bewildering diversities lies probably in the character of her inhabitants, both in hills and the plains, a character marked by exclusiveness, dependence and independence, contributed by her geography.

Notes

1. Preeti Prabhat, *Matrimonial Alliance and Ancient India Polity*, D.K. Print World, New Delhi, 2007, p. 27.
2. Edward Gait, *A History of Assam,* p. 257.
3. *Ibid.*, p. 98.
4. *Ibid.*, p. 81.
5. S.K. Bhuyan, *Anglo-Assamese Relations of Assam with the East India from 1771 to 1826,* Department of Historical and Antiquarian Studies in Assam, Guwahati, 1949, p. 16.
6. George Coedes, *The Making of South East Asia*, English (Tr.) By H.M. Wright, Routledge & Kegan Paul, London, 1966, p. 102.
7. S.K. Bhuyan, *Deodhai Buranji*, DHAS, Guwahati, 1988, p. 22.
8. S.K. Bhuyan, *Studies in the History of Assam, op.cit.*, p. 3.
9. S.K. Bhuyan, *Deodhai Asam Buranji*, DHAS, Guwahati, p. 92.

10. *Ibid.*, p. 91.
11. *Ibid.*, p. 91.
12. Amalendu Guha, "The Ahom Political System: An Enquiry into the State Formation Process in Medieval Assam (1228-1714)," in *Social Scientist,* Vol. 11, No. 12, Dec, 1983, p. 15.
13. S.K. Bhuyan, *Anglo-Assamese relations, 1771-1826*, DHAS, Guwhati, 1949, p. 16.
14. S.K. Bhuyan, *Assam Buranjis or A History of Assam*, DHAS, Guwhati, 1930, p. 24.
15. S.K. Bhuyan, *Atan Buragohain and His Times,* Lawyer's Book Stall, Gauhati, 1975, p. 29; S.K. Bhuyan, *Satsari Assam Buranji, op.cit.*, p. 24.
16. S.K. Bhuyan, *Tunkhungia Buranji*, Oxford University Press, 1933, pp. 37-38; S.K. Bhuyan, *Atan Buragohain and His Times,* Laweyer's Book Stall, Guwahati, 1975, pp. 70-71.
17. S.K. Bhuyan, *Tungkhungia Buranji,* Oxford University press, 1933, pp. 51, 97; S.K. Bhuyan, *Assam Buranjis or A History of Assam*, *op.cit.*, p. 78; *Idem*, ACHAB, pp. 294-295.
18. S K. Bhuyan, *An Assamese Nur Jahan: Or A Sketch of the Life of Queen Phuleswari Devi*, Published by the author at Gauhati, Assam, 1926. pp. 29-30.
19. Alexander Mackenzie, *North-East Frontier of India*, *op.cit.*, p. 92; see Golap Chandra Barua, *Ahom Buranji From the Earliest Times to the End of Ahom Rule, op.cit.*, p. 45; S.K. Bhuyan, *Deodhai Assam Buranji*, DHAS, Guwahati, 1988, pp. 6-7.
20. S.K. Bhuyan, *Satsari Assam Buranji, op.cit.*, pp. 79-80; S.K. Bhuyan, *Assam Buranjis or A History of Assam*, *op.cit.*, pp. 41-42.
21. S.K. Bhuyan, *Assam Buranjis or A History of Assam*, *op.cit.*, pp. 39, 64; S.K Bhuyan, *Deodhai Assam Buranji*, *op.cit.*, p. 44.
22. S.K. Bhuyan, *Assam Buranjis or A History of Assam*, *op.cit.*, p. 48.
23. Amalendu Guha, "The Ahom Political System," *op.cit.*, pp. 14-15.
24. Christopher von Furer Haimendorf, *Return to the Naked Nagas*, *op.cit*; From the Ahom *Buranjis* and the Oral tradition of Konyak and Ao the King had married two Naga girls: see A. Mackenzie, *The North-East Frontier of India*, *op.cit.*, pp. 91, 93, 101, 145-148; Amalendu Guha, "The Ahom Political System," *op.cit.*, pp. 14-15.
25. C.L. Imchen, "History of the Relations between the Nagas and the Valley Kingdoms," *op.cit.*, p. 115; N. Nyejat Konyak "Understanding Ahom-Konyak Relations Through Folk-Narratives" in *North-East India History Association* (NEIHA), 38th Session, ISSN 2349 753X, 2nd-4th October 2017, pp. 164-172.
26. Alban von Stockhausen, "Watlong the Naga Queen: negotiating local identities through narratives," in *Asian Ethnicity*, Vol.17, No.3, 2016, pp. 353-369; Information recorded by the author from village elders, Shri Nyakwang of Shangnu village and Yanang of Ponkong village Mon District, on April 2018.
27. Information recorded by the author from village elders Shri Thanglong Konyak, Tinglong, and K. Weangna, Ex-chairman Mon Town Council, on January, 2018. For the names of person, the spellings as they are given in the context of each sources have been used.
28. Information recorded by the author from village elders Shri Thanlong Konyak Ex-chairman Mon Town Council, January 2018; The *Morung/Baans* were a self-governing institution aiming to impart social instructions and trained men to channel fertility into their community. However, women are forbidden to enter the morung except on certain ceremonial occasions. Among the Konyak villages of Nagaland, the clan, the *khel* and the village has its own *Morung/Baan*, which is determined by its historical heritage. If a certain clan has established a village the position of the clan in the village is held high esteem and wields greater authority in the village affairs. The Konyak villages have a girl's dormitory called *Ywo/Morung*.

29. *Angh* of Palang (head chief) Morung belongs to the chiefly house. The clan is the further extension of kinship system in Konyak society.
30. Information recorded by the author from village elders Shri Lihwang, T. Manching, Tonyei, Shahlem, S. Shaopa, Konang Enyei and Smt. Shongna of Wakching village Mon, Nagaland on 13th January 2018; see Christopher von Furer Haimendorf, *Konyak Nagas*, Rinehart and Winston, New York, 1969, p. 33.
31. Information recorded by the author from Wakching village elders Shri S. Shaopa, Wakching village Mon, Nagaland on 13th January 2018; see Edward Gait, *op.cit.*; M. Alemchiba, *A Brief Historical Account of Nagaland*, Publisher Naga Institute of Culture Kohima, Nagaland, 1970, pp. 29-40.
32. A man at Wakching later told us that this Ahom wedding present was beaten to create a sound when heavy thunderstorms or winds approached the village. This had been the only 'use' of the object for the villagers; Government of Nagaland, Revenue Department, "Naga *khat's* in Sibsagar, No. 55, 1928; The question of management of the Naga *khats* was discussed at length in Mr Gunning's note of 12-1-1918. From letter No. 4400 Rc, 5-12-1921; Based on Sir William Reid's orders dated 17-11-1921; P. D. Gogoi, "The Konyak Naga: A Case Study of the Hahchra Naga Village," in Proceedings of *North-Eastern India History Association,* Twentieth Session, Dibrugarh, Assam, p. 195; Whatever is collected from the Assamese villages is shared by all in a community feast. The term 'tax' is also no longer used; This was a practice which continued. Until September 1922, the Konyak Nagas were given right to collect taxes in Geleky (Sibsagar) which included taxes on the products of agricultural harvest, betel nut; fishing lake called *bheels* were allowed to them. Even *paik* (labourers) were attached to them. For the management of lands and transaction of business, officials versed in Naga dialect called Naga-*katakis* were appointed. see J.P. Mills, *The Ao Nagas, op.cit.*, p. 11; J.P. Mills, *The Lhota Nagas, op.cit.*, pp. 1-2.
33. A practice which continued under the British. Until September 1922, the Konyak Nagas were given right to collect taxes in Geleky (Sibsagar) which included taxes on the products of agricultural harvest, betel nut, fishing lake called *bheels* were allowed to them. Even *paik* (labourers) were attached to them. For the management of lands and transaction of business Ahom official versed in Naga dialect called *Naga-kataki's* were appointed. see J.P. Mills, *The Ao Nagas*, *op.cit*., p. 11; *Idem*, *The Lhota Nagas, op.cit*., pp. 1-2.
34. Sung by the descendants of Watlong family to the scholar in 2017 during her field trip, 2018.
35. Information collected from elders/singers Shri Mewang, Smt. Nangkham Anghya and Tulish Anghya of Wanching village Mon Nagaland on 4th January 2018; Information recorded by the author from Shri W. Shaopong, Lonkmong, Thanglong Konyak, Metjen Konyak of Tanhai village Mon, Nagaland on 5th January 2018.The Aoleang Monyu is the festival of Konyak and it happens in the first week of April; see J.H. Hutton, *The Angami Nagas*, Oxford University Press, 1969, pp. 384-385; Alban von Stockhausen, Watlong, the Naga queen: negotiating local identities through narratives, *op.cit.*, p. 356.
36. Metjen Konyak, "Ahom-Konyak Relations," in *Indian Journal of Tai Studies,* Vol. IX, October, 2009, pp. 142-43; The slab of rock is considered as an object of pride by the Konyak people. This stone symbolises their connection and good relations with the Ahoms.
37. Suresh Kant Sharma and Usha Sharma, *Discovery of North-East: Geography, History, Culture, Religion, Politics, Sociology, Education and Economy. North-East India.* Vol. 1, Mittal Publications, North-Eastern India, 2005, pp. 145-148.

38. Naginimora is one of the sub-divisions under Mon District where Watlong Wangya (chief's daughter) was buried. it shared border with Bihubar, nearest railroad station is Simulguri, Assam; Metjen Konyak, "Ahom- Konyak Relations," *op.cit.*, pp. 142-143.
39. Information recorded by the author from Shri. Macdo, a chairman of Koro village, Wokha, on 11.10.2018.
40. *Ibid.*
41. Wozamo Odyuo, "The story of ancient Ahom and Lotha-Naga friendship," in *Nagaland Post*, 11 October 2014, p. 3.
42. Information recorded by the author from Shri. Alemtet Pongen a village elder of Chuchuyimlang village on 12th April, 2015.
43. The anklet is now a family heirloom of *Pongen* clan of Chuchuyimlang which is preserved and kept with Shri and Smt. *Alemted Pongen* who is the descendant of Imdangmeren Pongen. They wore this anklet during festivals and when they visited the descendant of the Ahom Raja at Jorhat, erstwhile Ahom capital.
44. Langpangkong range is situated in the foothill area towards Assam had a close contact with the Ahoms in the pre-colonial period.
45. Information recorded by the author from Shri. S. Nokon Longchar, 81-year-old, village elders of Leremin village (Mokokchung), on 29th March 2018.
46. Information recorded from Shri. S. Nokon Longchar, 81-year-old, village elders of Leremin village (Mokokchung), on 29th March 2018 by the author.
47. Information received from Shri Yemti Longkumer, an 82 year-old, Former Nagaland Public Service Commission, at Dimapur, on 23rd-25th March 2018; Also see, Aokumla Walling, "Oral Traditions and Archaeology Reconstructing the Pre-Colonial History of Ao Nagas with Special Reference to the Naga Ahom Relationship," Ph.D. thesis, Department of AIHC and Archaeology, Deccan College Post Graduate and Research Institute, 2016, pp. 66-70.
48. Information recorded from Shri. Yemti Longkumer, 81-year-old, ex-NCS, of Leremen village, Nagaland, 23/3/2018.
49. Information recorded by the author from Shri. A Pokyam Walling, 79-year-old, village elder of Nokpu village (Mokokchung district, Nagaland), 20th April 2018.
50. Information recorded by the author from Nokpu village council which recounts their oral tradition records a forty-five *putu* cycle. All the Ao village are governed by the *putu menden* (*putu*-generation, *Menden*-seat). It is the highest seat of authority in the village and all the villagers abide by it. The *putu menden* consists of men from the last stage of the morung, it is represented by all the clans in the village for the social and political administration of the village. It has the power to judge, enfore laws and regulations, it acts as the executive and administrative power in the village for the welfare of the villagers. This system of governance was first established by the Ao forefather in Chungliyimti village.
51. Information recorded by the author from Senti Walling, Nokpu village Mokokchung district, 20th May, 2018.
52. Information recorded by the author from Nokpu village elders Shri. Imli Imchen (60-year-old), Shri. Tarip Ao (60-year-old), Shri Ajung (52 year-old), Shri Imijung Yanger (60-year-old), Shri Aliba (42-year-old), Shri Chuba Walling (42-year-old), I Niken G.B. (64-year-old), Shri Temsu Longkumer (64-year-old), Shri Chujang Imchen (52-year-old), Shri Toshi (39-year-old) on 29-3-2018.
53. Information recorded by the author from Smt. Senti Walling of Nokpu village on 2017.
54. V. Elwin, *Nagaland*, *op.cit.*, p. 19; Mazhar Asif, *Tarikhe-e-Aasham*, Department of Historical and Antiquarian Studies, Guwahati, 2009.

55. J.N. Phukon & Girin Phukon, "Social Dynamics of material culture of the Ahom," in *Indian Journal of Tai Studies*, Vol. XI, 2011.
56. A. Guha, *Medieval and Early Colonial Assam: Society, Polity, Economy*, South Asia Books, New Delhi, 1991, p. 112.
57. Kanaklal Barua, "Pre-Historic Culture in Assam," (eds.), S.K. Sarma. & Usha Sharma, *Discovery of North-East India*, Vol. 5, *op.cit.*, p. 315.
58. Jadunath Sarkar (tr.), "Fathiyah-i-Ibriyah," in *Journal of Bihar and Orissa Research Society* (JBORS), Vol. I, 1915, p. 193.
59. Nagamese is an Assamese-based pidgin with loan words from Hindi, Bengali, and English but only a few words from various Naga languages. It emerges in Nagaland due to acculturation cultural diffusion imitation, contact and communication, cultural growth and development.
60. S.E. Peal, "Notes on a Visit to the Tribes inhabiting the hills south of Sibsagar, Asam (with five plates)," in *Journal of the Asiatic Society Bengal,* Vol. XLI, 1872, pp. 9-31
61. S.K. Bhuyan, *Anglo-Assamese Relations, op.cit.,* p. 39.
62. *Ibid.*, p. 53.
63. Maya Simionescu, and Eugen Simion, *Scientific Lingua Franca and National Languages at the Crossroads*, in ALLEA Biennial Yearbook, 2004, pp. 129-133; Critical Topics in Science and Scholarship Amsterdam: A.L.L.E.A. They had opined in antiquity, the role of a lingua franca which was played by old Greek, whereas in the Middle Ages it was Latin, followed by French, Germany, and Italian making a deep impact on culture, science and diplomacy.
64. Studies on translation and multilingualism; Lingua Franca: Chimera or Reality? European Commission Directorate-General for Translation, 2011; Access on 21:02.2015 http://www.e;;.org.pl/sites/ell.org.pl/files/lingua-franca-en.pdf, p. 8.
65. Sarah Holcombe, The Politico-Historical Construction of Pintupi Luritja and the Concept of Tribe, in *Oceania*, Vol. 74, No. 4, June 2004, p. 257.
66. Salikoko S. Mufwene, *The Evolution of Language: Hints from Creoles and Pidgins in Language*, Evolution and the Brain, James Minett & William Wang (eds.), pp. 1-33. City University of Hong Kong Press, 2009. Accessed on 02.01.15. htt:// mufwene.chicago. edu./publications. The Evolution of Language Hints from Creoles and Pidgins. Pdf, p. 19; Information recorded by the author from C.L. Imchen, a Sociology professor at NEHU, Shillong, 17.12.2015.
67. Meeta Deka, "Historical Matrix of Nagamese as a Communilects in Northeast India," in *Proceedings of North East India History Association,* Mirza, pp. 152-163.
68. Salikoko S. Mufwene, *op.cit.*, pp. 1-133.
69. John M'Cosh, *Topography of Assam,* Logo press, New Delhi, 1837, p. 156.
70. Also, Christoph von Furer Haimendorf mentions that many people fluently speak Nagamese in the Naga Hills. The influence of the Christian Missionaries and the British occupation in Nagaland had a significant impact on the vocabulary of Nagamese; W.C. Smith, *The Ao Naga Tribe of Assam: op.cit.*
71. Sajal Nag, *Contesting Marginality, Ethnicity, Insurgency and Sub-Nationalism In North-East India, op.cit.*, p. 40.
72. P. D. Stracey, *Nagaland Nightmare, op.cit.*, p. 16.
73. Information recorded by the author from Shri. Girin Phukon, (90-year-old), a retired professor of political science (Dibrugarh University), Moranhat, January 2019.
74. Sokhep Kri (ed.), *Gazetteer of Arunachal Pradesh,* Vol. I, Government of Arunachal Pradesh Gazetteers Department, 2010, p. 208.
75. H. Blochmann, "Koch Bihar, Koch Hajo, and Asam, in the 16th and 17th Centuries, according to the Akbarnamah, the Padishahnamah, and the Fathiyah i Ibriyah," in *Journal of Asiatic Society of Bengal*, 1872, p. 55.

76. Edward Gait, *A History of Assam*, *op.cit.*, p. 171.
77. S.K. Bhuyan, *Assam Buranjis or A History of Assam*, *op.cit.*, p. 61.
78. Hunter, *A Statistical Account of Assam*, Vol. I, *op.cit.*, pp. 44, 250; Allen, *Assam District Gazetteers,* Vol. II (Sibsagar), p. 172.
79. The Nagas are fond of using rice in their cuisine alongside various types of meat and they also make beverage using rice. Different Naga tribes prepare the fermented rice beer, namely *–Yi/Mejemtsu* in Ao dialect and *Yutho* in Konyak dialect, a little differently than others, the taste is somewhat sour, the beverage has a fruity aroma and it is served in bamboo made glasses.
80. Vizier Sanyu, *A History of Nagas and Nagaland Dynamics of Oral Tradition in Village Formation*, Commonwealth Publishers, New Delhi, 1996, p. 51.
81. S.K. Bhuyan, (ed.), *Asam Buranji*, Intro, xv.
82. Lila Gogoi, *The History of the System of Ahom Administration*, *op.cit,* p. 98.
83. Pratap Chandra Choudhury, *The History of Civilisation of the People of Assam to the Twelfth Century A.D.*, Spectrum Publications, Guwahati, first published 1959, (Reprint 2017), p. 338.
84. R.G. Woodthorpe, "Notes On the Wild Tribes Inhabiting the So-Called Naga Hills, On Our North-East Frontier of India," part I. in *The Journal of the Anthropological Institute of Great Britanin and Ireland*, Vol. 11, 1882, pp. 56-73; see S.E. Peal, "Notes on a Visit to the Tribes Inhabiting the Hills South of Sibsagar Assam," J.L. 1872-XLI (i), 9-31.
85. Bengal Government Paper, "Edgar's Note on the Angami and others Naga Tribes," Government of Nagaland, No. 876, 1871.
86. Kanaklal Barua, "Pre-Historic Culture in Assam," (eds.), S.K. Sarma. & Usha Sharma, *Discovery of North-East India,* Vol.5, Mittal Publication, 2005, p. 315.
87. Information received from Girin Phukon, (88-year-old), Political Science, Department of Dibrugarh University, Moranhat, on 17 January 2019; see William Robinson, *A Descriptive Account of Assam, op.cit.*, p. 227.
88. B.K. Barua, *Cultural History of Assam*, Vol. I, Lawyer's Book Stall, Guwahati, 1951, p. 105.
89. E.A. Gait, *A History of Assam*, *op.cit.,* p. 271.
90. William Robinson, *A Descriptive Account of Assam, op.cit.* p. 234.
91. Foreign Department, Report on the Trans-Dikhu Tour, File No. 469, Government of Nagaland, 1913, p. 11.
92. M. Horam, *Naga Polity,* B.R. Publishing Corp. Delhi, first print 1975, (Reprint 1992), p. 29.
93. G.M. Godden, "Naga and Other Frontier Tribes of North-East India," in *The Journal of the Anthropological Institute of Great Britain and Ireland,* Vol. 26, 1897, p. 13.
94. W.C. Smith, *The Ao Naga Tribes of Assam*, *op.cit.*, p. 37.
95. J.P. Mills, *The Ao Nagas*, *op.cit.*, p. 92.
96. *Ibid.*, pp. 90-91.
97. William Carlson Smith, *The Ao Nagas Tribes of Assam, op.cit.*, p. 46.
98. J.P. Mills, *The Ao Nagas*, MacMillan, London, 1926, pp. 90 91.
99. Based on field observation at Moranjan village, Moranhat, Upper Assam, from 17th November to 18th December 2015.
100. John, E., *Village Life in Modern Thailand,* University of California, 1958, p. 77; Frank M. Lebar, *Ethnic Groups of Mainland Southeast Asia,* Human relations Area files press, New Haven, 1964, pp. 191-224.
101. Thomas Vattoth Sdb, *The Wanchos in Transition,* Published by Don Busco Youth & Educational Services, Dimapur Nagaland, 2008, p. 253.

102. The Genealogy of Sri. Dulan Bailung are still preserved at Institute of Tai Studies and Research, Moranhat, Charaideo district, Assam. Accessed on 2017. According to the Ahom customary laws, only the priestly (i.e., Bailung, Deodhai, clan maintain the Ahom family genealogies.
103. Information recorded by the author from Mrs. Shonying Konyak at Tingya, Nagagaon village, Sivasagar, Assam on 26th November 2019; Also, field observation at Hahchara Konyak village (Sibsagar district), 18th March-20 June, 2018.
104. Information recorded by the author from Smt. Tinghat Konyak a school teacher at Tingya, Nagagaon village, Sivasagar, Assam, on 26th January 2019; Also, field observation at Hahchara Konyak village (Sibsagar district), 18th March-20 June 2018.
105. J.H. Hutton, "The Mixed culture of the Naga Tribes," in *The Journal of the Royal Anthropological Institute of Great Britain and Ireland,* Vol. 95, No. 1st Jan-Jun, 1965, p. 16.
106. Information recorded by the author from Shri. Tinghat Konyak a teacher from Naogaon Hatsara on 26th to 29th January, 2019; also field observation at Moranjaan villages on 19/12/2019.
107. B.K. Boruah, *Nagamese: The Language of Nagaland,* New Delhi, 1993, p. 7; Sajal Nag, *Contesting Marginality: Ethnicity, Insurgency and Sub-Nationalism in North-East India*, Manohar, New Delhi, 2002, p. 40.
108. Marcel Mauss, *The Gift: The Form And Functions of Exchange In Archaic Societies*, Routledge classics, London and New York, 1954.
109. Information recorded by the author from Shri Shomwang Wangham (chief) of Jaboka (Yansa), village on 3rd December-2017.
110. Bronislaw Malinoswski, *Argonauts of the Western Pacific: An Account of Native Enterprise and Adventure in the Archipelagoes of Melanesian New Guinea*, Routledge & Kegan Paul, London, first published 1922 (Reprint 1953), p. 96.
111. Information recorded by the author from Banfera (Rusa) chief Shri. Panwang Wangpa on 5th-October 2019.
112. Based on field observation and information recorded from Smt. Kohai, of Jaboka village, Tizit Nagaland in 2017.
113. Micheal Taussig, *The Devil and Commodity Fetishism in South America*, University of North Carolina Press, 1980, p. 71.
114. 113. *Ibid.*, p. 71.
115. Dolly Kikon, *Living with Oil & Coal Resource Politics & Militarisation in Northeast India*, Yoda Press, New Delhi, 2020, p. 111.
116. Information recorded by the author from Shri. Noknagam Wangsu, member of village elders at Jaboka village, Mon district on 27th February 2016.
117. G.A. Grierson, *Linguistic Survey of India*, Vol. II, Published by Government Printing, Calcutta, 1904.
118. *Idem*, *Linguistic Survey of India*, Vol. I, 1927, part. I; *Idem*, Linguistic Survey of India, Vol. II, 1904; E.T. Dalton, *Descriptive Ethnology of Bengal*, Appendix, 1873, pp. 69-70.
119. S.K. Bhuyan, *Studies in the History of Assam, op.cit.*, p. 39; The traditions of *Mita* and *Miteni* still survive among the Konyak and Ahom.
120. S.K. Bhuyan, *Studies in the History of Assam, op.cit.*, p. 46.
121. Temsula Ao, *The Ao Naga Oral Tradition*, *op.cit.*, p. 10; see, B.B. Ghosh, *Nagaland District Gazetteer*, Mokokchung District, 1979, p. 40.
122. Temsula Ao, *Ibid,* p. 10.
123. R. Chumbeno Ngullie & N. Venuh, "Socio-Political Institution of the Nagas in the Eighteenth Century," in Tejimala Gurung (ed.), *The Falling Polities Crisis and*

Decline of States in North-East India in the Eighteenth Century, DVS, New Delhi, 2018, p. 175.

124. S.K. Gogoi, "Religion of the Ahom: A Sociological Study," (Thesis) Dibrugarh University, 1995, p. 126.
125. *Ibid.*, p. 126.
126. 125. P. C. Choudhury, *The History of Civilisation of the People of Assam to the Twelfth Century, op.cit.*, p. 321.

Conclusion

Conventional and colonial studies on the hill tribes of northeast India have often tended to demonise the tribes and as lying outside the purview of state and civilisation. The tribes were considered as holding on to their isolation in the hills occasionally coming down only to raid the plains where they struck terror and devastation. Such a perspective had largely to do with earlier methodology and over dependence on colonial and ethnographic sources and failure to critique it. The recent advances in historical discipline, adoption of a multidisciplinary perspective and the inclusion of a wider array of sources have led to a more nuanced interpretation of earlier positions.[1] The field work undertaken for the present study by way of documentation of oral sources and material artefacts has added to the corpus of information on the subject. These indicate that despite a history of conflict there also existed alongside a greater tradition of co-existence and interdependence in the relation between the Nagas and the Ahoms.

During the medieval period, the Ahom state was the most dominant kingdom in northeast India. The Ahom state has been described as representing a quasi-feudal structure at the height of its state formation process. The Ahoms who came as a migratory body during the thirteenth century from Upper Burma established their kingdom in the Brahmaputra valley which lasted till the first half of the nineteenth century. The success of the Ahoms in the state formation process has been explained as due to many factors such as extension of wet rice cultivation, an organised system of labour utilisation through the *paik* and *khel* system, a wise policy of acculturation and assimilation, matrimonial alliances, etc. One of the most important features of the historical development during the period was the policy evolved by the Ahoms to deal with the hill tribes surrounding the kingdom and the relations which the hill tribes developed with the Ahom kingdom.

The Ahoms *Buranjis* refer to the Konyak, Ao, and Lotha Nagas by various names depending on the location from where they came.

Taking into account the early colonial records, the oral narratives and archaeological sources the names mentioned in the *Buranjis* have been identified with the above Naga groups or villages. The Lothas were referred to as Paniphatias, the Torphatias, the Doyingias; the Aos as the Hatigurias, the Assiringias, the Dopdarias; and the Konyaks as the Namsangias, the Borduarias, the Tablungias, the Jaktungias, and the Moolungias etc.

The areas inhabited by the Patkai Nagas were of strategic importance to the Ahoms for trade, transit and economic purposes. Initial relations were of conflict as evident from the expeditions sent by the Ahoms. The Ahoms later moved down to the valley which became the main base of their rule. The hills were never totally isolated or secluded as colonial historiography had made out to be. The foothill plains served as an outlet for the tribes to come down for procuring items. For the Naga tribes the interaction with the valley plains remained due to geo-political and economic factors. In particular, the passes (*duar*s) facilitated interaction and socio-economic dependence between the hill and plain dwellers. The Patkai Naga (now known as the Konyak, Wancho, Nocte Tutsa, Tangsa) served to foster commercial and cultural exchange with the Ahom Kingdom. Although this relationship was not always peaceful or without conflict, their political-economic links with the Ahoms extended over nearly 600 years. The area inhabited by the Patkai-Nagas was strategically important as it served as transit and trade route from ancient times. The routes to Burma (the Naras of Mogaung) lay through Naga country and it was very important both for strategic and other reasons. Henceforth, the Ahom never allowed the disturbances in this region to gain gigantic proportions so as to jeopardise their kingdom. Hence the policy that the Ahoms followed in dealing with the Nagas was quite clear.

As already stated, one of the important aspects of the Naga–Ahom relations were the socio-economic and political interests of the ruling Ahoms and the economic necessity of the Nagas residing in the hills to whom the plains served as an imperative outlet for raids and exchanges. Besides, the location of several salt springs in the Naga area gave the Patkai Nagas an upper hand in their dealing with the valley and other Naga groups in the interior. The Ahom state had to depend on the foothill salt wells for the supply of salt. Bengal salt came to be imported only after the extension of Ahom rule to Lower Assam. Over a period of time the Ahoms came to obtain possession of some of these salt wells and also the right to certain other wells by fighting with the Nagas.

Raiding was an integral feature of tribal society conducted for various purposes. However, raiding was not carried out randomly at all times. One of the main purposes of maintaining amicable relationship by the Ahoms with the Nagas was to prevent or reduce the raids by the hill tribes in the plains. The Ahoms tried to prevent the tribesmen from distressing the plains by granting them *posa* from the Ahom villages, *Naga khat,* fishing waters, and even assigned *paiks*', (*bahatias*) to provide them with part of their subsistence in each *duar'*s. Nevertheless, it was not guarantee against tribal raids. Inspite, of the concessions made to the tribes in various ways, most of them often violated their agreements, raiding villages within the Ahom kingdom, then the Ahom Raja retaliated by withholding the payment of annual grants which led to counter punitive expeditions resulting in the destruction of granaries and dwelling houses of the plain people. Often the conflict transpired as result of bargaining by the tribes relating to the grants. As a result, closing the markets and the *pass (duars)* and also sending punitive expeditions against the Naga, destruction of granaries and dwelling house of the tribes were the methods used by the Ahom state to punish the Nagas. Therefore, the primary objective of the Ahom rulers was to maintain the reconciliation with the hill men by adopting a policy of reciprocity. Henceforth, the tribes enjoyed the privilege of grants of *posa*, *khats,* etc, to restrain from aggression the Ahom villages. The introduction of the '*posa*' system in each *duars'* by assigning *katakis'* to maintain as a mode of channel to communicate with the Nagas, thus regularised the claim of the hill people to share in the produce of the fertile lands of the *duar* areas. However, whenever the Ahom administration became weak and *posa* was not delivered properly, this led to discord and conflict with the Nagas.

To deal with the Nagas the Ahom state appointed *kataki's* or moderators. They maintained a communication channel between the Ahom state and the Naga chiefs.' The *katakis'* managed and supervised the *khats' and bheels'* (land and fisheries held by the Nagas) and made what they could gain from it in return. The *katakis'* emerged to be an important intermediary between the Naga and the Ahom people. A lot depended on the sagacity, goodwill and trust generated by this representative in the relationship with the Nagas. Very often the post tended to be hereditary.

The passes (*duars*') facilitated contact and a socio-economic dependence between the foothill Nagas such as the *Namsangias*, *Bordurias*, *Assigingia* and the Ahom villages. One of the most important mechanisms through which Naga-Ahom relations was institutionalised was through the *duars'* (passes), where *hats* or markets were established by the Ahom state. The tribes came down to the plains through these passes. Some important *duars'* between the Dikhu and Doyang rivers in the Naga Hills were, *Assirangia duar, Namasangia duar, Dopdar duar, Doyang duar, Hathiguria duar, Paniphat duar, Jabokaduars, Naganimora duar, Geleki duar* and *Tiru duar*. Each *duar* had a *hat* attached to it opened on the eastern and western frontiers by the Ahom kings. These markets were connected with the Ahom capitals

Pre-modern market such as *hats* has been reconsidered as a meeting point where interaction happen to transfer of goods to fulfil the needs with no profit-making interests. The foothills were the special zones where inhabitants from the hills and the valley transacted in the markets that functioned once or twice a week catering to their local needs. Such markets or market places were not autonomous of socio-political relations or concern.

The areas in the *duars* which were visited by the Nagas, did not develop into bigger *haat*/markets, because the tribes did not bring large quantities of merchandise nor did they take away large quantities of commodities except ones they received by way of *posa*. The study further reveals that the tribes were not significantly dependent on the plains-men so far as staple food stuffs are concerned, for nowhere has there been any mention of rice, pulses or such other food items in the lists of *posa* to be delivered to the tribes. The lists of *posa* include such things as garments of various description, a few animals, iron products and salt. However, many scholars and historians seem to project as if the tribes were dependent for food on the plains which according to the *Buranji* are not true. The hill people were allowed to visit the *khat* and collect *posa* between the months November to May, i.e., harvesting seasons in the plains is not much for the tribes to collect the harvest but this is the fair-weather period and also the time when the plains men can weave the cloths and make other things ready for *posa*. This indicates that the Nagas enjoyed operational power in this track before the British occupation of the Ahom kingdom.

Salt manufacture, its control and distribution was a major political and economic issue in the hill and valley relations during the medieval period. The *Buranjis* and colonial writers have only mentioned in general the region from where the salt came from but the specific clans and villages who were involved in the manufacture and trading in salt have not been identified.

The Naga chiefs were often in the habit of visiting the Ahom kingdom and also the Nagas often sought the military help of the Ahom government in their inter-tribal warfare as also evident from the Naga oral narratives.

The Ahom rulers harnessed the twin strategy and practice of adoption and marital alliances with the Kachari, Miris, Nagas, and the Daflas. Their actions were motivated mainly by considerations of practical necessity and political expediency. The number of the Ahoms as a conquering tribe was very small. With such small numbers they found it, impossible to maintain their gradually expanding dominion. Therefore, they were compelled to increase their community by admitting non-Ahoms of both the plains and hill tribes into their fold. The Ahoms succeeded in assimilating with the tribes from the plains and paved the way for the growth of a wider Ahom community in the valley kingdom. The relations of the Ahom rulers took a completely different form with those of the plain tribes. Whereas the latter were conquered, occupying the territories of the hill-tribes did not happen. The Ahom rulers routinely recruited efficient tribesmen to important administrative post. One such instances as discussed earlier was the appointment of a Barphukan who was the son of a Banfera Naga. Often the adopted children were placed in high positions. References of many marital relations between the Nagas and Ahoms are found in the chronicles and Naga oral narratives.

Through such contacts and socio-economic interactions *Nagamese* developed as the medium of communication between the Nagas and the plainsmen. It evolved out of frequent social interaction primarily for economic and trade purpose. The use of *Nagamese* language, served as the lingua franca transgressing the boundaries of the multiple tribes among the Naga tribes and also used as a second language for communication between the other communities. The regular contact with the tribes made them quite familiar to the plains people. The plains people gave indigenous names to the different tribes they came in contact and till today they are popularly known by those names.

The trade between the hills and valley were based on reciprocity and hence, not very flourishing trade, as it was managed by the local inhabitants. The hill and plain territory has been described as a country where there was no extra-ordinary prosperity or distressing undernourishment occurs.

The plains at the foothills provided the tribes their natural outlets. As mentioned earlier, the Ao and Lotha tribes would come down to the foothills to barter their forest products, agricultural and handicraft products for salt, etc., which were not available in the hills. The plains were also happy to get the products from the hills. Hence the relationship between the Naga-Ahom resulted in interdependence and mutual cohabitation between the two communities. This was maintained through the principle of reciprocity by negotiating through the *katukis*.

The *duars* served as a passage to mutual connectivity for the Naga-Ahom in which they bartered, exchange gifts, visited each other during festivals. Subsequently, small and medium markets thrived, through the socio-economic contact and exchange. Other Naga tribes like Ao, Rengma, Chang, Sangtam, Khiamniungan became the regular customers with the neigbouring Nagas, for instance, Konyak, Lotha, and Ao who had a direct contact with the Ahoms. Interaction and integration was evident between the Nagas and Ahoms. However, when the British took over the *duars'* they imposed restriction by imposing Inner Line Permit in 1873, thus restricting outsider from collecting commodities or moving freely into the Naga areas. Besides, there was a major setback in the politics of salt commodity, when the British East company took control of salt monopoly in Assam, which led to the consequence for the decline of the sale of Naga traditional salt which was replaced by large scale import of Bengal salt.

The Ahom exercised its power as a dominant power in the region to regulate and obtain a share of the resources generated in peripheral and divergent economies and adopted a policy of political isolation in the latter period from any foreign power over its geographical space and natural resources. Encompassing all the varied aspects of the society such as social, cultural, linguistic, religious, political and economic which was greatly influenced by the Brahmanical culture and the neighbouring hill tribes in the process of state formation Medieval Assam, the Ahom state emerged as a very stable power; contributing to the consolidation of Assam and maintenance of a tactful policy towards the Naga.

The Ahoms beginning from the thirteenth century increased their numerical fold by adoptions, intermarriages and incorporated the non-Ahoms within their fold. They gradually assimilated with the local populace in religious, social and cultural aspects. It was a social necessity to do so in the interest of consolidation, process of adjustment with the different ethno-cultural groups and to hold on to their political hegemony. This process of assimilation contributed to the growth of the Ahom state. Friendship with the tribes was an important feature of their policy. The Naga (Ao, Lothas, Konyak) oral narratives also talk about Nagas seeking help from the Ahom Raja for settling their internal disputes. The Ahoms understood the importance of adopting a practical policy towards the Naga tribes.

It may be noted that in such times of weakened Ahom administration, for instance at the time of Moamaria rebellion and Burmese invasions, the Naga villages became a zone of refuge. The Naga inhabited areas were not simply a region of resistance to the valley people; but also a place of refuge or survival for the Ahoms. It provided shelter for the Ahoms in times of turmoil, external aggressions and calamities. For instance, during the sixteenth, seventeenth and eighteenth centuries when the Kochs, Mughals invaded Assam and during the Moamaria Rebellion and Burmese invasions many fled and took refuge in Konyak and Ao villages. The inhabitants of the plains whoever was willing to stay in the hills, were received into the fold of the Ao and Konyak Nagas, which indicates acceptance of outsiders into the community. Such instances were mentioned in Ahom *Buranjis* and in oral narratives among the Nagas. The Ahoms who came and settled in the hills were integrated into the Naga society. The same however does not appear to have occurred in the case of the Naga. For instance, the Konyaks who migrated and settled in the plains, while adopting certain cultural traits of the plains continued to hold on to their customary laws, institutions and practices such as *morungs,* traditional festivals etc.

The Ahoms never sought to occupy or envisaged a plan of annexing any of the hilly regions to their kingdom. As long as their political and economic interests were met, the Nagas were left undisturbed without interloping from the Ahoms, unless some parties asked for help. It was difficult to fight in the hills and there was little to gain in the shape of war booty except some mithuns, buffaloes etc. The Nagas on the Indo-Burma frontier also did not ally themselves with the enemies of the Ahoms beyond the Patkai range to jeopardise the Ahom kingdom. For the Ahoms, they needed the goodwill of the Naga; in case there was turmoil in Ahom kingdom, they needed a safe passage to take refuge, besides the Ahom needed the Nagas for economic and political purposes.

The Ahom state being the most powerful power in the region, the Nagas also had to deal astutely with their neighbour. They also sought to maintain a policy of coexistence and reciprocity. The Nagas while going down to the plains always brought with them forest products, baskets, and vegetables etc as gifts to be given to the Ahom villagers. Many foothills Nagas had strong cultural and kinship ties with their plainsmen friends. Geographical proximity and economic exigencies made the hills and plains inevitably dependent on each other.

The Naga-Ahom relations during the period were never static. As the Ahom polity evolved towards greater feudalisation of its state structure – its relation with the hill tribes also evolved The two contrasting entities- a valley based state power and a hill based non-state entity provided much of the dynamics of socio-political and economic change in the history of the region during the period. The Ahom state and the hill tribes had to adapt, compromise and evolve strategies which enabled their independence and mutual existence. In the downfall of the Ahom kingdom, it was not the hill tribes who were responsible. The decline was largely owing to the crisis the Ahom social formation was facing by the eighteenth century. The ever reiterated command given by the British to their frontier officers and commandants:

Conciliate these savages if you can. Be persistent in demanding the surrender of murders, but endeavour so to approach the tribes, that a basis may be opened for friendly intercourse in the future.[2]

Notes

1. See Willem Van Schendel, 'The Invention of the 'Jummas': State Formation and Ethnicity in Southeastern Bangladesh,' *Modern Asian Studies*, Vol. 26, No. 1 (Feb. 1992), pp. 95-128; Milton Osborne, *Southeast Asia: An Introductory History*, (First edition 1979), Allen & Unwin, Australia, (10th edition) 2010; James C Scott, *The Art of Not being Governed: An Anarchist History of Upland Southeast Asia*, Yale University Press, 2009, Indian reprint by Orient Black Swan, Hyderabad, 2010; Bengt G. Karlsson, "Evading the State: Ethnicity in Northeast India through the Lens of James Scott," in *Asian Ethnology,* Volume 72, 2 Number 2013.
2. Alexander Mackenzie, *The North-East Frontier of India*, Mittal Publications, New Delhi, 1884, (Reprint 1994) p. 369.

Works Cited Bibliography

Archival Sources

Assam State Archives, Guwahati, Assam

1. Board of Revenue Naga Hills (1770-1789).
2. Bengal Government Papers.
3. Foreign Political Proceedings (FPP), Pol. A, (1770-1931).
4. Political Proceeding, No. 58-61, 18th January-May (1841-1847).
5. Assam Secretariat, File No.177J, Nos.1-6, Serial No. 06, 1882.
6. Assam Commissioner papers, No.419, Major white's sketch report on our relations with the Natives chiefs of Upper Assam, 1838.

National Archives of India, New Delhi

1. Department Branch (1880).
2. Foreign Department proceedings, Extension of the eastern boundary of the Naga Hills District. Restriction regarding trans-frontier tours, External-A, Government of India, No.130- 131, March 1904.
3. Foreign Department, Report on the Trans-Dikhu Tour, 1913.
4. Foreign Departments, External A, Pros. No. 155-167, February, 1890.
5. J.T. Barnard, Report on a second expedition to the "Triangle" for the Liberation of Slaves, season 1927-28.
6. External Affairs Department, Tour of the Konyak Foothills of the Political officer, Tirap Frontier Tract, 1946.

West Bengal State Archives, West Bengal

1. Bengal Government papers (1900-1931)
2. Revenue Proceedings Bengal (1826-1936)
3. Bengal Political Consultations (1835).

Nagaland State Archives, Kohima

1. Judicial (criminal) Department (1840).
2. General Department, Demarcation of the Sibsagar and Naga Hills boundary, 1953.
3. General Department, Slavery in the Un-Administered Area between Assam and Burma, 1913.

4. Foreign Political Proceedings (1880-1944).
5. Judicial Department.
6. Confidential Letters, Nagaland (1900-1921).
7. Revenue Department, No. 780 R. DY REV/55, Government of Nagaland (1828-1922).
8. Government of Nagaland, 34 Culture and Traditional values of the Nagas, File No. 124, Nagaland state Archive, Kohima, 1971.
9. External Affairs Department, Tour of the Konyak Foothills of the Political officer, Tirap Frontier Tract, 1946.

(Select Proceedings: Journals, Political, Judicial, Revenue and Foreign).

Report of visit by Captain Welsh to the Singpho and Naga Frontier of Luckhimpore, No. 225, January 4, 1842.

Report on the Exploration Survey in the Naga Hills (east), 1874, pp. 1-4, on 7th August 1874.

Lieutenant W.A. Holcombe, presented a detailed report of his survey operations to the Deputy Commissioner of Lakhimpur.

Report on the Trans-Dikhu Tour, File No. 469, Government of Nagaland, 1913. Foreign Proceeding, Report of a visit by Captain Vetch to the Singpho and Naga

Frontier of Luckhimpore, 1842.

Foreign Proceeding, Report on the Trans-Dikhu Tour, Government of Nagaland, File No. 469, 1913.

Foreign Political Proceedings (FPP), various years (1800-1940).

Foreign Political Proceeding by T. Brodie, Reports on, No. 6, 26th February 1844.

Foreign Proceeding Periodical (FPP), by Jenkin No. 46, 28th March 1838.

Foreign Proceeding Consultations, No. 16, 21, National Archive of India, December, 1835. Foreign Political Proceedings by T. Brodie, Principal Assistant, No. 5, 15th September, Seebsaugar, 1841.

Bengal Political Consultations, No. 17, 24 November 1835.

Political Department, Expedition from the Upper Chindwin District into Unadministered Naga territory, (Branch Political), 1926.

Appointment and Political Department, Political A. Amendment of the Eastern Boundary of the Naga Hills Districts by inclusion of the Bhitar Namsang Area, File No. 453 Government of Nagaland, 1936.

Letter No. LR-8/71-72/1996 dated 14th July 1972 by Shri S.C. Dey Commissioner of Nagaland, Kohima, address to the Chief Secretary of Nagaland Kohima.

Letter No. 1149-R dated 20th April 1921 Guwahati from B.C. Allen Esquire B.A. (ICS).

Commissioner of the Assam Valley District Division to the Deputy Commissioner of Sibsagar Guwahati, Letter No.1149, 19th January 1921.

Letter No. 4400-R dated Shillong, the 5th December 1921 from the Chief Secretary of the Government of Assam to Commissioner of Suma Valley and Hill divisions in response to Letter No. 899-T dates the 24th October 1921.

Letter No. LR-9-73-74/1046 dated Mokokchung the 26th March 1974 sanction of Rs 1823 for Payment of Revenue to Naga *khat* owners Notified by L. Toshi Ao. Deputy Commissioner of Nagaland and Account branch of D.C. office for release of payment of *khat* revenue.

India, Political Consultation, No. 99, 11 February, 1835.

Letter No. LR-6/63-6/723-26 dated Mokokchung the 25th March 1964. Notified by M.L. Kampani, Deputy Commissioner of Mokokchung. Copy marked to the Chief Secretary of Nagaland, Shillong and Bill Section in duplicate/sanction and release of payment of Revenue of *khat's*.

Revenue Proceedings, Bengal, 1836; 1 March, No. 40; Brodie to Jenkins, 14 November 1835. Revenue Proceeding Bengal 1 March, No. 40, Matthie to Jenkins 15 February 1836.

Selected translate Buranjis (Published and Unpublished)

Assam Buranji, *A Chronicle describing the events of the period from Suhungmung to Gadadhar Singha (1681-1696)* (tr.), No. 7, Vol. V, Pt. VII, DHAS, Guwahati.

Assam Buranji, *A History of Kamrupa with Reference to Its Relations with Neighbouring Kingdoms* (tr.), No. 22, Vol. V, Pt. II, DHAS, Guwahati.

Barua, G.C. (ed.), *Ahom Buranji from the Earliest Times to The End of Ahom Rule,* Spectrum Publication House, Guwahati, 1985.

Bhuyan, S.K. (ed.), *Tungkhungia Buranji 1681-1826 A.D.*, Oxford University Press, 1933.

.................., *Lachit Barphukan And His Times,* DHAS, Gauhati, 1947.

.................., *Satsari Assam Buranji,* Gauhati University, Assam, 1960, (Reprint 1974).

.................., *Kachari Buranji,* Department of Historical and Antiquarian Studies, Guwahati, 2010.

.................., *Deodhai Assam Buranji*, Department of Historical and Antiquarian Studies, Guwahati, 1988.

.................., *Assam Buranji or A History of Assam*, Department of Historical and Antiquarian Studies, Gauhati, 1930.

.................., *Jayantia Buranji,* Department of Historical and Antiquarian Studies, Gauhati, 1937.

Bulletins and Souvenir

Bhuyan, S.K., *Bulletin* No.1, Government of India, DHAS, 1st edition (Reprint 2010).

Hazarika, B.B. (ed.), *Golden Jubilee Celebrations (1928-1978) Souvenir,* DHAS, 1928-79.

Persian Sources

Asif, Mazhar, *Tarikhe-e-Aasham*, Department of Historical and Antiquarian Studies, Guwahati, 2009.

Bhuyan, S.K. (ed.), Mughal Chronicle "*Shihabuddin Talish*," Department of Historical and Antiquarian Studies, Guwahati, 1993.

Gazetteers and Ethnographic Accounts

Allen, B.C., *Gazetteer of Naga Hills and Manipur*, Mittal Publications, New Delhi, 1905, (Reprint 2002).

.................., *Gazetteer of the Khasi & Jaintia Hill, Garo Hills, Lushai Hills,* Delhi, 1980.

Bagchi, R.N., *Gazetteer of India, Arunachal Pradesh, Tirap District,* 1980.

Bareh, Hamlet, *Nagaland District Gazetteer: Kohima*, Publisher Government of Nagaland District Gazetteer Unit,1970.

Butler, John, *A Sketch of Assam*: *with some Account of Hill Tribes*, Smith, Elder and Co., London, 1847.

Butler, J., *Travels and Adventures in the Province of Assam: During a Residence of Fourteen Years*, Smith Elder & Co., London, 1855.

Buchanan, H, *An Account of Assam,* Department of Historical and Antiquarian Studies Assam: Guwahati, 1987, (First complied between 1807-1814), (ed.), S.K. Bhuyan, p. 47.

Carnegy, p. T., *Annual Administration Report of the Naga Hills Political Agency for 1876-11,* Foreign Department Press, Calcutta, 1877.

Choudhury, S.Dutta (ed.), *Gazetteer of India, Arunachal Pradesh Tirap District*, Publisher Directory of Information and Public Relations, Government of Arunachal Pradesh, Shillong, 1980.

Clark, E.W, "Mission to Assam," in *Baptist Missionary Magazine,* 52(I), 125-6, 1872.

David, A.W, *Census of India*, Assam I, 1891.

Dowd, W.F, *Education in Impur Fields' Impur*, Assam, Dated February 5, 1918.

Friminger, Walter K.(ed.), *The Sylhet District Records,* Vol. II (1786-1788), Shillong, 1917.

Gait, E.A, *Assam Census Report 1891,* Vol. I, Printed at the Assam Secretariat Printing office, 1892.

Ghosh, B.B., *Nagaland District Gazetteers, Wokha District,* 1979.

.................., *Nagaland District Gazetteers*, *Mokokchung District,* 1979.

Gurung, Tejimala, "Crisis of Sustenance and Decline of the Ahom State in Eighteenth Century Assam," in J.B. Bhattacharjee and David R. Syiemlieh (eds.), *Early States in North East India,* Regency publication, 2013.

Hamilton, F., *An Account of Assam*: With Some Notices Concerning the Neighbouring Territories/ first comp. in 1807-1814, Department of Historian and Antiquarian Society, Gauhati, 1884, (Reprint 1963).

Hamilton, Walter, *The East-India Gazetteer*, Vol. I, B.R. Publishing Corporation, Delhi, Reprint 1984 (1828).

Haimendorf, C.V.F., *Konyak Nagas*, Rinehart and Winston, New York, 1969.

.................., *Return to the Naked Nagas*, Vikas Publishing House, New Delhi, 1976.

.................., *The Naked Nagas*, Methuen & Company, London,1939.

Hodson, T.C., *The Naga Tribes of Manipur*, Macmillan, London, 1911.

Hunter, W.W., *A Statistical Account of Assam*, Vol. I, Trubner and Co., London, 1897.

Hutton, J.H., *The Sema Nagas*, MacMillan, London, 1921.

.................., *The Angami Nagas*, Macmillan, Bombay, 1969. Iyer, Krishna and

Ratnam, Bala (eds.)., *Anthropology in India*, Bharatiya Vidya Bhavan, Bombay, 1961.

Johnstone, J., 'My Experience in Munnipore and the Naga Hills,' in V Elwin (ed.), *Nagas*, 1969.

Jenkins, Francis, *Relations with the Hills Tribes on the Frontiers of Assam,* 1853, Mills Report.

Kri, Sokhep, *Gazetteer of India, Arunachal Pradesh State Gazetteer*, Vol. I, Government of Arunachal Pradesh, Gazetteers Department, 2010.

Mackenzie, Alexander, *The North-East Frontier of India*, Mittal Publications, New Delhi, 1884, (Reprint 1994).

.................., *History of the Relations of the Government with the Hills Tribes of the North-East Frontier of Bengal*, Calcutta,1884.

M Dorson, Richard, (ed.), *Folklore and Folklife: An Introduction,* University of Chicago Press, 1972.

Michell, F. John, *Report on the North-East Frontier* of India: *A Topographical, Political, and Military Report*, Intelligence Branch, Quarter Master-General's Department in India, Vivek Publishing House, Delhi, 1973.

M'Cosh, John, *Topography of Assam*, G.H. Huttmann, Bengal Military Orphan Press, 1837.

Mills, J.P., *Reports on the Provinces of Assam,* CXXIV, Calcutta, 1854.

.................., *The Wild Tribes of the Naga Hills*, Vol. 7, Calcutta, 1926.

.................., *The Rengma Nagas*, MacMillan, London, 1937.

.................., *The Lhota Nagas*, MacMillan, London, 1922.

.................., *The Ao Nagas,* MacMillan, London, 1926.

Mills, A.J. Moffatt, *Report on the Provinces of Assam,* 1854, (Reprint 1984).

Owen, John, *Notes on The Naga Tribes in Communication with Assam,* British Library, Historical print editions, first editions, London,1844.

Pemberton, R.B., *Report on the Eastern Frontier of British India*, DHAS, Gauhati, 1966, pp. 84-85.

.................., *The Eastern Frontier of India*, Mittal Publications, New Delhi, 1835, (Reprint 1998).

Robinson, William, *A Descriptive Account of Assam with a Sketch of the Local Geography, and a Concise History of the Tea- Plant of Assam: to which is Added a Short Account of the Neighbouring Tribes, Exhibiting their History, Manners and Custom,* Sanskaran Prakahak, Delhi, 1975.

Reid, Robert, *History of the Frontier Areas Bordering on Assam*, The Assam Government Press, Shillong, 1942.

Scott, George, (ed.), *Gazetteer of Upper Burma and Shan States,* Part I, 1900.

Shakespear, L.W., *History of Upper Assam, Upper Burma and North Eastern Frontier,* Macmillan, London, 1914, (Reprint 2004).

.................., *History of the Assam Rifles*, Firma KLM Private LTD, Calcutta, 1977.

Waddell, L.A., *Tribes of the Brahmaputra Valley*, Spectrum Publisher, Guwahati, 1994.

Wade, J.P., *An Account of Assam* (ed.), B. Sarma, North Lakhimpur, 1927.

Secondary Sources

Acharyya, N. N., *Historical documents of Assam and Neighbouring States: Original Records in English,* Omsons Publication, 1966, (Reprint 1983).

.................., *History of Medieval Assam (13th to 17th Centuries),* Omsons Publication, New Delhi, 1966 (Reprint 1984).

.................., *A Brief History of Assam (From Earliest time to the Year 1983),* Omsons Publications, New Delhi, 1987.

………………, *North East as Viewed by Foreigner,* Omsons Publications, Gauhati, 1985, p. 135.

Althusser, Louis and *Reading Capital,* New Left Books, London, 1965.

Alemchiba, M., *A Brief Historical Account of Nagaland,* Naga Institute of Culture Kohima, Nagaland, 1970.

Ao, Temsula, *The Ao-Naga Oral Tradition,* Bhasha Publication, Baroda, 1999.

Ao, Tajenyuba, *British Occupation of Naga Country,* Naga Literature Society, 1993.

Bagchi, P. C., *India and China: A Thousand Years of Cultural Relations,* Hind Kitab Ltd. Bombay, 1950.

Basu, Nirmal Kumar, *Assam in Ahom Age: Being Politico-Economic and Socio-Cultural Studies,* 1970.

Barpujari, H.K., *Problems of the Hills tribes- Northeast Frontier,* Lawyer's Book Stall, Guwahati, 1970.

………………, *Assam in the Days of the Company,* Spectrum Publication, Guwahati, 1980.

………………, *The Comprehensive History of Assam,* Vol I, II and III, Publication Board of Assam, Guwahati, 1990.

………………, *American Missionaries and North-East India* (1836-1900 AD), Spectrum Publication, Guwahati, 1986.

Barua, Hem, *The Red river and the Blue Hill,* Lawyer's Book Stall, Gauhati, 1956.

Barua, B.K., *Cultural History of Assam,* Vol. I, Lawyer's Book Stall, Guwahati, 1951.

Barua, S.N., *Tribes of Indo-Burma Border: A Socio-Cultural History,* New Delhi, 1991.

Baruah, S.L., *A Comprehensive History of Assam,* Munshiram Manoharlal Publishers Pvt. Limited, New Delhi, 2013 (Reprint 2007).

Baruah, Swarna Lata, *Last Days Of Ahom Monarchy: A History Of Assam From 1796 to 1826,* Munshiram Manoharlal Publisher Pvt. Limited, 1993.

Baruah, Sanjib, *Between South and South East Asia: North East India and The Look East Policy,* Centre for North East India, South and Southeast Asia Studies, Guwahati, 2004, p. 19.

www.cenisea.org/publications/sanjib baruah.pdf.

Bendangangshi, *Glimpse of Naga History,* Published by Naga Patriots of Soyim, Mokokchung, Nagaland, 1993.

Bhattacharyya, S.N., *A History of Mughal North-East India Frontier Policy,* Chuckerverty Chatterjee & Co. Ltd, Calcutta, 1929.

Bhattacharjee, J.B. (ed.), *Studies in the History of North-East India,* North-Eastern Hill University, 1986.

Bhuyan, S.K., *Anglo-Assamese Relations, 1771-1826: A History Of The Relations Of Assam With The East India Company From 1771 to 1826,* Department of Historical and Antiquarian Studies in Assam, Guwahati, 1949.

………………, *Studies in the History of Assam,* Srimati Lakshewari Bhuyan company Bagan Road, Gauhati, 1965.

………………, *Atan Buragohain and His Times,* Lawyer's Book Stall, Gauhati, Assam, 1975.

………………, *An Assamese Nur Jur Jahan,* Published by the author at Gauhati, Assam, 1926.

………………, *Lachit Barphukan and His Times,* DHAS, Guwahati, 1947.

Bhuyan, A.C., *The Political History of Assam,* Sariaghat Press, Guwahati, 1977 (Reprint 1999).

………………, *The Administrative System of Assam,* Lawyer's Book Stall, Guwahati, 1992.

Boruah, B.K., *Nagamese the Language of Nagaland,* Mittal Publication, New Delhi, 1993.

Chakrovorty, B.C., *British Relations with the Hills Tribes of Assam since 1858,* K.L. Mukhopadhya, Calcutta, 1964.

Choudhury, N.D., *Historical Archaeology of Central Assam (From Earliest Time to 12th Century A.D),* B.R. Publishing Corporation, Delhi, 1985.

Choudhury, Pratab Chandra, *The History of Civilisation of the People of Assam to the Twelfth Century,* Spectrum Publication, Guwahati, 1959 (Reprint 2017).

Chatterji, Suniti Kumar, *The Place of Assam in the History and Civilisation of India,* Department of Publication, University of Gauhati, 1970.

Coedes, George, *The Making of South East Asia,* English Tr. By H.M. Wright, Routledge& Kegan Paul, London, 1966.

Danda, Dipali G., *Among the Dimasa of Assam: An Ethnographic Study,* Sterling, New Delhi, 1978.

Darity Jr. William A. *International Encyclopaedia of the Social Science,* Vol. II, Macmillan, USA, 2008.

Das, S.T., *Tribal Development and Social-Cultural Matrix,* Distributors, Delhi, 1993.

Das, N. K. and *People of India Nagaland,* Vol. XXXIV, Anthropological.

Dewan, Maniram, *Buranji Bibekaratna, Asamiya Bibhaga,* Dibrugarh Bisvabidyalaya, 2002.

Devi, Lakshmi, *Ahom-Tribal Relations: A Political Study,* Spectrum Publication House, Gauhati, 1968.

Dutta, Promatha Nath, *Glimpses into the History of Assam,* Vidyodaya Library Private Ltd., Calcutta, 1964.

N Elias, N., *Introductory Sketch of the History of the Shans in Upper Burma and Western Yunnan,* Printed at the Foreign Department Press, Calcutta, 1876.

Elwin, Verrier, *Nagaland,* Research Department Advisors Secretariat, Shillong, 1961.

.................., *A Philosophy for NEFA,* Directorate of Research Government of Arunachal Pradesh, first published 1957 (Reprint 1998).

.................., *India's North-East Frontier in the Nineteenth Century,* Oxford University Press, 1959.

.................., *The Kingdom of the Young: Abridged from the Muria and their Ghotul,* Oxford University Press, London, 1986.

Febvre, Lucien, *A Geographical Introduction to History,* Kegan Paul, Trench Trubner & Co. Ltd, New York, 1925.

Gait, Edward, *A History of Assam,* Lawyer's Book Stall, Gauhati Assam, 1906, (Reprint 1984).

Gammell, William, *A History of American Baptist Missions in Asia, Africa, Europe and North America,* Gould, Kendall and Lincoln, Boston, 1849.

Ganguli, M., *A Pilgrimage to the Nagas,* Oxford & IBH, New Delhi, 1984.

Ghosh, B.B., *History of Nagaland,* S. Chand, New Delhi, 1982.

Gohain, Uma Nath, *Assam Under the Ahom,* Spectrum Publication, Gauhati, 1942.

Gogoi, Padmeswar, *The Tai and the Tai Kingdoms,* Publication Board of Assam, 1968.

.................., *Tai Ahom religion and customs,* Publication Board, Gauhati, First Published 1976.

Gogoi, Jahnabi, *Agrarian System of Medieval Assam,* Concept Publishing Company, New Delhi, 2002.

Gogoi, Lila, *The Buranjis Historical Literature of Assam (A Critical Survey),* New Delhi, 1986.

Goswami, S.K., *A History of Revenue Administration of Assam,* Spectrum Publication, New Delhi, 1993.

Grierson, P. J Hamilton, *The Silent Trade: A Contribution to the Early History of Human Intercourse,* Edinburgh William Green & Sons Law Publishers, 1903.

Grierson, G.A., *Linguistic Survey of India (1898-1927),* Vol. 1, Part 1, Motilal Banarasidas, Delhi, (Reprint 1967), p. 42.

Guha, Amalendu, *Medieval and Early Colonial Assam: Society, Polity, Economy,* Publisher South Asia Books, New Delhi, 1991.

Guha, A., "The Ahom political system: an enquiry into the state formation process in medieval Assam, 1228-1714" *Social Scientist,* 11 (12), 1983.

Gudeman, Stephen and Rivera, Alberto, *Conversations in Columbia: The Domestic Economy in life and Text,* Cambridge University Press, London, 1990.

Holmes, Winfred., *Tekhi's Hunting: A Story of Naga Hills,* G. Bells and Sons Ltd, London, 1941.

Horam, M., *Naga Polity,* B.R. Publishing Corporation, Delhi, 1975.

.................., *Social and Cultural Life of Nagas (The Tangkhul Nagas).* B.R. Corporation, Delhi, 1977.

Holcombe, Sarah, The Politico-Historical Construction of the Pintupi Luritja and the Concept of Tribe, in *Oceania,* Vol. 74, No. 4, June 2004, p. 257.

Imchen, Panger, *Ancient Ao Naga religion and Culture,* Har-Anand Publications, New Delhi, 1993.

Jesse, F.Tennyson, *The Story of Burma,* Macmillan, London, 1946.

Johnstone, James, *Manipur and Naga Hills,* Gyan Publishing House, 5. Ansari Road, New Delhi, 2002.

Jacob, J., *The Nagas, Hill People of North East India Society, Culture and the Colonial encounter,* Edition Hanjsorg Mayer, West Germany, 1990.

Kalita, B.C., *Military Activities in Medieval Assam,* Spectrum Publications, New Delhi, 1986.

Kanchan, R.K., *Hindu Kingdoms of South-East Asia,* Cosmo Publication, New Delhi, 1990.

Kikon, Dolly, *Living with Oil & Coal Resource Politics & Militarisation in Northeast India,* Yoda Press, New Delhi, 2020.

Konyak, Yanang, A., *From Darkness to Light,* Christian Literature Centre, Gauhati, 1986.

Konyak, Metjen, L., *The Socio-Cultural and Political Significance of the Monarchical System of the Konyak Nagas,* Indian Society for Promoting Christian Knowledge, New Delhi, 2003.

Konyak, Chingang, *The Konyak Naga: Yesterday and Today,* Konyak Literature Committee, Dimapur, 2008.

Kumar, B.B., *The Tribal Societies of India: A Macro Perception,* Omsons Publication, New Delhi, 1998.

………………., *Naga Identity,* Concept Publishing Company, New Delhi, 2005.

………………., *Introduction to the Naga Tribes,* Prakashan Publication, Meerut, 1977, p. 53.

Leach, Edmund, *Political Systems of Highland Burma A study of Kachin Social Structure,* Fletcher and Son Ltd, Norwich, first published 1954 (Reprint 1964).

Lehman, F.L., *The Structure of Chin Society: A Tribal People Of Burma Adapted In A Non-Western Civilisation,* The University of Ilinois Press, 1963.

Lotha, Abraham., *History of Naga Anthropology, 1832-1947,* Chumpo Museum, Dimapur, 2007.

Lyall, Charles (ed.), *The Mikir;* from the papers of the late Edward Stack published by the Government of Eastern Bengal and Assam, D. Nutt, London, 1908.

Mauss, Marcel, *The Gift the form and reason for exchange in archaic societies,* Routledge classics London and New York, 1954.

Majumdar, D.N., *Races and Cultures of India,* Asia Publishing House, Allahabad, 1944.

Majumdar, R.C., *Hindu Colonies in The Far East,* General printers & publishers limited, Calcutta, 1944.

Misra, Udayon, *The Periphery Strikes Back: Challenge to the Nation-State in Assam and Nagaland,* Indian Institute of Advanced Study, Shimla, 2000.

Mufwene, Salikoko S., *The Evolution of Language: Hints from Creoles and Pidgins in Language,* Evolution and the Brain, James Minett & William Wang (eds.), City University of Hong Kong Press, 2009.

Nag, Sajal, *Contesting Marginality, Ethnicity, Insurgency and Sub-Nationalism in North-East India,* Manohar Publishers & Distributors, New Delhi, 2002.

Neog, Maheswar (ed.), *Studies in the Early History of Assam,* Asam Sahitya Sabha, Gauhati, 1973.

Nshoga, A., *Traditional Naga Village System and its Transformation,* Maulana Abul Kalam Azad Institute of Asian Studies, Kolkata, 2009.

Oppitz, Micheal, *Naga Identities; Changing Local Culture in the Northeast India,* Snoeck Zurich, 2008.

Prakash, Ved, *Encyclopaedia of North-East India,* Vol. 5, Atlantic Publishers and Distributors Ltd., 2007.

Ramuny, Murkot, *The World of Nagas,* Northern Book Centre, New Delhi, 1988.

Rattan, R.H., *Moina of Ancient Ahom-Nokpu Naga Relation,* Shree Venkateswara, New Delhi, 2004.

Raatan, T., *History of Religion and Culture of North East India,* Isha Publication, Delhi, 2011.

Raychaudhuri, Tapan and Habib Irfan (eds.), *The Cambridge Economic History of India,* Vol. I, c.1200-c.1750, Cambridge University Press, p. 478.

Rengma, G., *Political History of Rengma Naga,* 2006, printed at innovation, Dimapur, Nagaland, 2015.

Renford, R.K., *The Non-official British in India to 1920,* Oxford University Press, 1987.

Roland, Shimmi, Y.L., *Comparative History of the Nagas from Ancient Period till* 1826, Inter-India Publications, New Delhi, 1988.

Roy, C., *The Oraon of Chota Nagpur,* Bar Library Ranchi, 1925.

Roy, Sachin, *Aspects of Padam-Miniyong Culture,* Publisher North-East Frontier Agency, Shillong, 1960.

Rowney, H.B., *The Wild Tribes of India,* Thos, De La Rue & Co. London, 1882.

Sanyu, Vizier, *A History of Nagas and Nagaland (Dynamics of Oral Tradition in Village Formation,* Commonwealth Publishers, New Delhi, 1996.

Sarma, A.C., *Tai-Ahom System of Government,* B.K. Publishing House, Delhi, 1986.

Sardeshipande, S.C., *The Patkoi Nagas,* Daya Publishing House, Delhi, 1987.

Samanta, R.K. (ed.), *India's North-East the Process of Change and Development,* B.R. Publishing Corporation, 2002.

Sema, Hokishe, *Emergence of Nagaland Socio-Economic and Political Transformation and the Future,* Vikash Publishing House, Ltd, New Delhi, 1986.

Sen, Sipra, *Tribes and Castes of Assam:* Anthropology and Sociology, Gyan Publishing House, New Delhi, 1999.

Sdb, Thomas Vattoth, *The Wanchos in Transition,* Published by Don Bosco Youth & Educational Services, Dimapur, Nagaland, 2008.

Sharma, R.S. (ed), *Land Revenue in India: Historical Studies,* Motilal Banarsidass, Delhi, 1971.

Shimmi, Y.L. Roland, *Comparative History of the Nagas from Ancient period till 1826,* Inter-India Publications, New Delhi, 1988.

Singh, J.P. (ed.), *The Coinage and Economy of North Eastern States,* NSI, Varanasi, 1977.

Smith, W.C., *The Ao Naga Tribe of Assam: A Study in Ethnology and Sociology,* Macmillan, London,1925.

Sinha, Surajit, *Tribal polities and State system in Pre-Colonial Eastern and North Eastern India,* Centre for Studies in Social Science, Calcutta, 1987.

Singh, Kanwar Randip, *The Nagas of Nagaland Desperadoes and Heroes of Peace,* Deep & Deep Publication, New Delhi, 1987.

Singh, K.S. and Imchen, C.L., People of India Nagaland, Vol. XXXIV, Anthropological Survey of India, Calcutta, 1994.

Simionescu, Maya, and Simion, Eugen, *Scientific Lingua Franca and National Languages at the Crossroads,* in ALLEA Biennial Yearbook 2004.

Smith, W.C., *The Ao Nagas Tribes of Assam,* MacMillan, London, 1925.

Spengen, Wim van., *Tibetan Border Worlds. A Geo-Historical Analysis of Trade and Traders,* Kegan Paul International, London, 2000.

Stracey, P. D., *Nagaland Nightmare,* Allied Publishers Private Limited, New Delhi, 1968.

Taussig, Micheal, *The Devil and Commodity Fetishism in South America,* University of North Carolina Press, 1980.

Tekatemjen, *Studies on Theology and Naga Culture,* C.T.C. Aolijen, Mokokchung, Nagaland, 1996.

Terweil, B.J., *The Tais of Assam and Ancient Tai Ritual,* Gaya Centre for South East Asia Studies, 1980-1981.

Thong, Tezenlo, *Progress and Impact on the Nagas a Clash of World-views,* Ashgate Publishing Limited, England, 2014.

Thong, Joseph S., *Glimpse of Naga Legacy and Culture,* Published by Society for Naga Students Welfare, Kottayam Kerala, 2011, pp. 209-211.

Tonybee, Arnold J., *A Study of History,* Vol. XII, Oxford University Press, 1967.

Trivedi, V.R. (ed.), *Important Events of Assam,* Omsons publications, New Delhi, 1997.

Vansina, Jan, *Oral Traditional as History: A Study in Historical Methodology,* The University of Wisconsin Press, 1985.

Vasu, Narendra Nath, *The Social History of Kamarupa,* Vol. I, Northern Book Centre, New Delhi, first print 1983 (Reprint 1999).

Ward, A.W. *et.al.,* *The Cambridge Modern History: The Growth of Nationalties,* Vol. XI, 1990.

Walim, M.M., *History of the Konyak Baptist Church Association from 1950 to Present Time,* Published by author, Mon Theological College, Nagaland, 2005.

Waters, Thomas, *On Yuan Chwang's travel in India,* Vol. III, Part II, Varanasi, 1903.

West, A C., *Nineteen Century Naga-Material Culture,* Newsletter, 1985.

Wim, Van Spengen, *Tibetan Border Worlds: A Geo Historical Analysis of Trade and Trader,* Kegan Paul International, London, 2000.

Yonuo, Asoso, *The Rising Nagas: A Historical and Political Study,* Vivek Publishing House, Delhi, 1984.

Articles

Ahmad, Nisar, "Assam-Bengal Trade in the Medieval Period: A Numismatic Perspective," in *Journal of Economic and Social History of the Orient,* Vol. 33, No. 2, 1990.

Anju, Dai, "The Social and Economic Development of the Dai Community in Dehong," in *Proceeding of the International Conference on Thai Studies,* Kunming, 1990.

Barpujari, S.K., "Raja Purandar Singha's Management of Salt- Wells in the Naga Hills" in J.B. Bhattacharjee, (ed.), in *Studies in the Economic History of North East India,* Har- Anand Publications, New Delhi, 1994.

Barua, Kanaklal, "Pre-Historic Culture in Assam," (ed.), in S.K. Sarma. & Usha Sharma, *Discovery of North-East India,* Vol. 5, Mittal Publications, 2005.

Bhuyan, S.K., *An Assamese Nur Jur Jahan,* Published by the author at Gauhati, Assam, 1926.

Bhattacharya, P. C., "A Few Elements of the Indo-Mongoloid Boro Culture," in *the Journal of the Assam Research Society,* Vol. XVI, 1964.

Blochmann, H., "Koch Bihar, Koch Hajo, and Asam, in the 16th and 17th Centuries, according to the Akbarnamah, the Padishahnamah, and the Fathiyah i Ibriyah," in *Journal of Asiatic Society of Bengal,* 1872.

Bose, S.K. "The Ao Nagas and their Medium of Exchange," in Fozail Ahmad Qadri (ed.), *Society and Economy in North-East India,* 2006.

Butler, John, "Rough Notes On the Angami Nagas," Vol. XLIV, in *Journal of the Asiatic Society of Bengal,* Calcutta, 1875.

Chatterjee, Indrani (ed.)., "Slaver, Semantics, and the Sound of Silence," in *Slavery and South Asian History,* Bloomington & Indianapolis: Indiana University Press, 2006.

Deka, Meeta, "Historical Matrix of Nagamese as a Communilects in Northeast India," in *Proceedings of North East India History Association,* Mirza, 2017.

Godden, Gertrude, "Naga and Other Frontier Tribes of North-East India," in *The Journal of the Anthropological Institute of Great Britain and Ireland,* Vol. 26, 1897.

Gogoi, L., "The Age-old Amity of the Hills and the Plains," in *The Outlook on NEFA,* (eds.) by P. Chaliha, Assam Sahitya Sabha, Jorhat, Assam, 1958.

Gogoi, P. D., "The Konyak Nagas: A Case Study of the Hahchara Naga Village," in *Proceeding of North East India History Association,* 20th, Dibrugarh, 2000.

Gogoi, N.K., "History through Folk-Narratives Understanding Ahom-Tribal Relation," in *Indian Journal of Tai Studies,* Vol. IX, Moranhat, 2009.

Gordon, P., "Human Sacrifice and Slavery in the "Un-administered" Areas of Upper Burma During the Colonial Era," in *Journal of Social Issues in Southeast Asia,* Vol. 15, No. 2, October 2000.

Goswami, S., "The Eastern Nagas and the Salt Trade of Upper Assam," in *North East India History Association, 13th Session,* Aizawl, 1984.

Goswami, S.C., "Jabilee of the Naga Coin," in *Journal of Assam Research Society,* Vol. VII. Gauhati, 1939.

Grange, E.R., "Extract from the Narrative of an Expedition into the Naga Territory of Assam," in *Journal of Asiatic Society,* part I, 1840.

Grierson, A., "Linguistic Survey of India," Vol. I, part I, Tibeto-Burman Family, Calcutta, 1847, p. 42, quoted in NSF Seminar paper, 1995.

Guha, Amalendu, "The Ahom Political System: An Enquiry into the State Formation Process in Medieval Assam (1228-1714)," in *Social Scientist,* Vol. 11, No. 12, December 1983.

Gurung, Tejimala, "The Concept of Social Formation: A Study in its Theory and Practice in India," in *NEHU Journal of Social Sciences and Humanities,* Vol. XI, No. 2, April-June 1993.

………………..., "Emergence of the Ahom Monarchy in Upper Assam (13th-15th Century)," in F.A. Qadri (eds.), *Society and Economy,* Vol. 2, Regency Publication, New Delhi, 2006.

………………..., "Social Formation in Eighteenth Century Assam," Dept. of History, NEHU, Shillong, 1990.

Haimendorf, C.V.F., "Youth-Dormitories and Community House in India. A Restatement and a Review," in *Journals of Anthropos,* Bd, 45, H. 1/3, Published by Anthropos Institute, January and June, 1950.

http://www.jstor.org/stable/40450833, Accessed, 11-12-2015 09:15 UTC.

………………..., "Comparisons between the Mountain Peoples of the Philippines and some tribes of North-East India," in *The Geographical Journal,* Vol. 123, No. 3, Sept., 1971.

………………..., "Social and Cultural Change among the Konyak Nagas," *Highlander the Bulletin of the Cultural Research and State Museum Nagaland, Kohima,* Vol. 1, Cultural Research and State Museum, Nagaland, March 1973.

Halder, Tarun Kr., "Town, Market Centers and Trading Networks in Medieval Assam," in *International Journal of Applied Research,* 3(3), 2017.

Hodgson, B.G., "Route from Cathmandu in Nepal to Tazedo, on the Chinese Frontier," in *The Journal of the Asiatic Society,* XVII, 1832, pp. 513-534.

Holcombe, Sarah, The Politico-Historical Construction of Pintupi Luritja and the Concept of Tribe, in *Oceania,* Vol. 74, No. 4, June 2004.

Hornell, J., The Chank shell cult of India, *Antiquity* 16:113-33, 1942.

Hutton, J.H., "The significance of Head-Hunting in Assam," in *The Journal of the Royal Anthropological Institute of Great Britain and Ireland,* Vol. 58. July 1928.

………………..., "Head-Hunters of the North-East Frontier," in Journal of the Royal Society of Arts, Vol. 85, No. 4387, December 18, 1936.

Imchen, C.L., "Naga Myths of Origin and Historical Reconstruction," in C.A. Mawlong and Mignonette Momin (eds.), *Society and Economy in North-East India,* Vol. 1, Regency Publications, New Delhi, 2004.

………………..., "History of the Relations between the Nagas and the Valley Kingdoms," in Fozail Ahmad Qadri (ed.), *Society and Economy in North-East India,* Vol. 2, Regency Publication, New Delhi, 2006.

Jamir, Tiatoshi and Manzil Hazarika (eds.), *50 years After Daojali-Hading: Emerging Perspectives in the Archaeology of Northeast India,* Research India Press, New Delhi, 2014.

Jamir, Tiatoshi, "Late first millennium BC to second millennium AD agriculture in Nagaland: a reconstruction based on archaeology botanical evidence and radiocarbon dates," in *Current Science,* Vol. 104, No. 10, 25, May 2013.

Jamir, Tiatoshi *et.al.,* *Archaeology of Naga Ancestral Sites: Recent Archaeology Investigating in Phek and Kiphire District of Nagaland,* Vol. 2. Heritages Publishing House ,Dimapur, Nagaland, 2014.

Jha, Braj Narain, "Politics of Posa: A Case Study of Pre- and Post-independence scenario in Arunachal Pradesh and Assam," in *Proceeding of the Indian History Congress,* Vol. 57, 1996.

Jenkins, H.L., "Notes on the Burmese Route from Assam to the Hookoong Valley," in *Hill Tracts Between Assam and Burma Selection of Papers,* Vivek Publishing Company, Delhi, 1978.

Katz, Milton, "Gennain South-Eastern Asia," in *American Anthropologist, New Series,* Vol. 30, No. 4, December, 1928.

Kakoty, Sanjeep, "Agrarian Dynamics and Technology in the Ahom State," in Fozail Ahmad Qadri (ed.), *Society and Economy in North-East India,* Vol. 2, Regency Publication, New Delhi, 2006.

Kalu, Ogbu U., "Myth in Africa: A Study of its Aesthetic and Cultural Relevance," in *The Journal of Religion in Africa,* Vol. 19, Fasc. 1 Feb., 1989.

Kanungo, Alok Kumar, "Naga Ornaments and the Indian Ocean," in *Indo-Pacific Pre-History Association Bulletin* 26, 2006.

Keththolesie, "British Administrative policy in the Naga Hills," in *International Journal of Languages, Education and Social Science,* (Vol. 17, Issue 01), June 2015, www.illess.com, Accessed, 15-10-2014 09:30 UTC.

Khongreiwo, Rammathot, "Raids, Customary Laws and Slavery: Re-interpreting Pre-colonial Naga Warfare," in *NMML Occasional Paper, History and Society New Series* 39, Nehru Memorial Museum and Library Teen Murti House, New Delhi, 2003.

Kikon, Dolly, "Borders, Bagaans, and Bazaars, Locating the foothills along the Naga hills in Northeast India," in *Essay Biblio,* May-June 2008.

Konyak, N. Nyejat, "Understanding Ahom-Konyak Relations through Folk-Narratives" in *North-East India History Association* (NEIHA), 38thSession, ISSN 2349 753X, 2nd-4th October 2017.

Kroeber, A.L. and Talcott Parsons, "The Concepts of Culture and Social System," in *American Sociological Review,* XXIII, October, 1958.

Longchar, A.Wati, "American Baptist Missionaries' Role in Abolishing Slavery in North East India," in *Encounter between Gospel and Tribal Cultures,* A. Wati Longchar (ed.), Tribal Study Centre, etc., Jorhat, Assam, 1999.

Longchar, L.K., "The Missionary Position and the Nagas," in *Morung Express,* Dimapur, 28th October 2008.

Luthra, P.N., "North-East Frontier Agency tribes: impact of Ahom and British policy," in *Economic and Political Weekly* 6 (23), pp. 1143-1149, 1971.

Malinowski, B., "The Primitive Economic of the Trobriand Islanders," in *The Economic Journal,* Vol. 31, No. 121, Mar 1921.

Mills, J.P., "Certain Aspects of Naga Culture," in *Journal of the Royal Anthropological Institute of Great Britain and Ireland,* Vol. 56, Royal Anthropological Institute of Great Britain and Ireland, 1926.

http://www.jstor.org/stable/2843597, Accessed, 07-09-2016 05:25 UTC.

Mills, J.P., "Assam as a field for Research," in *The Journal of the Assam Research Society,* Vol. 1, No. 1, 1933.

Misra, Sanghamitra, "The Nature of Colonial Intervention in the Naga Hills, 1840-80," in *Economic and Political Weekly,* Vol. 33, Dec, 19-25, 1998.

Momin, Mignonette, "Contextualizing Origin Myths of Northeast India," in *Proceeding of North East India History Association, Twenty second session,* Darrang College, Tezpur, 2001.

Momin, Mignonette, "Acquisition and Distribution of Wealth: An enquiry into the rise of Pragjyotisa-Kamarupa," in Mignonette Momin and Cecile A. Mawlong (eds.), *Society and Economy in North East India* (Vol. 1), Regency Publications, New Delhi, 2005.

Mumtaza, I.S., "Some Source Material on the Ahom-Jayantia Trade Relations," in *Proceedings of North East India History Association 20th Session,* Dibrugarh University, Dibrugarh, 2000.

Muntaza, I.S., "Posa: Was it a Black-mail," in *Proceeding of North East India History Association, 14th session,* Jorhat, Shillong, 1993.

Nag, Sajal, "Contesting Exclusion, Resisting Inclusion: Contradictory Trends in Historical Research in North East India (1800-1900)," in Sabyasachi Bhattacharya, *Approaches to History,* ICHR, 2005, (Reprint 2015).

Peal, S.E., "Notes on a visit to the tribes inhabiting the hills south of Sibsagar Assam," in *Journal of Asiatic Society Bengal,* No. 1, 1872.

Phukan, J.N., "Relations of the Ahom Kings of Assam with those of Mong Mao (in Yunnan, China) and Mong Kwang (Mogaung in Myanmar)," in *Proceedings of the India History Congress,* Vol. 52, 1991.

Phukon J.N. & Phukon, Girin, "Socio-cultural Heritage of the Ahom," in *Indian Journal of Tai Studies,* Vol. X, Moranhat, Assam, 2010, p. 17.

Rao, Narayan Singh, "A Note on the History of the Longchang Tangsas of Arunachal Pradesh," in *North East India History Association proceedings 27th session,* Mizoram University Aizawl, 2006, pp. 128-129.

Rohman, F.A., "Folk-Narratives and Social Reality in Northeast India," in *Proceeding of the National Seminar on Oral Literature of Northeast India with special reference to Arunachal Pradesh,* Department of Tribal Studies, Itanagar, 1998.

Sharma, Manorama, "Trends, Possibilities and Problems in History Writing in Pre-Colonial North East India Economy and Society," in F.A. Qadri (ed.), *Society and Economy in North-East India,* Vol. 2, Regency Publications, New Delhi, 2006.

Idem, 'Trends of History Writing in North East India Assessment of works on the Pre-Ahom-18th Century,' in D.R. Syiemlieh and Manorama Sharma (ed.), *Society and Economy in North East India,* Vol. 3, Regency Publications, New Delhi, 2008.

Sadir, M., "The Ahoms: Their origin, manners and customs," in *Journal of the Royal Society of Arts,* Vol. 62, No. 3197, 27th February 1914.

Saha, N., "Naga: Konyak," in K. S. Singh, N. K. Das and C. L. Imchen (eds.), *People of India: Nagaland,* Vol. XXXIV, Anthropological Surveys of India, Seagull Books, Calcutta, 1994.

Sarkar, Jadunath, "Assam and the Ahom in 1660 A.D," in *Journal of the Bihar and Orissa Research Society,* Vol. 1, 1915.

Sarkar, Jadunath (Tr.), Shihabuddin Talish, Fathiya-i-Ibriya, 1663, "Assam and the Ahoms in 1660 A.D." in *Journal of the Bihar and Orissa Research Society* (JBORS), Vol. I, 1915, p. 118.

Singh, Chandrika, "Nagaland: From a District to a State: Culmination of Democratic Political Process," in *Indian Journal of Political Science,* Vol. 41, Indian Political Science Association, December 1980.

http://www.jstor.org/stable/41855059,Accessed:16-05-2016 06:14 UTC.

Stockhausen, Alban von, "Watlong, the Naga queen: negotiating local identities through narratives," in *Asian Ethnicity,* Vol. 17, No. 3, 2016

Thakur, Amrendra Kr., "Pattern of Pre-Colonial Trade and Polity Formations in Arunachal Pradesh: A Study of their Relationship" in *Proceedings of North East India History Association,* Imphal Session, 2002.

Idem, "Polity of Pre-Colonial Arunachal Pradesh: Interactions in Trade, Culture, State and Buddhism," in S. Dutta and B. Tripathy (eds.), *Buddhism in North-East India,* Indus Publishing Company, New Delhi, 2006.

Tinker, Hugh, "A Forgotten Long March: The Indian Exodus from Burma, 1942," in *Journal of Southeast Asian Studies* 6:1, 1975.

Wangsa, Peihwang, *Christianity and Social Change: A Case Study of Konyak,* Barkataki and Company Pvt. Ltd, Assam, 2000.

Wangjin, W., "Ideologies, Identities and Memories: Interpreting Stone Structure of the Konyak and Angami Nagas," in Tiatoshi Jamir and Manzil Hazarika (eds.), 50 Years After Daojali-Hading; Emerging Perspectives in the Archaeology of Northeast India, in *Research India Press,* New Delhi, 2014.

Wandell, L.A., "Tribes of the Brahmaputra valley," in *Journal of the Asiatic Society of Bengal,* No. 1, 1900.

Wilcox. R., "Memory of the Survey of Assam and the Neighbouring Countries, executed in 1825-1828," in *Selection of Papers Regarding The Hill Tracts Between Assam And Burmah and On The Upper Brahmaputra,* Bengal Secretariat Press, Calcutta, 1873, (Reprint 1978).

Woodthorpe, R.G., "Notes on the Wild Tribes Inhabiting the So-called Naga Hills on our North-East Frontier of India Part. II," in *Journal of the Anthropological Institute of Great Britain and Ireland* 11, 1882, p. 63.

Unpublished thesis

Borthakur, Manjula, "The Periodic Market System: A Comparative Study of Tribal and Peasant Economic with Special Reference to N.E. India," Ph.D. Dissertation, North Eastern Hill University, Shillong, 1993.

Enie, Lichumo, "Trade Relationship between Nagaland and Ahom," Ph.D. Dissertation, Department of History and Archaeology, Nagaland University, Kohima, Nagaland, 2016, p. 38.

Geoffrey, Marrison Edward, "The classification of the Naga languages of North-East India," Ph.D. Dissertation, Department of Phonetic and Linguistic, School of Oriental and African Studies, University of London, 1967.

Gogoi, Janhnabi Nathe, "Agrarian, System of Medieval Assam," PhD Dissertation, Dept. of History, Dibrugarh University, Assam, 1993.

Gurung, Tejimala, "Social Formation in Eighteenth Century Assam", Ph.D, Dissertation, Dept. of History, NEHU, Shillong, 1990.

Mundunsungkham, "The Casket of Gold; Aspects of the Economy, Society

Liza Talukdar, and Culture Under the Ahom rule circa 13th-18th," M.Phil., Dissertation, JNU, New Delhi, 2004.

Sanglier, Chubala, "Society and Economy of the Nagas From pre-Colonial to Colonial Period," Ph.D. Dissertation, Nagaland University, Lumami, 2012.

Wangjin,W., "On phenomenon, different perceptions: the case of stone structures of the Naga Hills and in Vidarbha," M.Phil. Dissertation, Jawaharlal Nehru University, New Delhi, 2011.

Walling, Aokumla, "Oral Traditions and Archaeological Reconstructing the Pre Colonial History of Ao Nagas with special reference to the Naga Ahom Relationship," PhD Dissertation, Department of Deccan College Post Graduate and Research Institute, 2016, pp. 46-47.

Appendices

Appendix - I

Chronology of Ahom Kings

List of Rulers		Period of Reign	Capital
1.	Suteupha	1228-1268 A.D.	Chairaideo
2.	Suteupha	1268-1281	Chairaideo
3.	Subinpha	1281-1293	Chairaideo
4.	Sukhrangpha	1295-1364	Chairaideo
5.	Sutupha	1364-1376	------
6.	Interregnus	1376-1380	------
7.	Tyaokhamti	1380-1389	Chairaideo
	Interregnum	1389-1397	--------
8.	Sudanpha	1397-1407	-------
9.	Sujangpha	1407-1422	Sargua
10.	Suphakpha	1422-1439	Sargua
11.	Susenpha	1439-1488	Sargua
12.	Sehenpha	1488-1493	------
13.	Supimpha	1493-1497	Sargua
14.	Suhummung (Dihingia Raja)	1497-1539	Sargua, Bakata
15.	Suklenmung (Gargayan Raja or Deka)	1539-1552	Gorgaon
16.	Sukhampha (Khora Raja)	1552-1603	----
17.	Susenpha (Burha Raja or Pratap Singh)	1603-1641	Gorgaon
18.	Surampha (Bhaga Raja)	1641-1644	---
19.	Sutyinpha (Naria Raja)	1644-1648	----
20.	Sutamla (Jayadhwaj Singha)	1648-1663	----
21.	Supungmung (Chakradhwaj Singha)	1663-1669	---
22.	Sungyatpha (Udayaditya Singha)	1669-1673	---
23.	Suklampha (Ramadhwaj)	1669-1673	----
24.	Suhung	1673-1675	---
25.	Gobar Raja only for 20 days	1675	----
26.	Sujinpha (Arjun Dihingia Raja)	1675-1677	----
27.	Sudaipha (Parvatia Raja)	1677-1679	----

28.	Sulipha (Ratnadhwaj) Lora Raja	1679-1681	Gorgaon
29.	Supatpha (Gadadhar Singha)	1681-1696	Gorgaon
30.	Sukhrungpha (Rudra Singha)	1696-1714	Gorgaon, Rongpur
31.	Sutanpha (Siva Singha)	1714-1744	Rongpur
32.	Sunenpha (Pramatha Singha)	1744-1751	Rongpur
33.	Surampha (Rajeswar Singha)	1751-1769	----
34.	Sunyeopha (Lakshmi Singha)	1769-1780	----
35.	Suhitpangpha (Gaurinath Singha)	1780-1795	Rongpur, Jorhat
36.	Suklingpha (Kamaleshwar Singha)	1795-1811	Jorhat
37.	Sudingpha (Chandrakanta Singha)	1811-1818	Jorhat
38.	Purandhar Singha	1818-1819	----
39.	Chandrakanta Singha (Second time)	1819-1821	---
40.	Jogeswar Singha (Puppet Monarch in the hand of Burmese ruler)	1819-1821	Jorhat
41.	Burmese Rule	1819-1824	Jorhat
42.	British Conquest Lower Assam	1824	Jorhat
43.	British Conquest of Upper Assam (Purandar Singha)	1825	Jorhat
44.	February 24, Treaty of Yandabo, by which the king of Burma ceded Assam to the British	1826	Jorhat
45.	Purandhar Singha (puppet to British) resumption of the territories by the East India Company	1833-1838	Jorhat

Appendix - II

Buranjis Name for Various Naga Tribes

Buranjis Nagas Name	Modern Naga Names
Abor	Adi (Assam, Arunachal Pradesh)
Aka or Hruso	West Kameng (Arunachal Pradesh)
Aitoniyas	Now a sub-tribe of Ahom
Banjapree	Changlang, district (a tributary to both Paneedwar and Borduriya)
Banferas (Tirap)	Runu Wanchos (In the olden days there were many villages under Runu chief)
Banfera	Oanoogaon (Arunachal Pradesh)
Banfera	Nokrang
Banfera	Nuagoan
Banfera	Niausa-Kanubari (Londing district)
Bam-sang	Wancho (Arunachal Pradesh)
Bekagaon	Changlang, district (a tributary to both Paneedwar and Borduriya)
Bekagaya	Changlang district (a tributary to both Paneedwar and Borduriya)
Burdwar	Burdwar

Burdwar	Jakum
Burdwar	Kaeemaee
Burdwar	Loongtoong
Burdwar	Boonteen
Burdwar	Bansgsang
Burdwar	Sunkan
Burdwar	Dadum
Borduriya (Sa-la)	Arunachal Pradesh
Burkoorma	Changlang, district (a tributary to both Paneedwar and Borduriya)
Ching-paw or Ching-pô	Singphos (Arunachal Pradesh and Burma)
Daflas	Nyishi (Arunachal Pradesh)
Khampti	Tai Khampti (Arunachal Pradesh)
Khatreegaon	Changlang, district (a tributary to both Paneedwar and Borduriya)
Miris	Mishing (Arunachal Pradesh, Assam)
Hooroogaon	Changlang district (a tributary to both Paneedwar and Bordwar)
Namsang	Ting-yan
Namsang	Kanjang
Namsang	Soobang
Namsang	Doodam
Namsang	Magaon
Namsang	Horoomoorma
Namsang	Khetreegaon
Namsang	Lamcha
Namchangiyas	Nocte (Tirap, Arunachal Pradesh)
Panibatia	Hill Mishing (Arunachal Pradesh)
Paneedwar	Paneedwar (Arunachal Pradesh), these are tributary to both Paneedwar and Burdwar)
Pooloong	Changlang, district (a tributary to both Paneedwar and Borduriya)
Pongchau-Wakka (Tirap)	Pongchau-Wakka (Longding district)
Paneedwar	Singpoongiya
Paneedwar	Hooroogaon
Paneedwar	Banjapree
Paneedwar	Tapeegaon
Paneedwar	Bekagaon
Paneedwar	Burkoorma
Paneedwar	Bekagaya
Paneedwar	Khetreegaon
Paneedwar	Pooloong

Rusa	Tohuh, Hobso Rusa (Osim and Kukuh, Rang lua, Tanglun)
Singphoi	Changlang (Arunachal, Burma)
Singphoongiya	Changlang (a tributary to both Paneedwar and Bordwar)
Tangsa	Changlang, Arunachal Pradesh
Tarbatia	Miris (Arunachal Pradesh)
Tapeegaon	Changlang, district (a tributary to both Paneedwar and Borduriya)
Nagaland	
Akok	Lotha
Aliba	Ao (Under Hatigurias duar)
Anzang	Rengma (Nagaland)
Bhandari	Lotha
Changdang	Ao (Under Assiringias duar)
Chungliyimsen	Ao (Under Hatigurias duar)
Chungtia	Ao (Under Hatigurias duar)
Chamgpang	Lotha
Chaktung	Wakching (Nagaland)
Chingtak	Tanhai (Mon, Nagaland)
Changnoee	Changnoee
Changnoee	Kamloong
Changnoee	Booragaon
Changnoee	Thuoloong
Changnoee	Muoloong
Changnoee	Haroogam
Changnoee	Lumcha
Changnoee	Monyegaong
Changnoee	Noagong (Konyak)
Hatigharia	Ao (Nagaland)
Jaboka	Ya-nu Konyak (Nagaland)
Jaboka	Horoo-oothoo or Lungthing (Konyak)
Jaboka	Bur-oothoo (Konyak)
Jaboka	Byagaon (Konyak)
Jaboka (Yansa)	Yanu (Konyak)
Jak-tung	Konyak
Jaktoong	Konghou (Konyak)
Jaktoong	Tingtak (Konyak)
Jaktoong	Loongma (Konyak)
Jaktoong	Totak (Konyak)
Jaktoong	Tophang (Konyak)
Jaktoong	Chingkong (Konyak)

Jaktoong	Seyong (Konyak)
Japu	Ao (Under Hatiguria duar)
Kanloong	Zankham (Konyak)
Kacha	Ze-me, Empeo, Arung
Kineonger	Ao (Under Hatigurias duar)
Khensa	Ao (Under Hatigurias duar)
Kooloong	Kooloong
Koolong	Bur Moothoon
Koolong	Horoo Moothoon
Koolong	Nuagaon
Kubza	Ao (Under Hatigurias duar)
Lakhuni	Ao (Under Hatigurias duar)
Longkhum	Ao (Under Hatigurias duar)
Longjang	Ao (Under Assiringias duar)
Lukmah	Konyak
Kharee	Ao (Under Assiringias duar)
Konghon	Konyak
Lakhuti	Lotha
Longchum	Lotha
Mangmentong	Ao (Under Hatigurias duar)
Mekuli	Ao (Under Hatigurias duar)
Mikirs	Arlengs (Kabirs Anlongs)
Mo-shang	Konyak
Mooloong	Poiloong
Mooloong	Lakma
Mooloong	Mooloong
Mooloong	Burgaon
Mooloong	Naogong
Muton	Konyak
Mu-lung	Konyak
Pangti	Lotha
Rabha	Kachāri (Nagaland, Arunachal Pradesh, Assam)
Sa-vin	Konyak
Samsa (Longjemdang)	Ao (Under Hatigurias duar)
Simi or Süma	Sema (Zunoboto district, Nagaland)
Sum-dum	Konyak
Sangloi (Chang-nu)	Konyak
Tablung	Wanching (Konyak)
Tabloong	Namsang (Konyak)
Tabloong	Nangta (Konyak)
Tabloong	Kansang (Konyak)
Tabloong	Konyak

Tabloong	Rungoja (Konyak)
Tabloong	Rangam (Konyak
Tabloong	Nengsa (Konyak)
Tabloong	Nengnain (Konyak)
Tabloong	Chinloee (Konyak)
Tabloong	Chenglong (Konyak)
Tabloong	Chinkong (Konyak)
Tabloong	ChingPhoee (Konyak)
Tamlu	Ching-meg-nu or Nangta (Konyak)
Tsuroi	Lotha
Waromong	Ao (Under Assiringias duar)
Yanmhon	Lotha
Yingsung	Lotha

Appendix - III

List of Hats and Markets in the Valley

S.l. Name of hats and markets	Places where held	Whether daily/ weekly/ fortnightly
1. Badati hat	Badati (Lakhimpur)	Weekly
2. Bhnaguri hat	Bahgora Dhunaguri (Lakhimpur)	-do-
3. Laholiah hat	Laholial (Lakhimpur)	-do-
4. Bangalmora hat	Bangalmara (Lakhimpur)	-do-
5. Tinthengia hat	Tinthengia/Karunabari	-do-
6. Krhutoli hat	Kehutoh (Lakhimpur)	-do-
7. Laluk hat	Laluk (Lakhimpur)	Daily
8. Tunijan hat	Tunijan (Lakhimpur)	Weekly
9. Dongibal hat	Dongibal (Lakhimpur)	Weekly
10. Bihpuria hat	Bihpuria (Lakhimpur)	Weekly
11. Dhalpur Sombaria hat	DhalpurDakua (Lakhimpur)	Weekly
12. Dhalpur Sombaria hat	Narayanpur Dihrong	-do-
13. Barbali hat	Barbali (Nagaon)	-do-
14. Simaluguri hat	Simaluguri (Sivasagar)	-do-
15. Jamuguri hat	Jamuguri (Golaghat)	-do-
16. Rongati hat	Rongati (Lakhimpur)	-do-
17. Joyhing Koliamari	Nakari Mauza Fortnightly	
18. Ananda Bagan Bazar	Ananda Bagan (Lakhimpur)	Weekly
19. Bamunbari	Bamunbari (Dibrugarh)	Weekly
20. Rajgarh	Rajgarh (Dibrugarh)	-do-
21. Borbam Budhbaria hat	Borbam (Sibsagar)	-do-
22. Tingkhong	Tingkhong (Dibrugarh)	-do-
23. Merbil	Merbil (Dibrugarh)	-do-
24. Joypur	Joypur (Dibrugarh)	-do-
25. Kathaloni	Near Arunachal Pradesh	Fortnightly
26. Namsang hat	Namsang (Arunachal Pradesh)	-do-

27. Joypur	Joypur T.E.	-Weekly-
28. Hapjan	Hapjan Parbat (Dibrugarh)	-do-
29. Balimara	Balimara T.E. (Dibrugarh)	-do-
30. Dilli	Dilli T.E. (Dibrugarh)	-do-
31. Rukong	Rukong T.E. (Dibrugarh)	-do-
32. Namrup	Namrup T.E. (Dibrugarh)	-do-
33. Lengrijan	Lengrijan T.E. (Dibrugarh)	-do-
34. Tinali	Tinali T.E. (Tinsukia)	Weekly
35. Tingkhong	Tingkhong T.E (Dibrugarh)	Fortnightly.
36. Dillibari	Dillibari T.E. (Dibrugarh)	-do-
37. Nilmoni	Nilmoni T.E. (Dibrugarh)	-do-
38. Sarojani	Sarojani T.E. (Dibrugarh)	-do-
39. Karangani	Karangani T.E.(Dibrugarh)	-do-
40. Rajgarh	Rajgarh T.E. Tingkhong (Dibrugarh)	-do-
41. Longboi	Longboi T.E. (Moran), Dibrugarh	-do-
42. Borbam	Borbam T.E. (Sibsagar)	-do-
43. Kenduguri	Kenduguri T.E. (Dibrugarh)	-do
44. Pithaguti	Pithaguti T.E. (Dibrugarh)	-do-
45. Diroi	Diroi T.E. (Dibrugarh)	-do-
46. Ouphulia	Ouphulia T.E. (Dibrugarh)	-do-
47. Salmari	Salmari T.E. (Dibrugarh)	-do-
48. Achabam	Achabam T.E. (Sibsagar)	Weekly
49. Umatara	Umatara T.E. (Dibrugarh)	Fortnightly
50. Desam	Desam T.E. (Dibrugarh)	-do-
51. Dhemaji Brihaspatibaria *hat*	Khublia G.E. (Lakhimpur)	Weekly
52. Chisi Charili *hat*	Bhebeli G.P. (Dhemaji)	-do-
53. Bathua Thanmukh *hat*	Bathua Thanmukh G.P. (Lakhimpur)	-do-
54. Batgharia *hat*	Hatigarh G.P. (Dhemaji)	-do-
55. Butikur *hat*	Naruathan G.P. (Dhemaji)	-do-
56. Kalakhowa Chariali	Kalakhowa Chariali (Dibrugarh)	Weekly
57. Ghoronia T.E. Priviate Mkt	Within T.E. (Dibrugarh)	Fortnightly
58. Lepetakata T.E. Private Mkt.	-do-	Bi-Weekly
59. Dewanbari T.E. Private Mkt.	-do-	Fortnightly
60. Medla Grant T.E. Pvt.Mkt	-do-	-do-
61. Barbarooah hat	Barbarooah (Dibrugarh)	Weekly
62. Jamirah T.E. Pvt. Mkt	Within T.E. Area	Daily
63. Barbarooah T.E. Pvt.Mkt.	-do-	Fortnightly
64. Jakaisessa hat	Jakai (Dibrugarh West)	Weekly
65 Margherita hat and Makt	Margherita (Tinsukia)	Weekly hat
66. Ledo hat and Market	Ledo (Tinsukia)	Daily Mkt.
67. Tirap hat and Market	Tirap Gate	-do-
68. Borgolai hat and Mkt	Borgolai (Tinsukia)	-do-
69. Powai	Powai T.E. (Tinsukia)	-do-
70. Dehing	Dehing T.E. (Tinsukia)	-do-
71. 7th Miles Bazaar	Na-Sadiya (Tinsukia)	Weekly
72. Sunpura	Sunpura (Tinsukia)	do
73. Kundil	Kundil (Sadiya)	Daily

74.	Chapakhowa	Chapakhowa (Tinsukia)	Weekly
75.	Dholla	Dholla (Sadiya)	-do-
76.	Jonai (M/Sellek)	Jonai (Murkongsellek) Dhemaji	Daily
77.	Ghoramara hat	Romai (Dibrugarh)	Weekly
78.	Nagagboolie	Nagaghoolie T.E. (Dibrugarh)	-do-
79.	Tingrai Bazar	Tingrai Tinali (Tinsukia)	-do-
80.	Guijan Bazar	Guijan (Tinsukia)	-do-
81.	Guijan Bazar	Guijan (Tinsukia)	-do-
82.	Makum	Makum (Tinsukia)	Weekly
83.	Makum	Makum	Daily
84.	Sukanpukhuri	Sukanpukhuru T.E.	Fortnightly
85.	Dighaltarrang	Dighaltarrang T.E. (Tinsukia)	-do-
86.	Daisajan	Daisajan T.E. (Tinsukia)	-do-
87.	Tiphuk	Tiphuk T.E. (Sibsagar)	-do-
88.	Baghjan	Baghjan T.E. (Tinsukia)	-do-
89.	Deamulie	Baghjan T.E. (Tinsukia)	Weekly
90.	Rupai	Rupai T.E. (Tinsukia)	-do-
91.	Hansara	Hansara T.E. (Tinsukia)	Fortnightly
92.	Samdang	Samdang T.E. (Tinsukia)	-do-
93.	Bessakupie	Bessakupie T.E. (Tinsukia)	Fortnightly
94.	Pabhajan Bazar	Pabhajan T.E. (Tinsukia)	-do-
95.	Dhoedaam Bazar	Dhoedaam T.E. (Tinsukia)	-do-
96.	Raidang Bazar	Raidang T.E. (Tinsukia)	-do-
97.	Limbuguri Bazar	Limbuguri T.E. --	-do-
98.	Dhella khat Bazar	DhellaKhat T.E. (Sibsagar)	-do-
99.	Sanmari Bazar	Sanmari T.E. (Tinsukia)	-do-
100.	Katchujan Bazar	Katchujan T.E.(Tinsukia)	-do-
101.	Gelapukhuri Bazar	Gelaphkhuri T.E. (Tinsukia)	-do-
102.	Nakhrai Bazar	Nakhrai T.E. (Tinsukia)	-do-
103.	Gongabari Bazar	Gongabari T.E.(Tinsukia)	-do-
104.	Rongagora Bazar	Rongagora T.E.(Tinsukia)	-do-
105.	Guijan Bazar	Guijan T.E. (Tinsukia)	-do-
106.	Bagapani Bazar	Bagapani T.E. (Sonitpur)	Weekly
107.	Holonghabi Bazar	Srikrishna T.E. --	--
108.	Borhapjan Bazar	Borhapjan T.E. --	--
109.	Betjan Bazar	Betjan T.E. --	--
110.	Anandabag Bazar	Anandabag T.E. --	--
111.	Nalani Bazar	Nalani T.E. --	--
112.	Bazaltali Bazar	Bazaltali T.E. --	--
113.	Hapjan Bazar	Hapjan T.E. --	--
114.	Haveda Bazar	Haveda T.E. --	--
115.	Sewpur Bazar	Sewpur T.E. --	--
116.	Padumani Bazar	Padumani T.E. --	--
117.	Doolahat Bazar	Near Doolahat T.E. --	--
118.	Dejoo Bazar	Near Dejoo T.E. --	--
119.	Silonibari Bazar	Silnoibari T.E. --	--
120.	Lakwa	Charaideo --	Daily

121. Sapekhati	Borhat (Charaideo)	--	-do-
122. Longpotia	Longpotia (Sibsagar)	--	--
123. Milonyoti	Milonjyoti (Sibsagar)	--	--
124. Sonari	Rajapukhuri (Charaideo)		--
125. Towkok	Towkok (Charaideo)	--	--
126. Bhojo	Bhojo (Charaideo)	--	--
127. Nazira	Sukafa (Sibsagar)	--	Weekly
128. Lengibor grant	Lengibor (Sibsagar)	--	--
129. Mahmora (Sonari)	Sepon (Sibsagar)	--	--
130. Kakotibari	Kakotibari (Sibsagari)	--	--
131. Bharalipukhuri	Bharali pukhuri (Sibsagar)		--
132. Desangpani	Sonari (Charaido)	--	Weekly

Appendix - IV

Katakis Under the Ahom Government (Clan-wise)

1. Ahom Katakis: Chiring, Chengali, Naga, Saupengia, Bantalia, Bakatial, Baghachowal and Ramu
2. Brahmin Katakis: Kalia, Kaupatia, Kahial, Sitalial, Chandi, Bah-baria, Boka, Uria, Nirah, Patra Kalai, RatnaKandali, ChotaKandoli, Birina, Chaturbhuj, Godadhar, Ekadah, Thakuria, Borguru and Haramial.
3. Gargayan, Namtial, Thakuria, Bangal, Gajpuria, Chaliha, Duara, Salaguria, Abhoypuria, Manipuria, Bania, Tiru, Cheng, Pakhi, Tangani, Tekela and Bharalar Kataki.

Maps and Photo

Fig. 1. Traditional Basket Making, Yansa (Jaboka) 2016.

Fig. 2. Shri Asen, 99-Year-Old, Last Surviving Head-Hunter of Yaboka Village and a Traditional Log Drum, Mon District, 2018.

Fig. 3. Community Feast After the Community Labour and a Traditional Thatch House, Nokzang Village, Mon District. Source: Photo by scholar, 2018

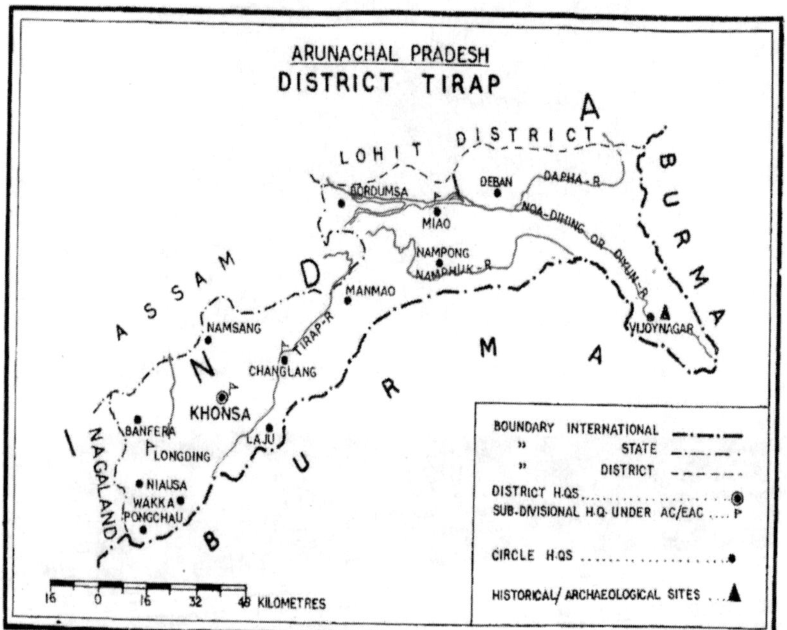

BASED UPON SURVEY OF INDIA MAP WITH THE PERMISSION OF THE SURVEYOR GENERAL OF INDIA.

Fig. 4. Traditional Earthen Pot Making at Tanhai Village, Mon District, 2017.

Fig. 5. Namtalao Haat (Sonari Town) 2017, originally started by Ahom Raja.

Fig. 6. Farmers Loading their products in a pick-up lorry to sell in a haat market, Sakho, Tingalibam near Charaideo.

Source: Photo by scholar, 2018.

Fig. 7. A Traditional Medicine Vendor in Rajapar Haat, Assam, 2019.

Fig. 8. A Konyak and Wancho Traders at Haatnu Haat (Chairaideo District), 2019.

Source: photo by 2017.

Fig. 9. A Konyak Man Going to *Haat* Market at Namtola (Sonari).

Fig. 10. Vendor at Geleky *Haat*. Source: Photo by scholar, 2016.

Source: Photo by scholar, 2016.

Fig. 11. Traditional Salt Packets for medicinal use.

Source: Photo by scholar, 2017.

A concrete salt well.

Source: Photo by Scholar, 2017.

Fig. 12. Descendant of Sentishila Walling.

Source: Photo by scholar, 2017.

Fig. 13. Naganijan Tea Estate.

Fig. 14. Assiringiah Duar.

Source: Photo by Haimendorf, 1939.

Fig. 15. Wangpa (chief) of the Konyak village of Banfera.

Source: Photo by Scholar, 2018.

Fig. 16. A Front View of the Wangpa (Chief) House, Shangnyu Village, Mon.

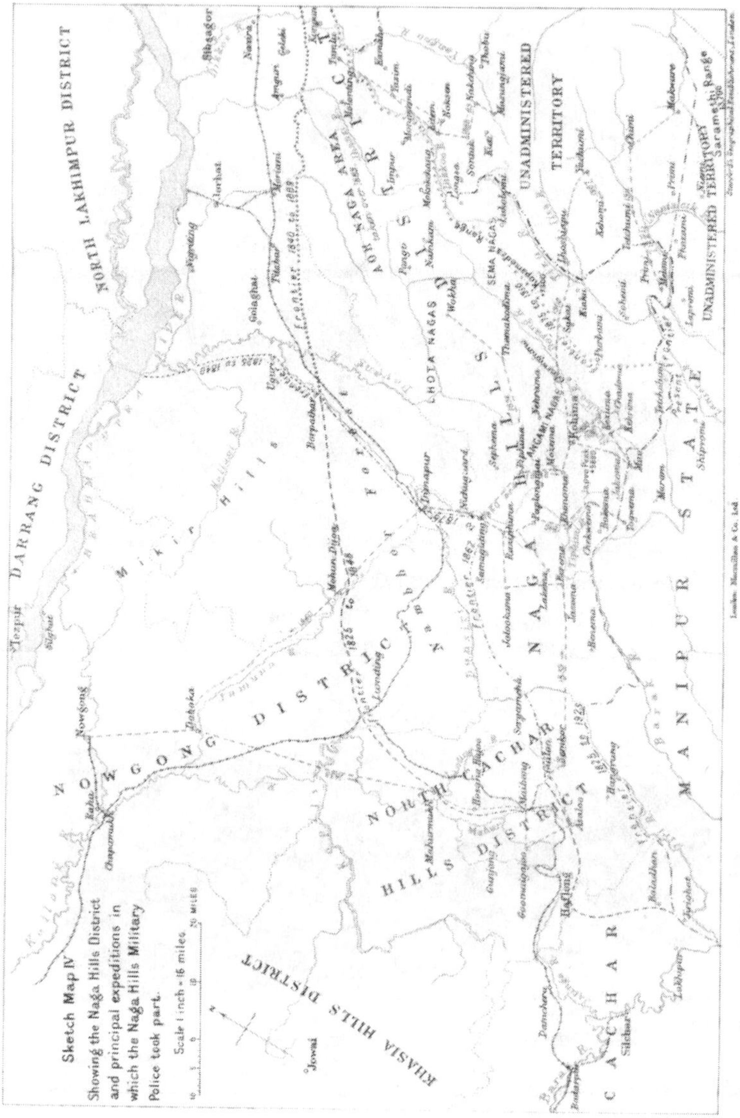

Source: Internet, 2022

Index

A

Abori Nagas, 22, 55

Abor Nagas of Bangang, 64

Afrikaan in South Africa, 168

Agricultural products, 113

Ahom Buranjis, 13, 57, 60, 64, 158

Ahom chronicles, 13

Ahomisation process, 146

Ahom king, 152

Ahom kingdom, 56, 60, 109, 110

Ahom king Gaurinath Singha, 171

Ahom king Kamaleswar Singha, 75

Ahom lar yimkong, 161

Ahom Lungwang (Raja), 67

Ahom Mahajon, 157

Ahom people, 113, 172

Ahom Raja, 26, 61, 62, 77, 92, 110, 111, 112, 122, 123, 148, 154, 155, 156, 158, 159, 161, 177, 183, 198

Ahom Raja Chaopha (Sukapha), 69

Ahom Raja Godapani, 110

Ahom Raja Pratap Singha, 70

Ahom Raja Suhenpha, 62

Ahom Raja Suhungmung (1497-1539), 114

Ahom Raja Suklenmung, 119

Ahom Raja Susenpha (1439-1488), 66

Ahom royal families, 146

Ahom rule, 95

Ahom rule to Lower Assam, 194

Ahom silk, 174

Ahoms married, 147

Ahom state, 70, 74, 193

Ahom valley kingdom, 103

Ahom villages, 22

Aitonia Nagas, 63

A.J. Moffatt Mills, 73

Alimenyinsem, 29, 113

Amalendu Guha, 146

Ambika Devi, 147

Angami areas, 154

Angh/Wangham, 32

Annual trading fairs, 105

Anokjangjen Yenden, 165

Ao-Ahom relations, 158

Ao and Konyak tribes, 158

Ao and Konyak villages, 160

Aoleang Konyak festival, 178

Arasentsur (soothsayer), 158

Archaeological investigation, 19

Arunachal Pradesh, 13, 15, 30, 36, 57, 62, 65, 67, 105, 115

Aso (generation), 24

Assam, 13, 35

Assam-Burma border, 62

Assam Company, 79

Assamese Bihu, 178

Assam Government till 1974, 125

Assam (Hindu culture), 74

Assam Valley, 23

Assirangia duar, 107

Assiring duar, 125
Assiringia khat, 124
Assiringia pass (duar), 92
Assiringias, 13
Assiring Pokhori, 125
Austric and the Tibeto-Burman, 184
Austric or Tibeto-Burman speakers, 173
Austro-Asiatic, 184

B

Bamboo bar, 127
Bamboo baskets, 176
Bamboo-pole, 127
Bamboo tube, 171
Banfera, 30, 71
Banfera Khunbao (chief), 63
Banfera Nagas, 63, 95, 197
Banfera (Wancho-Konyak), 62
Bar Gohain, 63
Barpatra Gohain, 63
Barter system, 107
B.B. Goswami, 15
Beepari/Bepari (male broker), 114
Bengal salt, 117, 198
Betel leaf, 127
Bhaiti-Raja, 57
Bhitar Namsang, 71
Bhogali celebrated, 166
Black beads, 42
Bogota Ali, 119
Bohag bihu in Assam, 167
Borahi women, 146
Borbarua Ali, 93
Borbarua Lenden, 161
Borduarias, 13, 31
Boree Nagas, 22
Boree Nagas (friendly), 55
Borhat-Namsang area, 115
Bori Dihing River at Rangarora, 119
Borpatra-Ali, 92
Bosfrontalis, 28
Brahmanical culture, 198
Brahmaputra valley, 15, 16, 35, 37, 55, 56, 57, 59, 60, 61, 74, 105, 107, 108, 115, 126, 162, 167, 179, 184, 193
Brahmaputra valley of India, 57, 58
British colonial rule, 17
British Government, 73
British Indian Penal Code of 1843, 132
British officers, 130
Broken men, 20
Buddhism of Burma, 183
Buffalo-fight, 110
Bura Gohain, 56, 62
Buranjis, 15, 23
Buri Dihing, 73
Burma, 20
Burma (Buddhist culture), 74
Burma (Myanmar), 55
Burmese aggression, 161
Burmese attack, 160
Burmese gong or Lah, 21
Burmese gongs, 34
Burmese invasions, 198
Burmese-Naga traders, 105

C

Cachar and Jantia, 55
Captain Brodie, 109
Captain Jenkins, 65
Cauca valley, 181
Cauca valley in Colombia, 181
Census of 1921, 88
Chairadeo district, 22
Chakhesang, 17
Chakhesang Nagas, 18
Chamua clan, 62
Changjanon, 31
Changki, 23, 30, 79
Changki villagers, 126

changklung, 129
Changlang, 30, 31, 37
Changlang and Longding, 62
Changlang district of Arunachal Pradesh, 30
Changsu, 40
Chaopha's (Sukapha) house, 69
Charaideo (Sonari), 75
Charingia duar, 107
Chatai Ali, 92, 93
China, 18
Chinghat Phukan and Laling Phukan, 66
Choubatobaayong, 161
Christianity, 172
Christian missionary, 117
Chuba-King, 26
Chuchuyimlang village, 158
Chulingyimti, 26
Chungli village, 26
Chungtia, 29
Clan land, 28
Cock-fights, 110
Come: ma (Ahom), 182
Commissioner of Assam, 124
Common land, 28
C.V. Haimendorf, 33

D

Dankhawali, 177
Dark blue dye, 40
Darrang district, 107
Deodhai, 56
Deodhai Asam, 110
Deputy Commissioner of the Naga hills, 89
Dhansari River, 37
Dhudar Ali, 92, 94
Dihingia, 56
Dihingia Raja, 56
Dikhu River, 24, 178
Dikhu valley, 36
Dikkoo (Dikhow) River, 23
Dobuka duar, 106
Dodhar Ali, 29
Dopdar duar, 106
Dopdarias, 13
Dopdoria duar, 125
Doyang and Dhansiri rivers, 157
Doyangia duar, 125
Doyang River, 23, 43
Doyang valley, 39
Doyingias, 13
Dupdorias, 23
Dup-duar-ias, 13

E

Eastern Konyak and Phom, 29
Eastern Naga, 65
Eastern Naga Hills, 31, 36
Eastern Nagas, 20, 22, 35, 55, 61, 65, 72, 104, 178
Eastern Naga salt, 111, 116
Eastern Naga salt wells, 87
Edward Gait, 14
Elephant-fights, 110
Elephant hunting, 111
Elongse, 18, 24
Emperor of Gaur, 76
English-Ahom-Konyak, 182
European (Lieutenant H. Brigge), 87

F

Ficussap, 28
First Anglo-Burmese War, 72
Fishing waters (bheels), 14
Foothill Nagas (Ao, Konyak, Lothas), 176
Foothill Naga villages, 112
Foothills markets of Brahmaputra valley, 112

G

Gadadhar Singha, 92, 114, 149, 152
Gaichak (bamboo wheel), 175
Garhgaon, 56
Garhgaon -Ali, 92
Gaurinath Singha, 117, 147
Gayal or mithun, 28
Geleky, 77
Ghor manu (family members), 181
Goalpara, 55
Godapani (Gadadhar Singha 1681-1696), 121
Golaghat, 37
Golaghat elaka, 78
Governor General of East India Company, 68
Grants of land (khats), 14

H

Handikoi family, 147
Hangnu River, 17
Haripara-Ali, 92
Hatidhar (elephant capturer), 110
Hatigorias, 13
Hatiguari duar, 125
Hatiguari duar (Bordobia), 125
Hatigurias, 13, 23
Hawk-fights, 110
Headhunting days, 33
Hill betel nut, 112
Hill products, 112
Hinduisation process, 146
Honoho hillock, 154
Hukong valley, 59

I

Imdangmeren Pongen, 159
Imkonglemba, 159
Immandangba of Khari village, 23
Imperial Burmese, 57
Indian subcontinent, 57
Individual land, 28
Indo-Mongoloid folk, 15
Indonesia, 16
Inner Line Permit in 1873, 198
Iron tools, 111
Irrawaddy and Chindwin valleys, 18
Irrawaddy river valley of Burma, 57
Island, 16

J

Jabilis, 29
Jabilis/Chabilis, 39
Jaboka, 71
Jaboka (Konyak), 111
Jaboka village, 180
Jaboka villagers (Konyak), 77
Jaboka village tradition, 112
Jabukas, 30, 31
Jaktoongias, 31
Japanese troops, 58
J.H. Hutton, 34, 170
Jhum cultivation, 19
Jhum field, 181
Jhum works, 21
Jitwangpeang, 151
Jorhat, 37
J.P. Mills, 25, 43

K

Kachari, 14
Kachari kingdom, 147
Kachari King Krishnachandra Narayan, 75
Kachari Raja Dersongpha, 104
Kachari rulers, 119
Kahulonglushi or Kahulong cultivation land, 165
Kailong, 31
Kalagaon, 37
Kamarbandha, 94
Kanubari, 31

Kanubari (Banfera), 109
Kareng-Ali, 92
Karengpa, 62
Kashinath Tamuli Phukan, 161
Khaat (gun powder), 35
Kha (Konyak-Wancho), 182
Khamjang Gohain, 87
Khats in Akuk duar, 77
Khaw nu (special rice), 166
Khiamunggan, 17
Khonsa, 37
Khora Raja (1552-1603), 88
Khrarukhung, 59
Khungro, 41
Khunkhatia, 59
King Godapani married a Nokpu girl, 165
King Pratap Singha, 70, 171
Kiswahili in Kenya, 168
Kithang or yankho, 38
Koch Raja Narayan, 66
Kongali celebrated in October, 166
Konyak, 15, 18, 19, 20, 21, 22
Konyak and Ao villages, 199
Konyak area, 23
Konyak (Jaboka) customs, 179
Konyak land, 149
Konyak Nagas, 21, 30
Konyak oral tradition, 95
Konyak ruling chief, 95
Konyak society, 34
Konyak village, 22, 109, 111, 153
Konyak-Wancho-Nocte-Tutsa, 35
Konyak-Wanchos, 90
Konyak (Yansa), 180
Koolem Motoniya, 104
Koro village, 154, 156
Kulingmen, 29
Kulingmen (Ao village), 113
Kurakhambang, 27

L

Lachit Barphukan, 91
lakhimi-ana in Assam, 167
Lakhugarh, 56
Lakhuti village, 78
Lakma, 31
Langbangkong, 29
Lingua-franca, 14
Longchakrep, 18
Longding, 31
Longding districts, 30
Longjakep, 24
Longkakpokla, 18, 24
Longkumer, 26
Longli lenden, 161
Longphok, 18, 24
Longsemdang, 89
Longterok, 24
Lonogoham, 77
Lota bih, 172
Lotha, 15, 17, 18
Lotha-Ahom friendship, 156, 157
Lotha area, 23
Lotha cotton trader, 109
Lotha Nagas, 87, 88, 129, 154
Lotha Pvuti, 73
Lothas, 41
Lothas Nagas, 37, 38
Lothas villages, 40
Lower Konyak, 30, 57
Lower Konyak Naga, 15, 30
Low-lying areas, 30
Lushai tribes, 132

M

Maan (Burmese), 153
Maan Singpho war, 165
Mahu (Konyak- Wancho), 182
Maibong, 28
Maikel, 18

Mai (Konyak- Wancho), 182
Majindar Barua, 76
Major Francis Jenkins, 72
Makhel, 18, 19
Malinowski, 179
Manas River, 55
Mangoldoi Sub-division, 107
Mangyanger, 26
Manipur, 18
Manipur to the Irrawaddy, 58
Manipur tribes, 19
Mao Nagas, 18, 19
Maotsu Ao festival, 159
Marangi Khowa, 61
Marangikhowa Gohain, 93
Marcel Mauss, 179
Matrimonial alliance, 14, 146
Medieval Assam, 198
Meijangkui, 34
Merangkhambang, 27
Merangkong village, 160
Merankong as Naogaon, 23
Merankong village, 28
Meteka-Ali, 92
Middleman for the interior Naga villages, 112
Miles Bronson, 36, 117
Minyumo-Nagami, 31
Mirjumla, 110
Mishimi, 55
Mita (friendship), 178
Mitani (friends), 181
Moamaria rebellion, 198
Moamaria Rebellion, 199
Moamariya revolt, 56
Mohammedan invasions, 63
Mohan, Bailung, 56
Mohnandha Ali, 93
Mohongia Baruah, 115
Mokokchung, 37
Mokokchung district in Nagaland, 158
Momai Tamuli Barbarua, 91
Mongkotepsü, 176
Mongsen, 23, 26
Mon in Nagaland, 36
Moolongs, 31
Mopongchuket as Molodubia, 23
Mopungchuket village, 162
Morajar Mouza, 93
Moranhat, Upper Assam, 74
Morung, 20, 22, 25
Moulmein (Myanmar), 18
Mughal and Burmese, 177
Mughal army, 75
Mughal invasion, 94
Munchee and China, 58
Muslim and Koch rulers, 167
Muttock Moran, 67
Muttock Moran Lungwang, 67
Myanmar, 18
Myanmar and Ahoms, 130

N

Naga-Ahom, 14
Naga-Ahom foothill areas, 103
Naga-Ahom political relationship, 94
Naga-Ahom relations, 68, 72, 87, 112, 121, 158, 167, 199
Naga-Ahom relationship, 61, 194
Naga-Ahom socio-cultural relations, 145, 170, 183
Naga Ali, 92, 93
Naga (Ao, Lothas, Konyak), 183, 198
Naga bih, 172
Naga-Burmese trade, 105
Naga claim, 17
Naga dogs, 28
Naga hills, 36, 65, 94, 104, 109, 110, 119, 132, 148, 181
Naga katakis, 14
Nagaland, 13, 30, 37, 65, 115, 131

Nagamese dialect, 33
Nagamese lingua franca, 182
Naganijan tea factory, 124
Naga pre-colonial past, 17
Naga Raja Thungbemo, 156
Nagas-Ahom often clashed, 87
Nagas (eastern Arunachal Pradesh), 57
Naga slaves, 131
Nagas (Lotha, Ao and Konyak), 88
Naga society, 20, 172
Nagas of Burma in Sagaing division, 104
Nagas of Sibsagar, 22, 55
Nagas on the Indo- Burma frontier, 199
Nagas tribes, 25, 74
Naga villages, 20, 74, 177
Naginimora (Lehkaan), 152
Namrupia, 56
Namsang, 37
Namsangia, 13, 30, 31, 59, 92
Namsoso Ali, 125
Nariya Raja (1644-48), 107
National Highway leading to Assam, 151
Natushi tenem, 164
Nawab of Lucknow, 76
Neo-Vaisnavism, 171
Nineteenth century, 15
Nocte-Borduaria, 66
Nokpu putu menden, 164
Nokpu village, 28, 89, 113, 122, 123, 124
Nonyang Lake, 58
North Cachar Hills, 28, 112
North-East India, 14
Northern Lothas, 41
North Myanmar, 59
Nou Heng (dry beef), 166

O

Okhyak (a traditional basket), 41
Ongpangsangba, 164
Osak (Strobilanctres Flaccidifolius), 175

P

Padshahnamah, 171
Palang Angh (chief), 150
Palang Morung, 148
Panee path duar, 125
Paneeput (Lotha), 108
Panger Imchen, 23
Pangti Rivers, 37
Pangti valley, 39
Pani-duar-ias, 13
Paniduarias, 13, 59
Paniphatias, 13, 194
Papukia, 59
Parvati, 56
Patkai Hills, 55, 57
Patkai mountain, 61
Patkai Nagas, 22, 61, 64, 194
Patkai Pass, 65
Patkai ranges, 57, 65, 68
Patkoi Nagas, 55
Persian sources, 15
Phak Keng (boiled leaves), 166
Phiro village, 154
Poharis (female broker), 114
Pongchau, 31, 37
Pongen clan, 158
Pramatheswari Devi, 147
Pramatta Singha, 147
Pratab Singha, 64, 91, 114, 147
Pre-colonial period, 17, 104
Pungkkong, 59
Puras of lands, 56
Purunder Singha, 119
Putu-generation, Menden-seat, 26
Putu menden, 26
Pvüti (village priest), 37

R

Raja Chandrakanta Singha, 162
Raja Godapani, 123

Raja Poorunder Singha, 73
Raja Pratap Singha, 89
Rajeswar Singha (1751-67), 107
Rengma, 13, 17, 40
R.G. Woodthorpe, 34
Rice beer, 38
Rongali celebrated in April, 166
Root of a small plant, 43
Rubiasikkimensis, 40
Rudra Singha (Ahom Raja), 56, 111, 113, 119, 159
Rule of exogamy, 20

S

Sadiya Khowa Gohain, 61
Salaguri-Ali, 92
Salal Gohain, 61
Sala, Marung and Sadiya, 61
Salt trade, 65
Salt wells, 65, 67
Samen Menchen, 26
Sanglap and Yansucho, 79
Sangtam tribe, 24
Saphakati (completely destroyed), 153
Second World War, 58
Sehenpha (1488-1493), 66
Sema Naga villages, 178
Sema to the south, 23
Senapati, Manipur district, 19
Sent to Harsavardhana, 126
Shihabuddin, 110
Shihabuddin Talish, 55, 75, 132
Shri. Girin Phukon, 74
Sibsagar and Chariado district, 92
Sibsagar and Lakhimpur, 64
Sibsagar district of Assam, 30
Siva Singha, 147
Slaves are not allowed to marry, 21
Soatingsheang, 153
Socio-cultural relations, 147
Socio-economic organisations, 20
Sonari Hindu girls, 147
Southeast Asia, 57
Southeast Asian countries, 173
Southern China, 173
Southern Lothas, 41, 42
Soyum village, 24
Stone monuments, 18
Strobilanthes flaccidi-folius (tchemo), 40
Suhenpha (1488-1493), 62
Suhungmung (Dihingia Raja 1497-1539), 63
Sukati-Ali, 92
Sukhampha, Khora Raja (1552-1603), 92
Sungkotenem Lake, 162
Suphakpha (1422-1439), 62
Sutsongrong, 175
Svarga Narayan, 63
Swargadeo Gadadhar Singha, 94
Swargadeo Pratap Singha, 93, 107

T

Tabloong, 72
Tablungia Nagas, 92
Tablungias, 13, 31, 59
Tai Ahom groups, 173
Tai language and religion, 184
Taimur- Ali, 92
Tai Research Institute Moranhat, 177
Tangjan, 31
Tangkhuls, 18
Tangsa, 30, 37
Tangsa and Konyak Naga, 13
Tangsa Nagas, 60, 62
Tao Nao (soya bean), 166
Taprongumi, 31
Tarik-i-Asam, 75
The Pangsao pass, 57
Thungbemo Kuresulan, 155
Tibetan trade, 105
Tibet side, 105

Tiger-bear contests, 110
Tipam chief's daughter, 62
Tirap and Changlang, 36, 64
Tirap and Changlang districts of Arunachal Pradesh, 104
Tirap District in Arunachal Pradesh, 31
Tirap Division of NEFA, 62
Tirap-Patkai, 57
Tirap-Patkai region, 68
Tirap valley, 68
Tista River, 31
Tizzy River, 17
Togat Ali, towards Amguri, Assam), 162
Trans-Dikhu villages, 105
Tsungremong, 27
Tuensang district, 24
Tuensang district of Nagaland, 30
Tungkhungia, 56
Tungkhungia Buranjis, 110, 110
Tutnu Jongsun wo, 67
Tutsa language, 115
Tutsa Lungwang (chief), 67
Tutsa village, 67
Tzula tzu (Dikhu River), 163
Tzusa village, 164

U

Upper Assam, 56
Upper Burma, 132, 193
Upper Konyak, 30

V

Vaishnavism, 166, 168, 172
Valley of Manipur, 155
Verrier Elwin, 131, 170

W

Wakching village, 148
Wanching Morung, 149
Wancho, 13, 22, 30
Wangham (chief), 36, 111
Wangham father, 32
Wanghampa (deputy chief), 33
Wangham, wangsa, 32
Wangpen mother, 32
Watlong Angya, 150
W. C. Smith, 170
White goats (nyanya), 39
Wild pigs, 28
Wokha district, 37
W.W. Hunter, 107

Y

Yangkang, 37
Yansa/Jaboka village, 90
Yanthow (muskets), 35
Yimkumli, 27
Yongmenala, 18, 24
Young girl at Ywo, 176

Z

Zeliang, 17
Zeliangrong, 18
Zingkaling Khamti in Burma, 105
Zunheboto, 37
Zu (rice beer), 180